Women and the State in Modern Indonesia

In the first study of the kind, Susan Blackburn examines how Indonesian women have engaged with the state since they began to organise a century ago. Voices from the women's movement resound in these pages, posing demands such as education for girls and reform of marriage laws. The state, for its part, is shown attempting to control women. The book investigates the outcomes of these mutual claims and the power of the state and the women's movement in improving women's lives. It also questions the effects on women of recent changes to the state, such as Indonesia's transition to democracy and the election of its first female president.

The wider context is important. On some issues, like reproductive health, international institutions have been influential, and as the largest Islamic society in the world, Indonesia offers special insights into the role of religion in shaping relations between women and the state.

SUSAN BLACKBURN is a senior lecturer in politics at Monash University, Australia. Her research has focussed on Indonesia and on international development. Her previous two books are *Jakarta: A History* (1991) and *Practical Visionaries: A Study of Community Aid Abroad* (1994). Her recent publications concern women in Indonesia.

T0370611

Women and the State in Modern Indonesia

Susan Blackburn

Monash University, Australia

CAMBRIDGE UNIVERSITY PRESS
Cambridge, New York, Melbourne, Madrid, Cape Town, Singapore, São Paulo, Delhi

Cambridge University Press
The Edinburgh Building, Cambridge CB2 8RU, UK

Published in the United States of America by Cambridge University Press, New York

www.cambridge.org
Information on this title: www.cambridge.org/9780521104555

First published 2004
This digitally printed version 2009

A catalogue record for this publication is available from the British Library

ISBN 978-0-521-84225-9 hardback
ISBN 978-0-521-10455-5 paperback

Contents

Acknowledgments

This book has been many enjoyable years in the making. Over that time I have collected an enormous amount of information yet still feel, as a non-Indonesian, that it is presumptuous of me to write about what Indonesian women want. During the New Order period I could reassure myself that Indonesian women could not produce such a book because of the restrictions of censorship and the education system, and the lack of support for research. All this is rapidly changing, so it is high time to publish my own reflections before Indonesian women write their own books on the subject.

Many people have helped me over the years. I have had excellent research assistants and wish to thank particularly Elizabeth Martyn and Helen Pausacker. Others who have helped and stimulated me include Sharon Bessell, Barbara Hatley, Elsbeth Locher-Scholten, Lynette Parker, Kathryn Robinson, Maila Stivens and Norma Sullivan, and numerous Indonesian activists including Nursyahbani Katjasungkana, Sri Kusyuniati and Damai Pakpahan. I learned a great deal too from the information and lively exchanges on the e-perempuan email discussion list. Jean Gelman Taylor provided helpful comments on the book manuscript. I am greatly in debt to librarians at Monash University, the Kalyanamitra resource centre and the Perpustakaan Nasional in Jakarta, and the KITLV in Leiden. I also wish to acknowledge the assistance of research grants from the Australian Research Council and Monash University.

Finally, I thank my partner, Roger Spegele, for constant and loving encouragement.

I dedicate this book to my mother, Jean Blackburn, who died in 2001 but whose example remains an inspiration to me.

Note on spelling and terminology

The spelling of Indonesian words and the naming of places and groups changed in the course of the twentieth century. To facilitate reading, this book will use current spelling, place names and terminology.

Glossary: abbreviations, acronyms and Indonesian terms

adat	Custom
bapak	Father
Aisyiyah	Women's wing of Muhammadiyah, modernist Islamic organisation
BTI	Barisan Tani Indonesia (Indonesian Farmers Front)
Dharma Wanita	Women's Service: organisation of wives of civil servants
Gapi	Gabungan Politik Indonesia (Indonesian Political Coalition)
Gerwani	Gerakan Wanita Indonesia (Indonesian Women's Movement)
Golkar	Sekretariat Bersama Golongan Karya (Joint Secretariat of Functional Groups)
hadis	Reports of the words and actions of the Prophet Muhammad
IBI	Ikatan Bidan Indonesia (Association of Indonesian Midwives)
ibu	Mother
ILO	International Labour Organisation
Istri Sedar	Aware Women
kampung	Lower-class urban residential area
kawin gantung	Suspended marriage
kiai	Islamic scholar
kodrat	Natural character/destiny
Kowani	Kongres Wanita Indonesia (Indonesian Women's Congress)
LBH-APIK	Lembaga Bantuan Hukum – Asosiasi Perempuan Indonesia untuk Keadilan (Legal Aid Foundation – Indonesian Women's Association for Justice)

LSM	Lembaga Swadaya Masyarakat (literally 'Self-Reliant Social Institutions'), a term used in the New Order period to refer to some kinds of non-government organisations
MMR	Maternal Mortality Rate
Muslimat NU	Muslimat-Nahdlatul Ulama (women's wing of NU)
Nahdlatul Ulama	Traditionalist Islamic organisation
P4A	Perkumpulan Pemberantasan Perdagangan Perempuan dan Anak-Anak (Organisation for the Eradication of Trade in Women and Children)
Pancasila	Five principles of Indonesian state ideology
PDI	Partai Demokrasi Indonesia (Indonesian Democratic Party)
PDI-P	Partai Demokrasi Indonesia – Perjuangan (Indonesian Democratic Party of Struggle)
perempuan	Indonesian word for woman, commonly used in the first four decades of the twentieth century and making a comeback since the fall of the New Order regime in 1998.
Perwari	Persatuan Wanita Republik Indonesian (Union of the Women of the Indonesian Republic)
pesantren	Islamic boarding school
PKI	Partai Komunis Indonesia (Indonesian Communist Party)
PKK	Pembinaan Kesejahteraan Keluarga (Family Guidance Movement)
PNI	Partai Nasionalis Indonesia (Indonesian Nationalist Party)
PPII	Perikatan Perkumpulan Isteri Indonesia (Federation of Indonesian Women's Associations)
priyayi	Traditional Javanese upper class
PSII	Partai Sarekat Islam Indonesia
selir	secondary wife
SOBSI	Sentral Organisasi Buruh Seluruh Indonesia (All-Indonesian Labour Unions Federation)
SPSI	Serikat Pekerja Seluruh Indonesia (All-Indonesia Workers' Union)
syariah	Islamic law
TBA	Traditional birth attendant
VVV	Vereeniging voor Vrouwenkiesrecht (Women's Suffrage Association)

wanita	Indonesian word for woman, in common use from the Japanese occupation onwards as a more 'respectable' word than *perempuan*, with connotations similar to that of 'lady' in English
WHO	World Health Organisation
Yasanti	Yayasan Annisa Swasti – Annisa Swasti Foundation

Introduction

During the New Order regime in Indonesia (1967–98), political life was entirely oriented towards the state. Women were affected as much as men. Whether or not it was possible for women's organisations to work on issues they considered important, and how successful they might be in such endeavours, depended heavily on whether the state looked upon them favourably. Then, in the space of only a few months, with the fall of President Suharto, the nature of political life changed dramatically, as the state grew weaker and civil society flourished in all kinds of admirable and repulsive ways – a mixture of mushrooms and toadstools bursting out of the debris of the authoritarian state. In 2001 the first Indonesian woman president took office, something unthinkable under the military-dominated New Order. Freedom of association was enjoyed by women and men, but women in particular soon began to feel the lack of state services and control of law and order. Sudden changes like these focus attention on the importance of the state for women.

This book investigates how the state and Indonesian women have engaged with one another over the past century. Because the state is such an important institution in people's lives, Indonesian women have had to come to terms with it. How have they done this, and with what results? How has the state responded and how has it sought to influence women?

Analysing the state's engagement with women is always a difficult task. Is the state autonomous in its treatment of men and women, or does it reflect the interests of certain groups in society? Although the state in Indonesia is dominated by men, it is not enough to say it reflects their interests rather than the interests of women. For a start, men, like women, are not a homogeneous group: the gender interests of men may vary with religion, ethnicity, class and age, to name just a few of the differences among men. States have to respond to many interests, both internal and external, which accounts for the complexity of decision-making. Nor is the state itself homogeneous, consisting as it does of a number of institutions with their own competing interests. Apart from the executive arm – the government – with its own contending ministries, the state also consists of the bureaucracy, the judiciary, the military and the police, which cannot always be relied on to administer government policies as they were intended. In the Indonesian case, moreover, the state has changed its nature over the course of the last century: starting out as a Dutch colony, it is now a fragile democracy. Not surprisingly, then, state attitudes to women have differed considerably. They are best appreciated by analysing particular issues, which is the approach taken in this book.

If the state requires dissection, so does the category of Indonesian women. Given the great diversity among Indonesian women, it is unlikely that one can identify common interests among them in their dealings with the state. It is necessary to ask which women's concerns are being advanced, by whom and why. A cognate question concerns women's agency in influencing policy; how much influence do they have, on what issues?

Indonesia is a large and extraordinarily diverse country. Its population of some 220 million people is spread over thousands of islands, the most important being the densely populated island of Java. There are about three hundred ethnic groups, none able to claim a majority. While about 90 per cent of Indonesians are nominally followers of Islam, significant minority religions exist and the extent to which religion dominates people's lives varies considerably. In the twentieth century, most Indonesians were poor and lived in rural areas, yet there were also wealthier urban groups and even aristocrats. All these factors cause divisions among women, making it difficult to say what might be 'women's issues' in relation to the state.

For the purposes of this book, 'women's issues' are those publicly defined as such by Indonesian women. Inevitably, in discussing the way in which women and the state have engaged with one another, the spotlight falls on a narrow group of women, the ones who are organised and articulate, capable of defining what women's issues are. For this reason women's organisations and their spokeswomen feature prominently in this book. I do not claim that these women are typical of all women, nor that they represent the interests of all women. Although it is possible to argue (as this book does) that when some women take up an issue, many women's lives are touched, it is not contended here that the issues featured in this book represent what all Indonesian women want. In fact it is recognised that the issues have been selected by certain groups of women as of concern to themselves or to their preconceived view of Indonesian womanhood. We have no way of knowing what other women may have wanted because they were not organised and had no public voice.

Unfortunate as that may be, it should not lead us to dismiss Indonesia's women's organisations as valueless because they are 'unrepresentative'. To do so would be to commit the same mistake as the colonial government, which derided nationalist leaders as unrepresentative of the masses of the 'Natives'. Rather, we should value the women's organisations as giving some insight, however limited, into the perceptions and feelings of certain groups of Indonesian women. From the point of view of the state, these organisations were the only ones that they could consult or that gave voice to the concerns of Indonesian women. As such they could not be discounted on matters about which they felt strongly, particularly if the state required women's cooperation. What this book tries to do is to validate these women and their organisations as political actors, while acknowledging their limitations – just as the Indonesian political party system must be recognised as deficient in its ability to channel people's demands to governments.

Despite the importance of the state, one should nevertheless be wary of attributing too much power to it. Women are embedded in gender relations that are only partly determined by the state. The power relations between men and women are produced and perpetuated by beliefs and practices about the appropriate behaviour and treatment of men and women in a particular society at a particular time. The bigger question is: What causes (and prevents) change in gender relations? Finding an answer depends on weighing up the respective influences of the actions of women, the state, or other forces such as socioeconomic and cultural change largely outside the control of state. Current literature about the value of reducing or restoring the role of the state can throw light on what the state should and can do about something as complex as the construction of gender relations. On occasion some efforts on the part of the state may be counterproductive. It may, then, be better for the state to leave the burden of effecting change to other forces in society and in the economy. From the point of view of the strategies pursued by women seeking to increase their power in gender relations, they need to consider how important it is to focus on influencing state policy and legislation as against changing social attitudes in other ways. Around the world women activists struggle with such dilemmas.

Central questions

A number of questions are addressed in this book. Whereas each chapter concerns a particular 'women's issue', the book as a whole attempts to answer various broad questions. Some of these questions focus on the state. When and why has the state in Indonesia been interested in women's issues? Which elements within the state have pursued which agendas and why, and has there been inconsistency within the state on these issues? Useful in finding answers to these questions are others concerning state ideology. In what ways has state ideology affected the construction of gender in Indonesia, intentionally and unintentionally? What causes changes in state ideology on gender?

Another group of questions relate to the women's movement in Indonesia in its dealings with the state. What role can a women's movement play in promoting the interests of women? What can it do by itself and what kinds of collaboration with the state are helpful? How can cooption by powerful states be avoided? How has the changing nature of the women's movement in Indonesia affected the kinds of issues placed on the public agenda, the actions taken on those issues and their outcomes?

Finally, questions are asked about the wider context of gender relations in Indonesia. What have been the outcomes of the state's interventions on women's issues? Who has benefited? What actions by the state can in fact advance women's empowerment? What has international pressure achieved in the way of advancing the 'women's agenda' in Indonesia?

Resolving all these issues is not helped by the fact that little has been written about Indonesian women from a political perspective at all. Explanations include the long neglect of the study of women in political science generally. By the time women began to enter the field of vision of political scientists and historians, the New Order regime had settled upon Indonesian society, with a fixed agenda that discouraged the study of politics or of women except in very restricted ways that accorded with its version of Pancasila, the state ideology.[1] This situation is rapidly changing, but in the past, conducting research on women from a political perspective was difficult. For instance, in the 1980s the Dutch researcher Saskia Wieringa found it quite dangerous to try to interview Indonesians about Gerwani, the banned pro-communist women's organisation (Wieringa 2002). Another obstacle has been the nationalist hegemony in Indonesian historiography. Women are only recognised, grudgingly, for their role in the nationalist movement.

While there are no studies of Indonesian women and the state that cover the duration of the twentieth century, this book builds on some very useful secondary sources. Anyone writing about the modern history of Indonesian women must pay homage to the pioneering work of Cora Vreede-de Stuers (1960), a Dutchwoman who studied the Indonesian

[1] The five tenets of Pancasila are belief in God, nationalism, humanity, sovereignty of the people, and social justice. Although intrinsically quite vague, these principles were interpreted by the New Order regime in such a way as to exclude all alternatives.

women's movement during the period of parliamentary democracy in the 1950s. In the last few years there has also been a revival of interest in the colonial period, signalled by the publication of books by Elspeth Locher-Scholten (2000) and Ann Stoler (1996). Recently, too, Saskia Wieringa has produced a landmark book on the remarkable women's organisation Gerwani, which was prominent in the 1950s and early 1960s. Her book also offers many valuable insights into earlier and later relations between women and the state (Wieringa 2002). While studies of women in the New Order abound, they focus on particular regions and particular issues, like birth control. But there are still many gaps in the secondary literature, even on important topics like gender and education in independent Indonesia.

Readers may be puzzled by the paucity of secondary sources by Indonesians used in this book. Occasional works, such as Sukanti Suryocondro's study of the women's movement (Suryochondro 1984), and Nani Suwondo's book on the legal position of Indonesian women (Suwondo 1981), stand out because of their rarity. Little has been written or published in Indonesia on women and the state. A litany of reasons could be cited: the education system under the New Order, which discouraged independent thinking and controlled the areas of research and publication; the decline of history as a subject and lack of funding for its research in the New Order, especially for topics relating to women which have low prestige; the loss of command of the Dutch language by Indonesians, leading to problems of accessing material from the colonial period; and the state of the publishing industry in Indonesia, with its small market for scholarly works, particularly on women. This all helps to account for why I, as an Australian woman, am writing this book rather than an Indonesian scholar. The situation is likely to change in the near future, as more Indonesians gain the opportunity to research and publish on the history and activities of their women's movement.

Primary sources have been used here where possible, especially the publications of Indonesian women and their organisations. I hope that the strong and varied voices emanating from these sources will encourage more writers to mine their full depths. These writings constantly remind us that the issues being discussed here are not the substance of dry political analysis but the deeply felt concerns of Indonesian women. Struggles for education and against polygamy have aroused particularly strong passions. Current high levels of violence in Indonesia cause deep anguish.

The lack of studies on Indonesian women and the state is surprising on at least two counts. Although there is considerable interest now in comparative essays on women and the state in Islamic countries

(e.g. Kandiyoti 1991; Moghadam 1994), Indonesia is almost always omit-
ted from such collections. Yet it is the largest Islamic society in the world.
Those observers who do register this fact often comment on how little
the Indonesian state reflects the interests of Islam, in its relations with
women as in many other matters. On certain issues, however, religion is
critical in restricting the autonomy of the state, as this book will show.

Secondly, it is worth studying Indonesian women in their interactions
with the state because of the strong social position that has frequently been
claimed for Southeast Asian women compared with elsewhere in Asia.
From early times visitors to Indonesia, as to other parts of the region,
have been impressed by the apparently high status of female inhabitants,
as evident in their frequent control of family finances and their high degree
of public visibility, particularly in commerce (Reid 1988). Nevertheless
it is striking that this celebrated high status has not translated into a
commensurate recognition by the state in Indonesia. Women have not
found it easy to enter the public political arena and articulate their needs
and concerns to the state.

The structure of this book

Chapter 1 provides historical background information about the evolution of state gender ideology in Indonesia and of the women's movement,
indicating the relationship between the two. Subsequent chapters focus
on issues on which Indonesian women and the state have engaged publicly and usually controversially over the course of the twentieth century.
Each of them is a weighty matter from the point of view of both parties,
involving differences of opinion about goals and means.

Each chapter will concentrate mainly on the period in which the issue
entered the public agenda and was taken up by the state, but it will
also discuss the lack of state (or women's) interest in the issue at other
periods, and whether or not the issue disappeared from the public agenda
after state action was taken. It will consider, too, what effects that action
has had for the construction of gender in Indonesia and for the lives of
Indonesian women generally. This will assist in evaluating the efforts of
the state (and of the women's movement) on behalf of women.

Each of Chapters 2 to 8 investigates who raised a particular topic
as a matter of interest to both the state and women, and why. From
the point of view of Indonesian women, two of these issues, education (Chapter 2) and suffrage (Chapter 4), were considered by women's
organisations to be the keys to combating the perceived evils of early
marriage (Chapter 3), polygamy (Chapter 5) and economic exploitation
(Chapter 7). Indonesian women themselves can be seen to have initiated

pressure on the state to engage with these issues. In some cases little pressure needed to be applied because the state itself took an interest in the matter: this could be said most accurately about the education of girls. On other issues the state was generally most reluctant to admit that the topic was one of public importance or that it was appropriate for the state to act: this applied to suffrage, polygamy, economic exploitation and violence against women. In some cases the Indonesian women's movement did not take a prominent initiating role: suffrage (Chapter 4), birth control and reproductive health (Chapter 6). It was the New Order state that pushed strongly for birth control, with support from foreign aid; in the case of suffrage and reproductive health, the initiative came from outside. External pressure was brought to bear, drawing attention to the need for action in areas that had otherwise been neglected by both the women's movement and the state. In the case of violence against women (Chapter 8), while women's organisations in the late twentieth century had been trying to put domestic violence issues on the public agenda, it was the breakdown of law and order from 1998 onwards that forced the state to confront the issue more generally.

Finally, the Conclusion draws together the threads of the individual chapters, reflects on their lessons and considers what the twenty-first century may hold in store for Indonesian women and the state. Completed in January 2004, this book is able to cover events only up to that date.

1   State gender ideologies and the women's movement

As a prelude to later thematically based chapters, this chapter examines the changing nature of the gender ideology of the Indonesian state during the twentieth century, and how it relates to the development of the women's movement. Some basic questions are raised about the influence of the state on that movement and about the extent to which the state reflects or seeks to change society's views of gender. Subsequent chapters will explore the ability of the movement itself to influence state gender ideology.

Gender ideology

Gender ideology spells out expectations of how men and women should behave according to their ascribed sex. In this book I use the term to refer to ideas about the construction of gender in Indonesia. Such ideas are being constantly contested from various quarters, because of the diversity of views about gender within and outside Indonesia.

In Indonesia, different ethnic groups have their own gender traditions. Some of the best known include the matrilineal system of West Sumatra (Minangkabau), where inheritance of property follows the female line: husbands are 'guests' in their wives' houses. Nevertheless, Minangkabau men still have their own power bases, since family and community decisions are formally made by male representatives of lineages – the brothers of female property-holders. By contrast, nearby Batak society in northern Sumatra is strongly patrilineal: women are unable to inherit and are economically dependent on men as well as excluded from public decision-making. And in Java, society is organised bilaterally: there is a greater degree of equality between the sexes, and women play a prominent role in commerce and agriculture, although tradition has excluded them from public political life. In addition to these variations on the role and power of men and women, some ethnic groups do not clearly differentiate between male and female: instead of a dichotomy there are held to be more than two sexes and a more fluid notion of sexuality. Bugis society in south Sulawesi, for instance, accepts transvestite male priests (*bissu*) as constituting a third sex with its own gender expectations.[1]

On top of and often conflicting with these ancient gender practices, various world religions, notably Islam, have imposed their own rules relating to how men and women should behave. Religious expectations have often been more rigid than the older notions of gender, but in some places compromises have been reached. Thus the matrilineal Minangkabau have been regarded as devout Muslims although their inheritance practices conflict with Islamic notions that inherited property should be divided among all children, with larger shares going to sons.

More recently, Indonesia experienced the influx of Western views of gender via the colonial system as Dutch rule spread across the archipelago from the seventeenth century onwards. This proved to be just the first instalment of 'modern' ideas that continue to be influential, as Indonesia has remained open to world trade and communications, foreign investment and foreign development assistance, and participation in international forums.

Ideas about gender in Indonesia in the twentieth century have thus made up a heady brew. There have been frequent inconsistencies and contradictions, the most obvious being amongst Muslims concerning acceptable behaviour for men and women according to religious teachings. What is striking about both the state and the women's movement is how much more limited their range of thinking has been about gender than that found in society at large. The New Order state in particular endorsed a restrictive and fairly consistent gender ideology. Within the women's movement also, the alternatives espoused have not been very numerous except at times when greater freedom of expression has been possible. Here the prevailing nature of the state has clearly been important for the development of gender ideology amongst women.

State gender ideology refers to the assumptions about gender on which the state acts and the way it attempts to influence the construction of gender in society. Sometimes these assumptions on the part of the state are overt, contained in official statements about policies relating to women. More often assumptions have to be deduced indirectly from actions and policies, for example by examining policies on the education of girls and boys. These reveal what the state believes is appropriate for men and women in that society, or what aspirations the state has for gender relations. Most commonly gender ideology is incoherent and inconsistent, reflecting the preoccupations of the different segments of the state and

---

[1] Examples of regional studies of gender in Indonesia can be found in Atkinson and Errington (1990).

pragmatic responses to pressure applied from different quarters. Indonesia has experienced many kinds of state – colonial, democratic and authoritarian, some of them more monolithic in their ideological stance than others.

Unpacking the state in Indonesia reveals a number of puzzles. The degree of homogeneity and autonomy of the state, already mentioned in the Introduction, is a question to which this book will return at various points. Different segments of the state apparatus will often have conflicting interests and objectives as far as gender (and many other matters) is concerned. During the New Order, for instance, the army influenced state gender ideology, but its vision of domesticated women diverged from that of the Department of Labour which increasingly sought to exploit women as a cheap workforce in the manufacturing sector. From the point of view of women, the more heterogeneous the state, the more points it offers for them to apply pressure. The disadvantage is that with a fragmented state, while it may be easier to stall unwelcome measures, it is harder to push through new policy initiatives. As we shall see, although the women's movement was able to get extensive discussion of marriage reform in parliament in the democratic 1950s, it had to await an authoritarian state that had its own reasons for backing marriage law reform before a Marriage Law was manoeuvred through the state system by the New Order Government.

The degree of autonomy of the state in pursuing gender policies is a central concern of this book. Did the colonial state reflect the interests of the Dutch, or more narrowly of Dutch men or Dutch capitalism, in the gender ideology it practised in the Indies? Certainly those interests were influential, but the colonial state also felt obliged, for pragmatic reasons, to consider other interests that might otherwise cause it trouble. On issues related to women, for instance, the concerns of Islamic groups had to be balanced against others.

Nor, once independence was achieved, could the state be said to reflect views about gender within Indonesian society at large, for the simple reason that those views vary considerably between different sexes, classes and religious and ethnic groups, not to mention other sources of diversity. Even to say, as a crude approach might have it, that the state reflects the views of men about gender is far from illuminating, considering the diversity among men. On a few matters it may be possible to talk about 'men's interests' in so far as male prerogatives may be challenged. The case of polygamy is one such instance, where Indonesian men proved most reluctant to allow restrictions to be placed on their right according to Islam to have more than one wife at a time. Nevertheless, the state did finally move to impose such restrictions.

Although the Indonesian state does not reflect the full diversity of masculine interests on gender, it can be said to reflect the gender ideology of a certain group of men. During the colonial period, middle-class Dutchmen dominated state thinking on gender, while since independence the fact that the state has been in the hands of wealthier men from predominantly moderate Muslim and Western-educated backgrounds is discernible in state gender ideology. That does not, however, exclude differences of opinion among that group and their need to consider the views of powerful elements like the Islamic movement or international organisations. To what extent the state has been in a position to impose its gender ideology on others has varied with the issue and the times, as later chapters will show.

The fact that the state reflects only certain interests is indicated by the gap between state rhetoric and the practice of many Indonesians as far as gender is concerned. For instance, throughout the twentieth century the Indonesian state upheld the notion of *kodrat*, or natural destiny, for men and women, projecting men as primary income-earners and women as child-rearers and housewives. Policies have been predicated on this assumption. Not only has this failed to serve the interests of most women or men, but it does not reflect their practices either. Most poor Indonesian women are income-earners along with their menfolk.

On any issue one can ask the question: To which groups within or outside Indonesian society has the state felt accountable, and why? At different times the state has been under pressure from external sources such as foreign-aid donors, and from a variety of internal social and economic groupings such as investors, Islamic groups and women's organisations. At other times the main dynamic has been struggles within the state itself. Understanding these dynamics will often be necessary in order to fathom state gender ideology and practice.

The Indonesian women's movement

The term 'women's movement' is used here to refer to the collective articulation of the desires of Indonesian women. Those who make up the movement are women's organisations concerned to advance the cause of women (in whatever ways they see fit), articulate individuals claiming to speak on behalf of women more generally, and the more indistinct body of supporters and sympathisers who may not formally be members of women's organisations. Organisations are at the heart of the movement because they express its concerns in the most sustained and organised way, speak directly to parties and governments on behalf of women, and are available for consultation on issues concerning them. States find it

convenient to deal with organisations acting as pressure groups that channel demands; hence the emphasis given to them in this book.

Use of the term 'women's movement' should not be taken to imply that
there is agreement among women, let alone among members of the movement, about detail or methods of emancipating women. The Indonesian
women's movement is very diverse and has varied in composition over
the last century. In it are to be found, for instance, religious organisations
like Muslimat NU, the women's wing of the large Islamic organisation
Nahdlatul Ulama (Revival of Religious Scholars), secular organisations
of the wives of civil servants, and small but very dynamic urban groups of
limited size but great expertise like Kalyanamitra, the women's resource
centre in Jakarta. There have been very substantial areas of conflict within
the Indonesian women's movement, particularly between religious and
non-religious elements, but it is still possible to speak of 'a movement'
implying a common effort to improve the situation of Indonesian women.
Identifying which women receive priority at any one time, and how the
movement discerns 'Indonesian womanhood', will constitute one of the
main tasks of subsequent chapters.

Compared to the population of Indonesian women as a whole, the
women's movement, despite its diversity, cannot be regarded as representing the full range of women. Some sections of Indonesian womanhood are
poorly represented, like farm workers, women in remote areas, women
of Chinese ethnicity and disabled or elderly women. The skewed nature
of the Indonesian women's movement is a consequence of the way it has
developed over the years and the constraints upon it and upon the women
outside its ranks. This book makes no claim that any particular women's
organisations nor their combined total can be regarded as speaking on
behalf of all Indonesian women. It merely asserts that organised women
are the voices the state hears and the women it has to contend with. The
state has to make choices, to decide whether or not organised women
represent forces important enough to be consulted, and whose voices to
heed in cases where women's voices conflict. The issues presented by the
women's movement to the state have been those of most burning interest
to the organisations active within it, and they in turn have been dominated
by Javanese middle-class women. How relevant these issues may also be
to other women varies with the subject under discussion, something to
be examined in this book. As the women's movement changes this century, one can expect other interests to be advanced, with the proviso that
organisations tend to be dominated by urban, better-educated people:
such are the strengths and weaknesses of organisations.

The Indonesian women's movement has received little attention from
scholars. Apart from Cora Vreede-de Stuers (1960), whose work focussed

on the colonial period and the 1950s, and Sukanti Suryocondro who gave a largely sociological account of the movement up to the 1980s (Suryochondro 1984) and a briefer analysis in the 1990s (Suryochondro 2000), there are only a few scattered studies which address the subject in a general way: Mangoensarkoro (1946), Kartowijono (1977), Lombard (1977), Suwondo (1981), and Abdullah (1993). Studies have been made of the women's movement at particular periods. Thus a short official publication was issued during the 1930s (De Inheemsche Vrouwenbeweging 1932); there are two studies of the Japanese Occupation (Mangunpuspito 1984; Rachmat-Ishaya 1990); books were commissioned by Indonesian authorities on the role of women in the Revolution (Nurliana, Manus, Ohorella et al. 1986); and Elizabeth Martyn has contributed an excellent thesis on the1950s (Martyn 2001). The women's movement during the New Order has received the most attention, although it is significant that more tends to be written about the impact of state gender ideology than about what women were actually doing (Douglas 1980; Suryakusuma 1987; Andriyani 1994; Lev 1996; Niehof 1998; Robinson 1997; Saptari and Utrecht 1997). Yanti Muchtar (1999) has contributed an insider's analysis of new women's organisations at the end of the New Order, and a short essay has been written about changes since then (Budianta 2001).

Rather than being a study of the women's movement per se, this book deals only with its relations with the state. As a result, sections of the movement that have attempted to stay aloof from the state receive less attention. This includes Islamic women's organisations, most of which have chosen not to engage with the state: they have claimed to be non-political. Obviously it is impossible to be truly non-political and Islamic groups have been influential in many ways, but they have rarely been outspoken on the issues under consideration in this book. That in itself is an interesting political phenomenon contributing to the tendency of devout Muslims to consider they are treated as a minority in the largest Islamic country in the world (Wertheim 1986). Muslim organisations have long been suspicious of the state in Indonesia, regarding the colonial state as heathen, and the Republican state as likely to coopt or damage them. Autonomy has its advantages for women's groups: it fosters an independent spirit and creates a sphere where women are more free to develop their own ideas. At least that is the theory: as far as Muslim groups are concerned women are often subject to control from male-led Islamic organisations. One consequence has been that for much of the time Islamic women have taken a back seat in the women's movement to the more publicly articulate and demanding secular women's organisations.

In characterising women's organisations, one inevitably encounters the vexed question of feminism. Whether or not the term should be attributed to particular groups or individuals is complicated by distinctions between self-definition and external labelling. Most Indonesians (like many other Asians) avoid the term feminism because of its Western connotations and history. The heavy influences of nationalism, Islam and New Order ideology have all worked to create difficulties for people who use or accept the feminist label. It was common during colonial times for members of the women's movement to deny that they espoused feminism, which they considered a Western phenomenon advocating competition with men, whereas Indonesian women's organisations were described as working with men for national independence. Within the Islamic movement, too, feminism has generally been regarded as a misconceived Western notion. The New Order dismissed feminism along with liberalism and other 'isms' as subversive and irrelevant to Indonesian culture, making it difficult for people to embrace the term. In recent times Indonesian women activists, particularly those with connections to the international women's movement, have been less reluctant to identify as feminists. Avoiding too much identification with Western variants, I apply the term feminism to ideas or people demonstrating a commitment to the elimination or alleviation of discrimination against women.

If the women's movement in Indonesia is so diverse, how is it possible to say that its followers are united in upholding 'the women's cause' of eliminating discrimination? Can an organisation of midwives, or of women studying the Koran, or a women's sporting group be said to be feminist or in any way part of a movement for a 'cause'? In this book I take a wide view of 'the women's cause', as wide as is taken in Indonesia where there has been little hesitation in regarding women's organisations as united under the banner of improving the lot of Indonesian women. Improvement may occur in many ways. Thus the three women's groups mentioned above, whatever their complete range of activities, may well wish to lower maternal mortality rates, to promote women's education and to improve women's access to sporting facilities. Nevertheless, there are clearly differences between these organisations and those more overtly aiming to fight discrimination against women. It is necessary to classify women's organisations in various ways to understand what unites and divides them.

One such classification is Maxine Molyneux' (2001) distinction between organisations that pursue women's 'practical' as opposed to 'strategic' gender interests. 'Practical' gender interests include the requirements of women to fulfil their gender roles as determined in any particular place or time, without challenging the gender status quo. Thus, in order to be good wives and mothers according to prevailing gender ideology, women may consider they need better health facilities for infants, or better domestic science education in schools. Some women's organisations may pursue these needs. Other groups may wish to challenge the dominant gender ideology in various ways, such as by demanding women's right to vote or to abortion, all in the name of eliminating the subordination of women. It is the latter group, those pursuing women's 'strategic' gender interests, that is commonly labelled as feminist because of its analysis of discrimination against women and of women's rights.

However, as Saskia Wieringa (2002) and others have noted, it is difficult to divide women's organisations according to whether they pursue either practical or strategic gender interests. Most organisations are concerned with both kinds of needs, and the mix will vary from time to time. Thus, as Wieringa argues, one of Indonesia's most radical women's organisations, the socialist Gerakan Wanita Indonesia (Indonesian Women's Movement – Gerwani), won much of its enormous support through activities to improve the daily lives of women, such as setting up child-care facilities. Although the distinction proposed by Molyneux may not precisely fit Indonesian organisations, it is a useful one to bear in mind when considering the kinds of 'women's issues' that will be discussed in the following chapters.

In her analysis of Indonesian women's organisations, Sukanti Suryocondro (Suryochondro 1984) distinguishes between them according to their membership: general, religious, wives of state officials, aristocrats, youth, professionals, students, regional and so on. She also considers it relevant to mention whether the organisation is affiliated or connected to a party, government department or other organisation (e.g. a women's wing of an Islamic association). These distinctions are significant when comparing the membership of the women's movement in different periods, and I will employ them in my historical section below.

For the purposes of this book I find the following categories useful. The distinction between *religious* (particularly Islamic) and *non-religious* is significant in understanding the activities and platforms of organisations, as alluded to above. As far as claims to representation are concerned, it is relevant to distinguish organisations that are *membership* based from those which are not. Membership-based organisations seek members from amongst the group they claim to represent, for example midwives or Christian women. Other organisations formed by a small group of people accountable only to themselves always have more difficulty in being accepted as representing anyone, and may well have problems even in relating to those whom they aim to assist, such as poor women. In political terms they are more easily dismissed by unsympathetic power-holders. The *class* basis of organisations is obviously a related issue here. Labelling organisations according to class helps in understanding their activities and achievements and serves to remind us of possible limitations placed on an organisation in claiming to speak for all women. Another and connected distinction is the *geographic* one of observing differences between urban and rural organisations and between organisations based on particular regions in Indonesia. Most women's organisations in the twentieth century were urban-based and Javanese, yet it is often forgotten what a difference this made to their ability to speak for all Indonesian women. These are some of the distinctions among organisations which will be referred to in this book and which are also relevant in understanding the interaction between the women's movement and the state.

As an aside, it is worth mentioning that there are few good studies of individual Indonesian women's organisations. The best and most comprehensive is Saskia Wieringa's book on Gerwani (Wieringa 2002). She has also made some illuminating comparisons between Gerwani and the New Order Government's creation, the Pembinaan Kesejahteraan Keluarga (Family Guidance Movement – PKK) (Wieringa 1992). Because of their mass membership aimed at mobilising ordinary women for change (political change in the case of Gerwani, 'development' in the case of the PKK), there are some interesting similarities between these two otherwise very different organisations. In many ways they had more in common with one another than with other women's organisations that have had more restricted membership and goals. PKK itself, and another large women's organisation created by the New Order, Dharma Wanita (Women's Service, for wives of civil servants), have been the subject of a number of studies, but none has attempted to review these organisations in their entirety (Bianpoen 2000; Buchori and Soenarto, 2000). Unfortunately, too, there are only fragments of studies of religious women's organisations, which have always been among the largest and oldest in the women's movement. A few brief histories of Christian women's organisations have been written (Manoppo-Watupongoh 1991; Poerwandari 2000). Some Islamic groups have published their own histories ('Aisjijah 1939; Madjelis Departement Pergerakan Isteri PSII 1940; Ma'shum and Sawawi 1996; Sejarah Muslimat 1979), and some essays have been written about them (Baidlowi 1993; Istiadah 1995; Marcocs-Natsir 2000; Marcoes 2002; Rahman 2000). Studies of women's organisations that ceased to exist after independence are even scarcer (Liem 1936; Schultz-Metzer 1936; Hamdani 1984). Much work remains to be done on regionally based women's organisations. Very few Indonesian women have attempted to give an inside view of organisational life; an exception is Andriyani (1996).

One of the central concerns of this book is to understand what have been considered 'women's issues' by both the state and the women's movement in the course of the twentieth century. The term is used here to refer to the issues that women's organisations and the state have considered important in relation to Indonesian women. Not all issues relating to gender are covered by this category, and a large part of the interest of this study is in analysing why some issues are regarded as 'women's issues' and others are not. Thus some actions of the state may be highly significant in affecting the construction of gender in Indonesia, but not seen in that light by Indonesian women (or indeed by the state). For instance, economic policies may bring about the rise of manufacturing employment for women, with important but unintended consequences for gender relations in some areas. I will explore the relationship between the way in which state policies affect gender relations and the ways in which the women's movement responds (or fails to respond) to such changes, as well as the way in which women have deliberately tried to influence state policies on gender.

The rest of this chapter sets out a brief historical overview of the relationship between state gender ideology and the Indonesian women's movement. The intention is to provide background for the thematic chapters that follow.

State gender discourse and its relationship to the growth of the women's movement

The colonial period, 1900–42

The adoption by the Dutch colonial government of the Ethical Policy in 1901 had important gender consequences in the Netherlands Indies. The Dutch took measures in the early twentieth century to promote girls' schooling and to protect women, measures that were, however, always limited by the lack of resources devoted to implementing them and conflicting interests faced by the authorities. Scrutiny of colonial policy by the Dutch parliament, especially after Dutch women gained the vote in 1919, meant that colonial policy had to take account of Dutch sensibilities about women's issues, but at the same time the colonial authorities naturally had to consider financial implications and the need to promote Dutch economic interests in the colony. Anne Stoler (1995) has drawn attention to the colonial bourgeois preoccupation with sexual morality, especially as the size of the European population in the Indies grew from the late nineteenth century onwards. International influences had also to be considered: the prestige of the Dutch as colonial rulers was at stake, and after the First World War scrutiny began to be applied by international institutions connected to the League of Nations. Special concerns for the Dutch authorities in relation to gender were the education of girls, intermarriage between Europeans and 'natives' and the upbringing of their offspring, and prostitution associated with the army. As Elsbeth Locher-Scholten (2000) has shown, most policies were compromised by the need to take economic interests into account.

The influence of colonial gender ideology on the rise of the Indonesian women's movement is palpable. Western education assisted women to speak out publicly, expressing their perceptions of women's needs. At first their views were very much in line with those spread by the Ethical Policy. The best-known exponent of early aspirations of 'modern' educated Indonesian women was Raden Ajeng Kartini (1879–1904), the daughter of a high-ranking Javanese *priyayi* (aristocrat). Kartini chafed against the restrictions facing upper-class girls and wanted to pursue her schooling beyond the elementary level her parents deemed suitable, since girls were destined to be married off in their teenage years. Although Kartini herself died young, the posthumous publication in 1911 of her letters to sympathetic Dutch friends (Kartini 1911) marked an important step in the recognition of Javanese women's feelings and needs. Kartini admired what she saw as emancipated European women and hoped that the Dutch education would spread ideas of women's emancipation.

As a young woman inspired by a Western education, Kartini was not unique. In the 1910s many such educated young women emerged in different parts of Indonesia to form and join modern women's organisations, mostly of a social nature but also engaged in welfare work and religious activities. Because their founders and members were educated young women, the organisations were limited to regions where modern education had taken strongest hold, notably in northern Sulawesi, and parts of Java and Sumatra. The first known women's organisation was Putri Mardika (Free Women), founded in Java in 1912 with the help of a male-led organisation, Budi Utomo (Noble Endeavour). Like most such groups, it was quite short-lived, but it did publish its own magazine of the same name for a few years. These early women's publications are a valuable source of insight into the thinking of Indonesian women (Salmon 1977). An organisation that has lasted since its creation in 1917 is Aisyiyah, named after one of the Prophet's wives and created in Yogyakarta as the women's wing of the large modernist Islamic movement, Muhammadiyah.

Not until the 1920s did some of these organisations come together in a coordinated way. What united them was as much nationalism as common identification as women. In 1928 a number of women's organisations cooperated to stage a national congress in Yogyakarta that led to the formation of a national women's federation. Lasting until the Japanese

Occupation in 1942, its members comprised religious and secular women's organisations that, although not overtly political, were sympathetic to the nationalist cause and saw themselves as part of the Indonesian nation. The federation's main expressed concerns were to promote the education of girls and improve women's legal position, including in marriage. At regular conferences, convenors struggled to maintain unity between organisations that differed, for instance, in their attitude towards polygamy, which Islamic associations refused to condemn. The more radical Istri Sedar (Aware Women) left the federation over this issue. It was a time, too, when political parties and major male-led religious organisations began to form women's wings that often engaged with other women's groups either in cooperation or controversy.

The nationalist orientation of the Indonesian women's movement excluded women deemed to be 'alien'. These included organisations of Eurasian and Chinese women, most of whom were born in the colony (Liem 1936; Schultz-Metzer 1936). Such women could only hope to be part of the nation if they abandoned their 'foreign' identities and identified as Indonesian. As a result, organisations specifically for such 'foreign' women played no role in the women's movement, before or after independence.

Although increasingly the women's movement identified with nationalism, a closer look at member organisations reveals quite strongly entrenched Western bourgeois notions of femininity, sometimes complementing pre-existing notions of gender (such as those of the Javanese *priyayi*) and sometimes coexisting uneasily with Islamic views or those derived from custom. Their publications project an idealised version of Indonesian womanhood, influenced by modernist Islam and Western middle-class modernity, that had little basis in the lives of most Indonesian women (Hatley and Blackburn 2000).

If the concern of most women's organisations to appear 'modern' could be attributed to colonialism, colonial policy could also be held partly responsible for the difficulty of women's organisations in reaching out to rural and poor women. By the late 1920s the colonial rulers had become very wary of any such trends on the part of nationalist-inclined groups, and police harassment deterred many women from trying to engage in anything that the Dutch might consider radical. The women's movement in the colonial period was limited to a very thin layer of largely urban, Western-educated, more prosperous women. Prominent leaders to emerge in these years included Suwarni Pringgodigdo and Maria Ullfah Santoso.

To give some notion of the composition and size of the organised women's movement at this time, it is useful to refer to a survey of the Indonesian women's movement by the Sundanese women's leader, Emma Puradireja, in early 1939 (Poeradiredja 1939). She divided the movement into two groups of organisations, those based on religion and those based on religiously neutral, nationalist principles. The former, drawing on well-established beliefs, reached a larger number of women, down to the village level, whereas the latter appealed mainly to urban, better-educated women. The largest of the religious type, she stated, were Aisyiyah (estimated to have 12,000 members), Pergerakan Perempuan Partai Sarekat Islam Indonesia (Women's Movement of the Party of Indonesian Islamic Union) (6,500) and Puteri Islam Makassar (Islamic Women of Makassar) (7,500). The first two were women's auxiliaries of male organisations. Of the non-religious organisations, the largest were Pasundan Istri (Pasundan Women) (1,250), Istri Sedar (600) and Istri Indonesia (Indonesian Women) (500 members). In addition there were hundreds of small organisations with up to about five hundred members each. Emma Puradireja's estimates reveal the small size of the women's movement and the fact that the largest organisations were those best able to reach a wide base through the infrastructure of religion.

The Japanese Occupation, 1942–1945

The Japanese, who defeated the Dutch and occupied Indonesia during the Pacific War, had definite views about gender that were exaggerated by the military character of the regime. Men had to join the defence forces and work for the war effort by providing labour and producing goods, while women were obliged to support their menfolk and, in the case of some younger women, serve the military as prostitutes.

During the Occupation, the Indonesian women's movement was totally dominated by the Japanese armed forces, which divided up the archipelago into three separate military administrations. Independent organisations were suppressed and women were drafted into movements intended to harness women to support the war effort. In Java and Bali the women's organisation was called Fujinkai and its president was a well-known women's movement leader, Sukaptinah Sunarjo Mangunpuspito. In Sumatra it was named Hahanokai and was led by Rasuna Said and Ratna Sari, former leaders of an Islamic organisation, Permi (Kahin 1999: 102). A number of writers have pointed to the way in which the Fujinkai was a forerunner of the 'wives' organisations' that formed the backbone of the official women's movement under the New Order. Based on an organisation in Japan, the Fujinkai saw women primarily as wives and mothers who should offer loyal support to their husbands, and the structure of the organisation paralleled that of the civil administration, with officials' wives taking leadership positions. The activities of the women's organisations created by the Japanese centred around nationalism and contributing to the economy. Younger women were expected to contribute to defence by joining the Barisan Srikandi (Srikandi Brigade) where they learnt about first-aid, self-defence and food preparation for the volunteer army.[2]

During the Japanese Occupation women were unable to make any demands on the state or to organise independently. In retrospect, however, it is clear that this was an important period for mobilising women into the nationalist movement and the formal workforce, and for providing a model for the state-dominated women's movement that re-emerged in the 1960s.

The 'Revolution': the struggle for independence, 1945–1949

On 17 August 1945, in the dying days of Japanese rule, nationalists led by Sukarno declared the independent Republic of Indonesia. In the subsequent period, labelled in Indonesian history the Revolution, the new Republican government struggled to impose control over the archipelago but had to confront the Dutch, who quickly returned to reclaim their colony. For many Indonesians, this was an era of contending governments, as the Republican and colonial states vied for control of territory and population. Although the Republic was weak, it had a clear, democratic and egalitarian stance on gender, as was manifested by a number of decrees and in the 1945 Constitution, which proclaimed all citizens were equal before the law. The nationalists who gained control of the Republican state apparatus in October 1945 were largely democrats and socialists strongly influenced by the West. The shaky coalition governments of these years contained the country's first female ministers, Maria Ullfah Santoso, Minister of Social Affairs, and S. K. Trimurti, Minister of Labour.

As soon as the heavy hand of Japanese control was lifted, independent women's organisations sprang up again, most of them dedicated to supporting the new Republic. One of the most important and enduring of these early new organisations was the non-religious Persatuan Wanita Republik Indonesia (Union of the Women of the Indonesian Republic – Perwari). Another lasting creation of the Revolution period was Muslimat NU, the women's wing of the large traditional Javanese Islamic organisation Nahdlatul Ulama. In 1946 some women's organisations

---

[2] Little has been written about the women's movement during the Japanese Occupation. Sources include Mangunpuspito (1984); Nurliana, Manus, Ohorella et al. (1986); Rachmat-Ishaya (1990); Ohorella, Sutjiatiningsih, Ibrahim et al. (1992).

formed a new nationalist-oriented federation, Kongres Wanita Indonesia (Indonesian Women's Congress – Kowani). In personnel and membership it was a successor to the women's federations of the colonial period. Although it has undergone some changes of membership and minor name revisions, Kowani has survived to the present day as the largest alliance of women's organisations, and as such it has regularly been consulted by governments on issues relating to women.

During the struggle for independence, the efforts of women's organisations focussed on survival of families in very difficult times and on support for the nationalist cause. Some women's fighting units were formed, but the more common activity was providing first-aid and food for soldiers and the Republic's civil service – in many ways a continuation of the activities of the Fujinkai and Hahanokai created during the Japanese Occupation.

Although during the Revolution the state was able to do little on behalf of women, this was a critical period for subsequent relations between the women's movement and the state after the transfer of sovereignty from the Dutch to the Republic was finally made in 1949. The women's movement earned credibility with the state on which it was subsequently able to draw. Principles of equality were laid down, and the fact that the Constitution of 1945 established Indonesia as basically a secular state (albeit with recognition of the importance of religion) was decisive in ruling out the possibility that Islamic *syariah* law would be applied, with all the implications that might have for women.

The democratic state, 1949–1958

After the transfer of sovereignty in 1949, a new constitution was adopted in 1950, giving Indonesia a parliamentary regime, with a figurehead president (Sukarno). The democratic orientation of the early governments of Indonesia meant they had to take account of women, who voted in the first general elections of 1955. The intentions of governments to promote equality were borne out in legislation that included equal pay for civil servants, and the promotion of mass education and adult literacy. Lack of resources, Cabinet instability and pressing national concerns such as regional rebellions meant that the implementation of many well-intentioned policies took a back seat, and on other matters, such as the marriage law, it is clear that the state did not have the will to proceed in the face of Islamic opposition. Probably the greatest contribution of the state in this period was the freedom it gave to women's organisations to establish themselves and participate in activities right down to the village level.

Apart from a general commitment to equality, no particular ideology of gender was imposed or inculcated by the regime, with the consequence that organisations were free to advance their own agendas.

Women's organisations flourished during this period, although their growth was restricted in large areas of the archipelago where education and communications were poor. The most active large organisations in the federation, Kowani, and the most vocal in representing women to the state were Perwari and Gerwani, a more radical organisation founded in 1950 that became closely aligned to the Communist Party, the Partai Komunis Indonesia (Indonesian Communist Party – PKI). Islamic organisations continued to have the largest memberships, but they tended to take a low profile on anything regarded as 'political'. Within Kowani there continued to be friction between religious and secular organisations over matters relating to marriage law.

In the 1955 elections women proved keen to vote but few were elected: 19 out of 271 members of the parliament, about 7 per cent of the total (Martyn 2001: 160). After such a promising start during the Revolution period, there were no more female ministers in the many Cabinets of the 1950s. The women's movement campaigned hard for a marriage law but was largely ignored by the unstable Cabinets of the period of liberal democracy in Indonesia in the 1950s.

Because the state had few resources to offer and exerted little power over them, most women's organisations during this period were not particularly state-oriented. They had their own activities and were very self-reliant, in an era when foreign aid was not available to Indonesian non-government organisations. Their leaders were nationally and sometimes internationally well known as forthright and experienced women. They included Suyatin Kartowiyono, Yetty Rizali Noor and Nani Suwondo of Perwari; Umi Sarjono and S. K. Trimurti of Gerwani; Maria Ullfah Santoso (later Subadio) in Kowani; Mahmudah Mawardi of Muslimat NU; and, outside the main women's organisations, individuals like the journalist Herawati Diah and Supeni of the Partai Nasionalis Indonesia (Indonesian Nationalist Party – PNI).

Since the return of democracy to Indonesia in 1998, this earlier period of freedom holds particular interest for students of the women's movement (Martyn 2001).

Guided Democracy (1958–1965)

The balance between the state and the women's movement changed significantly with the introduction of Guided Democracy in 1958, when

President Sukarno restored the 1945 Constitution that bestowed great power on the President. Up to then merely a figurehead (albeit a very influential one), Sukarno was now in a position to impose his 'revolutionary' ideology on his people. Highly rhetorical, his views were strongly infused with nationalism and anti-imperialism, influenced by Marxism but rejecting the divisive connotations of domestic class warfare. More important were the authoritarian aspects of his rule, which increasingly outlawed opposition, removed critics from official posts, censored newspapers and jailed dissidents.

As far as women were concerned, Sukarno set out his views in the polemical work *Sarinah* (Sukarno 1963). Women were to devote themselves to the nation, and concerns like national unity took precedence over women's issues. During Guided Democracy, there were plenty of occasions for shows of nationalist solidarity as Sukarno led campaigns against the Dutch over their refusal to hand over Papua to the Republic after 1949, and then against Britain and Malaysia in his 'Crush Malaysia' campaign. The President drew women into militant activities, such as drilling for national defence. During Guided Democracy the women's movement fell into line with his agenda, subordinating previous priorities to those of the President. In line with government moves against certain political parties, Kowani banned two Islamic women's organisations associated with those parties, and in its 1964 congress bestowed on the President the title 'Great Leader of the Revolutionary Women's Movement of Indonesia' (Suwondo 1981: 201–2). The president of Kowani during the Guided Democracy years was the forceful Hurustiati Subandrio, the wife of Sukarno's Foreign Minister. Even before the New Order, the movement had lost its independence.

The dominant women's organisation of the Guided Democracy era was Gerwani, which benefited from the favour bestowed by Sukarno on the PKI. During these years its leader was Umi Sarjono, and in 1963 it claimed 1.5 million members (Hindley 1964: 208). However, as Wieringa has shown in her detailed study of Gerwani, that favour came at the price of Gerwani's agenda on women's issues, which it had to subordinate to the President's (and the PKI's) nationalist and anti-imperialist agenda (Wieringa 2002).

As in the following period, during Guided Democracy organised women had little opportunity to voice their concerns to the state, which, in turn, showed little interest in considering their needs. Unlike the New Order period, however, during Guided Democracy the impact of the state on the lives of ordinary women was generally negative, due to the complete neglect of the economy in these years. By the end of the period, the country was deep in crisis.

The New Order, 1965–1998

Much has been written about the gender ideology of the New Order, including by the authorities themselves.[3] The New Order saw women as a significant structural group in society which needed to be brought into line with its search for harmony and development (Douglas 1980).Women should play their part in ensuring social stability, implementing development plans and reducing the birth-rate. In the early years of the regime women were seen solely as housewives and mothers. The term *kodrat*, meaning inherent nature, was frequently on the lips of government spokesmen in relation to women: their *kodrat* destined them to be carers and educators of the younger generation. Expectations by the state of motherly duty reached a new height. Social and political relations centred around images of *ibu* (mother) and *bapak* (father). While both figures were responsible for the welfare of the members of their groups (families, businesses, organisations, etc.), the *bapaks* enjoyed access to power and privilege that were denied to the *ibus* who performed endless practical and necessary tasks without any prospect of reward except through their husbands, in keeping with what Djajadiningrat-Nieuwenhuis (1987) refers to as 'ibuism'. Julia Suryakusuma (1987) has enlarged the notion of ibuism into 'state ibuism', which she considers the defining characteristic of the New Order gender ideology: it involved the propagation by the state of the nuclear family norm in which women conformed to the Western middle-class housewife role and selflessly served their husbands, family and the state. The concepts developed by Djajadiningrat-Nieuwenhuis and Suryakusuma have been widely accepted by commentators on gender in New Order Indonesia. The tensions within the New Order gender ideology, between its traditional and modern elements, and between its bourgeois ideals and the reality of Indonesian women's lives, will feature in the following chapters of this book.

The pinnacle of 'state ibuism' was the phenomenon known as the wives' organisations. As the number and size of such organisations grew, they came to dominate the women's federation, Kowani. The best-known and largest of these wives' organisations was Dharma Wanita (Women's Service), for the wives of civil servants. The activities of Dharma Wanita were linked to the development in the early 1970s of the state-sponsored Family Guidance Movement (Pembinaan Kesejahteraan Keluarga – PKK) which, under the central control of the Minister of Internal Affairs, had branches at every level of society led by the wives of state officials. PKK

---

[3] Although General Suharto did not officially become president until 1967, his regime had de facto control in Indonesia shortly after the so-called 'coup' of 1 October 1965.

was the means by which the state mobilised ordinary women behind its development efforts, obliging them to carry out tasks in a voluntary capacity.

In seeking the rationale for the New Order gender ideology, Dan Lev locates it primarily in the regime's desire for stability: after a period of great upheaval, the definition of women as wives and mothers served to consolidate family life and maintain the traditions that the New Order valued (Lev 1996). Because the family unit was regarded as a foundation stone of the larger 'state family', motherhood conceived in New Order terms was important to the regime. Suzanne Brenner goes further than Lev to argue that it was important for the New Order state not only to maintain stability but also to 'continually reestablish a climate of national crisis, raising fear of unseen danger, impending chaos, that threatens to descend on the nation if stability is not maintained' (Brenner 1999: 35). It was, after all, a state that had come into being in a time of crisis and justified a continuing military presence as necessary for national resilience. Hence the emphasis on the need for mothers to maintain vigilance over family morality and for the state to monitor family life. Official speeches and state-controlled media continually stressed the ideal wife and mother, aware of her *kodrat*, maintaining approved Indonesian traditions, carrying out her assigned development tasks and raising her children as good citizens.

While in many ways a culturally introverted regime, the New Order was nevertheless subject to outside influence on a number of issues, including the position of women. An important innovation of the New Order state, as far as gender is concerned, was its creation of the Ministry for Women's Role, which was first introduced as a junior ministry in 1978 during the International Decade for Women (1975–85). Up until that time there had been no female ministers. Clearly the Ministry represented the regime's answer to international pressure to be seen to take women seriously. Ministers for Women's Role presented the government line in international gatherings like conferences on women as well as in United Nations bodies like UNICEF. The Ministers themselves tended to have a background in Kowani. Although the Ministry was elevated to Cabinet status in 1983, it still lacked a line Department, which meant it had to depend on other departments like Health and Education for the implementation of its policies. A weak ministry, it was heavily criticised by more radical elements in the women's movement who identified it with what they called the *wanita* as opposed to the *perempuan* approach to women. The choice of Indonesian term for woman became an ideological marker, as the New Order consistently used the more 'ladylike' word *wanita* while its critics increasingly favoured the more 'down-to-earth' (and now resurgent) word *perempuan* (Muchtar 1999). The Ministry for Women's Role was, however, a good example of the institutionalisation of international norms. Over time some of its staff became attuned to international rhetoric on women's rights and acted as a 'Trojan horse' within the New Order bureaucracy, introducing new ideas that often conflicted with the rest of state gender ideology (Robinson 1997).

For the Indonesian women's movement, the fall of the Sukarnoist regime had immense consequences. In the anti-communist purge that followed the 'coup' of 1 October 1965, Gerwani was banned and its members arrested. The regime then moved to purge the women's federation and put it under close control. As mentioned above, the so-called wives' organisations took the lead in Kowani. Older organisations like Perwari were greatly weakened because they had depended for their membership on many of the women who were now forced to devote their organisational time exclusively to Dharma Wanita. The official women's movement obediently echoed the prevailing government line, presenting women's role as predominantly that of contributing to national development. Only those of its aims congruent with government policy were allowed to remain in its platform. Thus, for instance, it still campaigned for a marriage law, because that goal was acceptable to Suharto, who granted this wish in 1974 (see Chapter 5).

State gender ideology could not, however, govern the minds of all Indonesian women. The rapid economic growth that occurred during the New Order years gave rise to a cohort of better-educated young women. Some of them took a more independent view of their role in society and wished to raise a number of issues outside the list sanctioned by the government-dominated official women's movement represented by Kowani. Some of these women formed new independent organisations from the 1980s onwards and championed more radical issues such as the rights of women factory workers. They were joined by organisations with a strong human-rights bent (Eldridge 1995).

Unlike most member organisations of Kowani, these groups were not 'membership' organisations but rather what the Indonesians called LSMs (Lembaga Swadaya Masyarakat – Self-reliant Social Institutions). These were 'cause' groups with self-appointed governing bodies consisting of a small group of like-minded individuals. Many of these new groups had human-rights agendas, some of them offering legal assistance to victims of state policies like people evicted from slum sites. For such organisations, seeking a membership base was not the appropriate structure. For others working on behalf of poor people, it was not possible to enlist members among their clients, because the New Order policy referred to as 'floating mass' had depoliticised ('floated') the rural population in order to 'allow them to devote themselves to development', and any groups that tried to organise the people for obviously political goals risked being branded as communist and suppressed. Unlike 'membership' organisations that depended primarily on financial support from their subscribers, LSMs were often recipients of foreign funding, either from international organisations like UNICEF, from Middle-Eastern Islamic sources or from non-government aid organisations (NGOs) like NOVIB or Oxfam. This made them susceptible to government accusations of being foreign-influenced, and indeed the agendas of such LSMs were often oriented to the prevailing priorities of funding sources. However, the situation is more complex, since the leaders of such LSMs were themselves cosmopolitan people often committed to such agendas regardless of funding exigencies.

The new orientation of many LSMs is seen in their preference for talking about rights rather than the duties emphasised by the government. Prominent women's organisations to emerge from the 1980s onwards were the resource centre Kalyanamitra, the legal-rights organisation Lembaga Bantuan Hukum – Asosiasi Perempuan Indonesia untuk Keadilan (Legal Aid Foundation – Indonesian Women's Association for Justice – LBH-APIK), Yayasan Annisa Swasti (Annisa Swasti Foundation – Yasanti), which organised with women workers, the women's crisis centre Rifka Annisa and Solidaritas Perempuan (Women's Solidarity), which campaigned on behalf of women workers. Their leaders, like Sri Kusyuniati, Yanti Muchtar, Nursyahbani Kacasungkana and Ita Nadia began to be well known through the press, which welcomed their articulate and critical voices. (The media too was acquiring feminist journalists like Debra Yatim, Maria Hartiningsih and Julia Suryakusuma.) Not surprisingly, given their origins, these organisations were very Java-centred, although LBH-APIK gradually opened offices on some other islands. Their founders were tertiary-educated young women who were strongly critical of the official women's movement's subordination to the state. Even those like the leaders of Rifka Annisa who were strongly Islamic in orientation spoke the language of the international women's movement (Muchtar 1999).

The older religious membership-based organisations like Aisyiyah and Muslimat NU continued with their religious and social work through their extensive networks in the archipelago. They attempted to maintain their independence of the state by eschewing overtly political stances. The best-known older leader of an Islamic women's organisation at the height of the New Order was Baroreh Baried of Aisyiyah. Over time they too became more influenced by the feminist ideas circulating internationally from the 1980s. Young new leaders emerged from the ranks of the female youth sections of the Islamic organisations, determined to reinterpret religious texts in more woman-friendly ways. By the late twentieth century there were some formidable new spokeswomen of this kind, such as Lies Markus-Natsir and Siti Dzuhayatin. Women's organisations affiliated to NU and Muhammadiyah together claim more than 15 million members, making them far and away the largest organisations of Indonesian women (Marcoes 2002: 192–3).

In addition to the new organisations, the women's movement acquired in the late New Order period a number of intellectual spokeswomen as university education spread. Their rise went along with the opening of Women's Studies programmes at some universities, a development fostered by the Ministry of Women's Role. New voices in these years included the economic demographer Mayling Oey, the sociologists Mely Tan and Yulfita Raharjo and the psychologist Saparinah Sadli. (Significantly, the first two women are of Chinese descent: such women rarely featured in the leadership of organisations where to be identifiably Chinese would be a distinct political disadvantage under the racism prevalent in Indonesia.)

Transition to democracy, 1998–2003

When Suharto resigned in May 1998, the situation again changed dramatically. As in the 1950s, one of the most important contributions of the state to gender ideology at this time of democratisation was just to allow people to organise independently, indicating that the state did not wish to control their activities. Freed from the trammels of New Order ideology, the Ministry for Women's Role became more outspoken, critiquing government policies from the viewpoint of gender equality. The sympathy of the Wahid government (1999–2001) with gender issues was indicated by the appointment of the strongly feminist (and Islamic) minister Khofifah Indar Parawansa, who changed the name of the ministry to Ministry for Women's Empowerment. It was also highly significant that at the same time the Family Planning Coordination Board was moved into her Ministry (Parawansa 2002).

The fall of the New Order in 1998 saw the mushrooming of new women's organisations, notably in regions of the country where few had existed before. It was clear that the women's movement had outgrown Kowani, whose leaders acknowledged that much had changed. Without the backing of state sponsorship and power, Dharma Wanita and PKK have had to adapt to a world in which gender ideology has changed and the basis for their membership has become purely voluntary. This is a great boon for other groups that had felt constrained by the official women's movement. In December 1998 the Women's Coalition for Justice and Democracy, a new alliance, organised a women's national congress that recognised the different concerns and greater decentralisation of the women's movement in the post-New Order phase (Bianpoen 1998).

In the new era, women who took a more independent, feminist line in the last years of the New Order became even more prominent as governments conferred official positions upon them, and new opportunities for advocacy emerged. Those who gained prominence as activists for the first time in very recent years include the political scientist Chusnul Mar'iyah, her profession being a sign of the times.

Indonesia is undergoing a turbulent transition. Women's organisations have played an important role in many new developments including conducting voter education and campaigning against rising violence in the country. Both the Habibie and Wahid governments in 1998–2000 demonstrated considerable respect for the women's movement, as shown by Habibie's creation of the National Commission Against Violence Towards Women, headed by Saparinah Sadli, and Wahid's appointment of Khofifah Indar Parawansa to head the Ministry for Women's Empowerment. Nevertheless, the number of women in parliament actually fell in the 1999 elections, indicating that women had little pull within the political party system.[4] Nor did political parties show much interest in women's issues, and the first woman president, Megawati Sukarnoputri, inaugurated in 2001, herself shows little awareness or concern about the situation of women in her country. The women's movement still has a long way to go to gain influence over the political process. For one thing, it is hard for it to create a political constituency when it has had little experience in building a politically aware membership base. Failing to use its own members to act as an independent means of social influence, it is still too dependent on the state, which in turn is weak and preoccupied with matters other than the concerns of the women's movement.

Conclusion

Indonesia in the twentieth century alternated between periods of stability and turmoil. Turbulent periods are important in providing new opportunities for women in ways that can be capitalised on later in political terms: women learned new skills and were seen in different roles in times like the Japanese Occupation and the Revolution. Upheaval may also bring to the fore issues that were concealed in quieter times, like the grievances of

---

[4] Following the 1999 election, only 9 per cent of the parliament members were women, compared with a peak of 13 per cent under the New Order (*Jakarta Post* 10 March 2003).

people in neglected regions. Times of stability offer the best chance for careful policy-making and implementation, but whether or not women can utilise these opportunities may depend heavily on state gender ideology and on the strength of the women's movement itself.

In the twentieth century there is plenty of evidence of the impact of state gender ideology on the women's movement in Indonesia. When that ideology is restrictive, it becomes more difficult for women to form organisations and recruit members freely. Under the New Order the suppression of Gerwani ended for some decades the possibility of recruiting poor women into political organisations. At certain times, most notably during the Japanese Occupation, state control over the movement has been extreme. The state has also sought to influence the agenda of women's organisations, one of the most obvious examples being the New Order's imposition of 'the role of women in development' and in particular its mobilisation of women behind the Family Planning Programme.

On the other hand, it is harder to discern the influence of the women's movement on the state. While the state has been relatively independent of pressure from women's organisations, it has been far more responsive to other forces, in particular the Islamic movement which has frequently been at cross-purposes with the women's movement. Some significant changes, such as the introduction of the Minister for Women's Role during the New Order, have resulted from international rather than domestic pressure.

In the chapters that follow, gender issues of concern to either or both the women's movement and the state will be examined to determine more precisely the influence of state gender ideology, and the conditions under which women's organisations have succeeded in attracting state attention to their concerns. A further question will be to what extent state intervention or assistance is efficacious in producing the kinds of changes desired by the women's movement.

How effective the women's movement itself has been in improving the situation of Indonesian women is another question raised at several points in this book. The women's movement has been through a number of cycles and generations. During the colonial period, women's organisations, as a 'modern' phenomenon, attracted young, relatively well-educated women. Few such organisations survived suppression by the Japanese. While religious organisations have shown great staying power, others, like Perwari, seem to have a fixed lifespan as their members age. Groups associated with the officially approved New Order women's movement are seen to belong to the older generation and may not long outlive the collapse of their sponsor. While new organisations and leaders help revive the women's movement, lessons learnt by the older generation may well be forgotten, particularly when the state has attempted to repress memories. Fortunately some individuals, like Saparinah Sadli and Herawati Diah at the end of the century, soldier on to bridge the generations. As the following chapters will show, there has been no shortage of committed talent in the Indonesian women's movement.

2   Education

From Kartini on, Indonesian women have regarded education as basic to their advancement. The first area of public policy in which Indonesian women openly engaged with governments was the education of girls. It was and continues to be a matter of mutual interest. The main areas of contention have been the kind and amount of education that the state should fund for girls and the outcomes to be expected from it. While arguing over these matters, protagonists reveal their assumptions about gender relations. This chapter examines the nature of the debate, which was at its most prominent and heartfelt early in the century. The education issue was closely related to a number of other concerns of women, which are the subject of later chapters in this book, such as marriage, motherhood and employment. Later in the century, while access to schooling remained a prominent issue in the public arena, the ways in which education might influence the construction of gender received little attention, for reasons that will be discussed.

Education is a broad term. This chapter will focus on one section of it: schooling, in which the modern state has played a prominent role as provider. Before colonial rule, Indonesian girls were of course educated informally, supervised by parents who wanted them to be properly prepared for their role in the workforce and/or married life. Girls were, after all, married early, as the next chapter will discuss. Although schools existed, they were intended for boys, and it was rare indeed for girls to attend them. Most were managed by religious groups, to train boys in the reading of sacred texts, since religions were led by men (Reid 1988). This was to change with the establishment of Dutch colonial rule in the Indies.

Schooling serves many purposes. For the modern state, it must help build a suitable labour force and a stable, governable but flexible society. Nationalist movements opposing colonialism wanted schooling to promote commitment to national unity and independence and help mould skilled citizens capable of constructing a strong modern society. For individuals, education is variously a meal ticket, a socialising influence, an entrée to a wider cultural and intellectual heritage, a form of child care, a means of escape from economic and social constraints, and the locus of many other hopes and desires. What is interesting from the point of view of the construction of gender is the different purposes which education is expected to serve for men and women. In Indonesia, as in many other developing countries this century, the emphasis on schooling for boys has been on economic and political outcomes, both for themselves and for society, while for girls schooling has been legitimised more by reference to social and cultural outcomes. Anxiety about the education of girls revolves around their perceived responsibilities for maintaining tradition and raising the next generation. In other words, assumptions about the sexual division of labour are basic to views about educational change. Men are expected to provide the backbone of the formal workforce and public political life, while women's contribution in these areas is subsidiary and incidental to their primary role as housewives and mothers.

Feminists frequently support the education of girls because of its potential to confer greater autonomy on them, that is to empower them by providing access to employment and to knowledge of the world, boosting their self-confidence and assertiveness in dealing with others, and improving their capacity to communicate with others and thus possibly influence them. In this chapter a crucial question will be the extent to which Indonesians believed that emancipation was a goal of the education of girls. There is no logical reason why the state might not join with women in considering this as important: it is a matter for investigation.

The focus here is on the colonial period in Indonesia, because the foundations of later discourse were laid in the earlier part of this century. Modern education was a colonial import. During the colonial period in Indonesia as elsewhere, educational infrastructure was assembled, in people's minds as much as in school buildings, and proved to be as lasting as the railway system that was another legacy of colonialism. This is not to say that colonial views were simply perpetuated, for during this period the nationalist response also emerged: the origins of a nationalist education system also go back to colonial times. But the pioneers of nationalist education, being themselves in part the product of Western education, necessarily entrenched some aspects of that system. The question examined here is how the recipients and administrators of education systems envisaged gender construction, with emphasis on the earlier, formative period.

Of course, it is not possible to discuss gender in isolation from other important variables in the construction of identity, like class and ethnicity. In the colonial period the focus of the education debate was on the wealthier section of Indonesian society, since neither resources nor political will were available to extend schooling to the majority of the population in the countryside. The class and ethnic origins of early modern education have been of lasting importance for gender construction. Although Western schooling was initially more advanced in north Sulawesi because of the Christian missionary effort there, it was the more densely populated Java, and to some extent also Sumatra, which proved the focus of the debate about public schooling for girls, a debate which came to reflect an amalgam of Western bourgeois and Javanese *priyayi* values. Those values, and their implications for gender, have had a lasting effect on schooling for girls. Religion has been less important than class in influencing the discourse about the state's role in the education of women, because the state has taken responsibility only for secular education; religious groups have had their own education systems that have had varying degrees of support from the state. Since this book focusses on women and the state, this chapter will not consider religious education, which deserves a book in itself.

The Ethical Policy opens up state schools for girls

Modern-style schooling, providing secular instruction, did not really begin until the nineteenth century when the Dutch, having occupied most of the archipelago, introduced schools primarily to train men for colonial administration. The government funded a few schools in urban areas, mostly in Java, the main centre of population, teaching in Dutch and in Malay, the lingua franca of the archipelago. Institutions were also opened to train doctors, midwives and nurses. In addition Western education was offered in some private schools, including those established by missions. Most children attending these modern schools were from European or Eurasian families, who wanted their children educated in the Dutch fashion. Few Indonesian parents desired to send their daughters to school, considering the cost, traditional objections to the mixing of the sexes and the lack of employment opportunities for educated women. At the end of the nineteenth century there were only about 15,000 Indonesian girls in Western-style schools, about one-sixth of the total number of Indonesian pupils, in a population of some 30 million people at that time (Bemmelen 1982: 27).

The real expansion of modern education dates from the early twentieth century, promoted by the official adoption of the so-called Ethical Policy in 1901, whereby the Dutch recognised an obligation to improve the standard of living of their colonial subjects. The number and range of government-funded schools were greatly increased, although they still offered education to only a small minority of the population: the

main beneficiaries remained Europeans. The introduction of vernacular language schools for Chinese and Malay-speaking children, however,
expanded access at least to primary schooling. Under the influence of
Western education, Islamic schools too were being transformed during
the early twentieth century to take on more secular teaching like basic
mathematics and literacy in non-Arabic languages like Malay.

During the early decades of the twentieth century the state school system consisted of schools based on the Netherlands curriculum intended
primarily for European children, separate schools using the Dutch
medium for Chinese and 'Native' children, vernacular schools (teaching in, e.g., Malay, Balinese or Javanese) for village children and linkage
schools to enable Indonesian children to learn Dutch in preparation for
attending secondary schools and tertiary institutions where all teaching was in that language. The colonial system of formal education was
thus highly fragmented and not well articulated, so that it was difficult
for a child who attended a village school, where the teaching medium
was the vernacular, to access higher levels of education. Little advanced
education was available and a few hundred Indonesians, including some
women, attended universities in the Netherlands.

A major influence in colonial education policy at the beginning of the
century was J. H. Abendanon, the colonial Director of Education. Both he
and his wife, Rosa Abendanon, befriended the young aristocratic Javanese
woman Raden Ajeng Kartini, whose educational ambitions they encouraged. Kartini's father, the regent (highest rank among the *priyayi*) in
Japara, was unusual for his times in allowing his daughters to attend
Dutch elementary schools. However, when they reached puberty they
were confined within the house as was the custom in *priyayi* families
in the period leading up to early marriage – an insurance policy for the
virginity of the bride. Kartini pleaded with her parents to allow her to continue her schooling and wrote impassioned letters about it to her Dutch
friends. She is considered to have made out the most eloquent case for
the education of Javanese girls.

In 1903 Kartini privately memorialised the Dutch Government in
support of the education of the Javanese (Kartini 1974). Although not
arguing purely for girls' schooling, much of her proposal concerned this
cause. Tactically she saw the need to start with the education of 'the
daughters of the nobility'. The argument for educating them was primarily along moral lines, resting on their potentially civilising influence
as wives and mothers. Although in her personal correspondence with
Dutch friends Kartini argued the need for women to be educated for
reasons of autonomy, she was apparently not prepared to put that view
publicly.

The posthumous publication of Kartini's letters by Dutch friends in 1911 (Kartini 1911) served to fuel the campaign for girls' schooling. Since Kartini was seen by the protagonists of the Ethical Policy as a prime example of the kind of Javanese they wished to promote, she represents a fusion of the views of both educated Indonesian girls and elements within the colonial state.

As Director of Education in the Indies at the time, Abendanon championed the cause of the education of girls, but he had no success in convincing his superiors of the need to devote resources for this purpose (Wal 1963). Only a few Christian mission schools in Minahasa succeeded in attracting girls in considerable numbers. In order to fulfil Kartini's mission, Dutch friends moved privately to set up the so-called Kartini schools for Javanese girls from 1913 onwards.

Debates of the 1910s

Kartini's well-known trumpet call on behalf of Javanese women starts the twentieth-century gender discourse off on a high note. What happened in the world of girls' education in the following decades has received little attention, thus missing the excitement of these years. The second decade of this century in the Dutch East Indies was a period of social and political ferment, when many Indonesians were exploring new ideas, challenging old ones and dreaming of new futures. It is a period that has been examined by authors like Takashi Shiraishi (1990), who has given loving attention to the detail of turbulence among the intellectuals and political activists of Java. However, his account has entirely missed the equally passionate spirit that pervaded many women's circles at the same time. From the point of view of women, it was also an 'age in movement' as Shiraishi put it, and the main force at work was the same: Western schooling and contact with foreign ideas and ways of organising.

By the 1910s a growing contingent of Indonesian women had received schooling, although admittedly they still constituted only a tiny minority of the population. But like the men about whom Shiraishi wrote, they were pioneers, a remarkable collection of individuals. At this time the case still needed to be argued for educating girls, and educated young women played a prominent part in that public debate.

The right of girls to education is now so widely accepted that it is hard to recapture the subversive potential of its defence earlier this century, although it would help to remember that the battle is still being fought in some countries like Afghanistan, Pakistan and Bangladesh. Colonial supporters of education for girls did indeed regard it as radical in the Indonesian context, but just as we know now that Western education in the Indies created the largely unintended consequence of nationalism among its recipients, so it seems the European proponents of schooling for girls did not foresee its full consequences. Their words and actions had quite different reverberations in the Indies than they did back in Europe, giving rise to uncertainties, contradictions and conflicts, as well as emancipatory implications for many women of that time.

Part of the interest of this period, apart from its engaging freshness, its feel of a new wind blowing, is as a counterpoint to later periods of education of girls. It is hardly surprising that education at the turn of the century produced a Kartini – in fact far more than one Kartini. From the history of the education of women we expect it to be liberating, to shake old notions of the construction of gender. What is perhaps more surprising is that so few years of schooling could have such far-reaching effects. In Indonesia today schooling is almost universal at the elementary level, and although higher education is enjoyed by only a small minority, there is no great distinction between the access of men and women (Oey-Gardiner 1992). But few would argue that education in Indonesia now has the power to galvanise its beneficiaries into new thought and action in the way it did for a significant, tiny minority in the early part of the last century. Some would blame this on the New Order's vice-like hold over the education system, but the process can be traced further back in time, particularly as far as gender construction is concerned, to the period of the rise of nationalist education from the 1920s onwards.

The 1910s was a period when the Indonesian world of ideas was broken open by modern education, a time when almost everything was up for challenge, including the construction of womanhood. Although many Dutch people had firm notions of how they wished Indonesian society to be restructured, their views were not universally accepted by Indonesians and even those foreign ideas that were adopted often served as irritants in the situation where they were newly implanted. In this turbulent environment, Indonesian women also had a role to play in the search for new structures, new trajectories – as reflected in the debates of the time about education.

Declining Welfare Commission, 1914

Whereas Abendanon had been told by his superiors at the start of the century that Indonesians showed little interest in sending their daughters to school, by the 1910s everyone involved acknowledged that the situation had changed significantly. The number of girls attending government schools, although still minuscule in proportion to the population, was rising.[1] Apart from the private Kartini schools established by the Dutch, a number of Indonesians had also begun setting up their own separate schools for girls. The best-known of these were women: Dewi Sartika founded schools in West Java, while Rohana Kudus and Rahmah El Yunusiyyah worked in West Sumatra.

However, at the start of the decade the government still did not give financial support to schools for girls, expecting instead that girls would attend mixed schools, despite evidence that parents in most regions were opposed to coeducation. Nor did most parents, even in higher ranks in society, generally send their daughters to school. During the 1910s, therefore, the proponents of education for Indonesian girls had to put up a strong fight, which they did in numerous public forums. The first of these was the Commission Enquiring into Declining Welfare in Java and Madura (Mindere Welvaart Commissie – Declining Welfare Commission). It met over a number of years and published several volumes of its findings, including one in 1914 on the position of women (Netherlands Indies Government 1914). The Commission took evidence from many people, including written submissions from several Indonesian women.

Most of the women's submissions put great emphasis on the need to educate girls, resting their arguments on similar premises although there was considerable variation in the way these arguments were worded, largely reflecting class differences among the women. Three submissions came from women belonging to the royal houses of central Java, the so-called Principalities of Yogyakarta and Surakarta.[2] All three recognised that the purposes of educating girls of different classes must differ. Vocational education, although relevant for girls of lower classes who might be expected to earn their own income (for instance as teacher, doctor, nurse, typist or clerk), was not so important for wives of the nobility whose lives were restricted. These women appeared to envy the greater freedom of the lower classes and to hope that increasingly women would be able to support themselves. In the meantime, even if women chose marriage as their main goal, schooling could help prepare them for that task.

Priyayi woman contributors of lower rank were more outspoken in some respects, but in other ways they echoed Dutch-middle class views

[1] In 1909 only 3,097 girls attended village schools provided by the government; by 1914 that number had risen to 19,455 and in 1919 to 36,649 (Bemmelen 1982: 185).
[2] Raden Ayu Ario Surio Sugianto (daughter of Pangeran Gondo Sewojo from the Mangku Negoro House and married to a son of Mangku Negoro V), Raden Ajeng Karlinah (daughter of Pangeran Notodirodjo of Yogyakarta) and Raden Ajeng Amirati (daughter of Pangeran Ario Paku Alam VI).

of the period and clearly addressed themselves to the needs of that minority of women in their own social sphere. For instance, Raden Ayu Surio Hadikusumo, a sister of Kartini, argued that girls should be prepared at school 'to become competent in an occupation by means of which they can later become financially independent' *or* to learn how to be a good housewife, able to raise children, look after the health of the family and be 'a life-companion of an educated and civilised man'. However, as might be expected of a sister of Kartini, she did not lose the opportunity to criticise the 'social evils' which she believed that education of girls would help eliminate: child marriage and polygamy. She argued that educated girls would find themselves able to resist these pressures both because a 'financially independent' woman would not be pressured by her family to marry against her will, and because schooling would teach a woman to value herself, to 'learn that she is not an object but a person just as a man is, with the right to live' (Netherlands Indies Government 1914: Bijdrage van RA Soerio Hadikoesoema). The submissions of Raden Ajeng Martini and of Umi Kalsum echoed these sentiments. Compared with Kartini's 1903 submission, these women felt less constrained in arguing the autonomy case for the education of girls.

But the most interesting and forthright views were expressed by the three women who had carved out independent lives for themselves: Jarisah, a midwife from Bandung, Raden Dewi Sartika, head of a girls' school in Bandung, and Raden Ayu Siti Sundari, editor of a Javanese women's journal.

Jarisah made a strong argument for women to acquire the knowledge that was essential to their future lives. Women would need to learn to speak in public, because 'it is an inescapable fact that the ideas of men and women differ in many respects'. She pointed to a recent meeting of the social welfare organisation Maju Kemuliaan (Noble Advancement), where women repeatedly expressed their craving for knowledge 'so as no longer to be fooled by men about things which we women *can* and *must* know for ourselves'. Cases in point for this midwife, drawn from her own hard experience, were the ignorance of girls about sex and pregnancy, and the dangers of venereal disease. She endorsed views expressed in other submissions about the need for Javanese women to know more about housekeeping (especially in relation to hygiene and child-rearing), condemned easy divorce and polygamy, and concluded with a rousing appeal to men's desire for progress: 'Briefly and to the point, I give men this choice: Progress with free women or remain in darkness with slaves for wives. If they want the former, then outdated religious ideas may not be spared!' (Netherlands Indies Government 1914: Bijdrage van Mevrouw Djarisah).

From her experience of almost a decade of running private schools for girls, Dewi Sartika[3] put forward her view that the schooling needs of boys and girls did not differ much and emphasised the moral advantages of a sound education. This was clearly an important point for her to win in light of the criticisms she had to contend with. She described her trials in dealing with the opposition of the conservative Sundanese older generation to sending girls to school. That generation, she explained, educated their girls only to be good housewives, and this was done at home, before they were married off at an early age. These parents were reluctant to send their daughters to school because they did not see the use of it, they were afraid of letting the child out of their supervision, and they disliked the 'frankness' which they felt girls learnt at school and which would lead them into bad behaviour. All these fears she had spent years allaying.

Dewi Sartika's submission went on to express still stronger feelings about the purposes of educating girls. She wanted the opportunity to extend vocational education for girls to train them for jobs previously held only by men, such as civil servant, clerk and bookkeeper. By keeping women out of such occupations, she said, 'Thereby men have treated our women as a lesser class who, having learnt no trade, must earn their bowl of rice with coolie work in factories and businesses. As a woman it cuts me to the quick that such women, although performing the same duties as men, earn lower wages than them.'

Like others who contributed submissions to the Commission, Dewi Sartika was convinced education would slowly bring about the decline of bad practices affecting women like child marriage, prostitution and polygamy. She came as close as anyone to making an overt link between education and the autonomy of girls:

Raise the child to be an independently thinking individual, who values herself. Through the awakening of her self-awareness the woman will of her own initiative also take sides against arranged marriages, and against the dissipation and tyranny of her husband, factors which have made many a marriage into a disaster.

Men will learn to value her better. After long years the Woman will be able to become the equal of the Man. (Netherlands Indies Government 1914: Bijdrage van Raden Dewi Sartika)

The longest submission came from R. A. Siti Sundari, a feisty young Javanese woman about whom relatively little is known despite her input

---

[3] On Dewi Sartika (1884–1947) see Wiriaatmadja (1983) and Government of Indonesia (1967).

into a number of debates on women during the 1910s and 1920s.[4] According to her own account she had been the honorary editor of a fortnightly Javanese periodical, *Wanito Sworo* (Women's Voice), and had set up a private school for Javanese girls and women, the popularity of which proved how much separate schools were wanted.

Much of Siti Sundari's submission (Netherlands Indies Government 1914: Bijdrage van Raden Ajoe Siti Soendari) covered the same ground as Dewi Sartika. A new point raised by her was the desire of educated young men to marry educated wives, 'so that they can talk with them about things worth knowing and about politics', and because, having learned Dutch ways of living, they wanted wives who also had that understanding.

Like most other contributors, she differentiated between the kind of education appropriate for girls of different classes.

In my opinion, education for village children does not need to be too extensive, because it would not be useful for their way of life. If they just learn to read and write in Javanese and learn to know Latin letters, and to do arithmetic, that is sufficient. Besides that, daughters of village and *kampung* [lower-class urban residential area] people should be given training in cooking, making Native cakes, sewing, making batik and such matters which will later be of use, e.g. if they wish to set up a street-stall or feed boarders, or become a cook. And knowledge of these things will strengthen the marriage bond.

Siti Sundari clearly admired the ability of village women to gain independence through earning their own living. It meant they were less afraid of divorce, for instance, or of polygamy, which she regarded as an abomination.

Like Dewi Sartika, she concluded that education was the key to necessary social and moral changes in Javanese society: 'It is very difficult to change customs and usages grounded in religion. I have thought long and hard about it and have found no effective means of doing away with these unsuitable customs. Finally I know of no other weapon against rotten customs than in the first place: education.'

Although expressed much more colourfully and feelingly, the views of these independent-minded women were not far removed from those of progressive Dutch officials of the period. The chairman of the Declining Welfare Commission, H. E. Steinmetz, spent much of the volume on women cataloguing very similar opinions, culled not just from Java but also from European feminist writings, and combating conservative opponents of schooling for girls. For Steinmetz, however, such opinions

---

[4] According to *De Inheemsche Vrouwenbeweging* (1932: 8), she was the daughter of a teacher in Ponorogo. A contemporary article about her (Dekker 1914) claimed she was the daughter of a headmaster called Wirio Darmobroto, and her own school was at Pacitan.

were easy to come by in European circles of the time, while for the Indonesian contributors to the report these views had continually to be defended. Even what might appear to be uncontroversial views about teaching housekeeping and child-rearing to girls were potentially explosive issues in their day, representing as they did the likelihood that girls were being taught notions that contradicted the customs of their parents and relatives.

The Colonial Education Congress of 1916

The level of official Dutch interest in education in the colonies is reflected in the fact that two congresses on the subject were held in the Dutch capital, The Hague, in 1916 and 1919, taking submissions and hearing evidence from a range of witnesses. In both congresses sessions were devoted to the education of Indonesian girls. In general the contentious issues were which girls should be educated and how; it was accepted that the education of girls was desirable but since the resources and demand were not considered to exist for universal education, choices had to be made. Unlike the 1914 Declining Welfare Report, debate here covered the Outer Islands as well as Java, although as usual Java received the most attention.

Not surprisingly given the Dutch location, the views of Dutch educators and administrators tended to dominate these debates. The 1916 congress received strong input from A. Limburg, former director of a well-established school for daughters of chiefs and notables in Minahasa, a Christian area of North Sulawesi with the highest level of education of girls in the archipelago. In his view there was still no strong demand for the education of girls from the population at large, and for the time being he felt it should be limited to girls of higher classes, particularly considering the lack of resources (notably female teachers). He expected that such education would have liberating effects, causing girls to question old-fashioned customs as had been the case with Kartini, a name frequently evoked at these congresses. As for what should be taught to these girls, he advised that it should be largely of a practical nature: 'I would like to see them taught hygiene of body, house and yard, domestic science, handicrafts, singing, nursing of young children and the sick, good manners, and a feeling for all that is fine and good and true.' He advocated the kind of education he himself had been involved in providing: segregated schooling in the Dutch language for upper-class girls, preferably through boarding schools where there was more opportunity to mould susceptible young minds. The long-term aim of educating girls was clearly social change to produce women in the domestic Christian mould (Eerste Koloniaal Onderwijscongres 1916: 194–202, and Prae-Adviezen 1916: 181–94).

Slightly different ideas were expressed by prominent Dutch officials. A former inspector of native schools, C. Lekkerkerker, opposed separate schools for girls up to the age of ten or twelve on practical grounds (lack of female teachers) but admitted that for later years they were necessary. He was however concerned that the education system was becoming streamed along class lines (Prae-Adviezen 1916: 293–300 and Eerste Koloniaal Onderwijscongres 1916: 224–6). As might be expected, J. H. Abendanon strongly defended the education of girls. For those going on beyond lower education, he argued, the purpose was not just to make them into good housewives and wives but to give them 'the opportunity to mean something in society, not just for the upbringing of children but also to be able to be independently active' (Eerste Koloniaal Onderwijscongres 1916: 224–6). Abendanon's views were consistent with those of many feminist-minded Indonesians, from Kartini onwards.

A lengthy deposition was made to the 1916 congress by Miss M. S. van Willigen, a Dutch woman on leave from her teaching post in Java. Like many protagonists of female education, she emphasised its moral significance. Purely intellectual education 'laid the foundation for materialism of the grossest sort'. In the area of moral education 'woman has a great – the greatest – task to fulfil'. This was a strong premise for arguing against the commonly held view that the education of boys should precede that of girls. Basic to her was the role of mothers, who should be trained to provide education in the wider sense of upbringing.

In Miss van der Willigen's view, educated women would run their households economically, lead their children's education and provide a home which kept husbands from gambling and opium and the company of unworthy women. 'That is the great moral influence which will flow from the educated Native woman, who by nature has this inborn sweetness and civilisation, which is the strength of the weak' (Eerste Koloniaal Onderwijscongres 1916: 210). Such a woman, too, would never allow herself to be married off against her will, or be content to accept a place as a co-wife in a polygamous marriage, and would want the means to support herself so as to make her own way in life 'as so many of her European sisters do'.

It was clear that Miss van der Willigen espoused education of the kind that contemporary Dutchwomen of a liberal feminist persuasion wanted for girls anywhere. Like the administrators, however, she was prepared to concede that different kinds of schooling would have to be provided for Indonesian girls in different circumstances. Schools for girls of the 'popular class' should be separate from those for daughters of the more well-to-do and better educated. The education of the former should be of more limited duration and be practically oriented, in Malay, providing girls with skills they would need in later life, both in the home and in the workforce. For the latter, girls should get schooling of a higher intellectual level, in the Dutch language, but also with the addition of skills of practical use to women such as simple bookkeeping, health and child care, and 'naturally feminine handcrafts'. Most of these girls would remain at school until the age of twelve or thirteen and get a 'rounded' education which would suit them for marriage to lower-level officials. For those who wanted it, further education opportunities should be provided. Like Limburg, she emphasised the value of boarding schools both to encourage parents to send their girls to school and 'for character formation', which she clearly thought was lacking in Indonesian families.

Indonesian men had little to say about the education of girls at the 1916 congress. Their representatives were the nationalists Sam Ratulangi, from Minahasa where girls' education was already well advanced, and R. M. Suwardi Suryaningrat from Java, both of whom were students in Holland at the time. Suwardi's views are particularly interesting, given his prominence in Indonesian education thinking and policy, under the name he later assumed, Ki Hajar Dewantoro. One of a radical triumvirate of nationalists who were exiled to the Netherlands in 1913, during his six-year stay there, Suwardi and his wife obtained teaching qualifications and steeped themselves in ideas about alternative education, in particular those of Montessori, Frobel and Steiner (McVey 1967; Tsuchiya 1987). In the debate about girls' education the nationalist spirit was already strongly to the fore with both young men. For them, other issues had priority over the education of girls. Although in favour of it, they had little to offer as to its nature, extent or objectives.

Two Indonesian women made contributions to the 1916 congress discussion on women's education: Mrs Kandou from Minahasa, the first Indonesian woman to take out her education diploma in the Netherlands, and the indefatigable Siti Sundari, who had come to Holland in 1915 in search of training as a teacher (Poeze 1986: 111–12). Contemporary documentation revealed that she was a young widow who had left her child behind in Java (Deventer 1915).

Mrs Kandou wished to speak from the point of view of a Minahasan. Clearly she felt that remarks about the inferiority of women were out of place in Minahasa, where 'the customs and legends show us that women in the original conception of the people took a place in the family perfectly equal to that of men'. However, she did wish to plead for an extension of the schooling available to girls in that region. Although lower education had been available to girls there for four decades, they felt the lack of higher education, especially since it made it hard for well-educated young Minahasan men to find suitable wives among their compatriots (Eerste Koloniaal Onderwijscongres 1916: 223). Like Ratulangi, she felt coeducation was suitable for Minahasans and advocated providing higher schooling for girls of a general nature but including some attention to hygiene and household matters. Hers was a family-oriented view of the value of education for girls.

In her usual spirited manner, Siti Sundari defended girls' education. The arguments put forward in support of sending Javanese girls to school (and she claimed to be able to speak only for Javanese women) were threefold: that mothers as first teachers of children must be educated; that educated men would naturally want educated wives; and that it was necessary for the respect of the Javanese nation. In her view, girls should receive the same standard and quality of schooling as boys, involving general education like arithmetic, writing and reading, but in addition they should also learn 'women's work like sewing, cooking and batik'. They should be taught in Javanese but should also know how to speak Malay, and those who wished to continue with their studies should be taught Dutch. Like other speakers, she felt it was necessary to provide boarding schools for girls who were continuing beyond basic education, but her reasoning differed from that of the Dutch speakers. While they saw boarding schools as a way of moulding Indonesian girls to a more European pattern, she explicitly recommended that in these schools life should have a Javanese flavour, 'so that these girls do not take on different customs and lose their own nationality'. Her views here coincided with those of Suwardi Suryaningrat, whether under his influence or in reflection of the growing nationalism of the time. She concluded her speech by saying, 'At this moment the spirit of the late R.A. Kartini watches our endeavours: it illuminates us' (Eerste Koloniaal Onderwijscongres 1916: 232).

The congress of 1919 had little to add to the debate of 1916, largely because a number of contributors were more concerned about the fate of Eurasian girls than they were about vocational training for Indonesians, and no new ideas were put forward. No Indonesian women participated in this discussion. By this time, however, training facilities for Indonesian girls were opening up and the government was subsidising private girls' schools, albeit on a very limited basis (Bemmelen 1982).

The views of recently educated girls

The full flavour of the radical impact of Western-style schooling in the 1910s is really felt only by sampling the heartfelt writings of young women who had recently experienced that education. A good example of these views is to be found in *Sunting Melayu* (Malay Ornament), a weekly newspaper for women and edited by women, published between 1912 and 1921 in Minangkabau (West Sumatra).

This newspaper demonstrates that what might now appear at official level to be fairly conservative views about the education of girls translated in practice, in Minangkabau at least, into quite radicalising experiences for girls. Given our knowledge of Kartini's correspondence a decade or so earlier, this should not be surprising. For Minangkabau girls, debate about their education occurred in the context of conflict between the *kaum muda* (young group) and *kaum tua* (old group), those who challenged and supported *adat* (tradition) respectively. The patron of *Sunting Melayu*, Datu' Sutan Maharadja, whose daughter Zubaedah Ratna Juwita was one of the paper's editors, was a strong supporter of the education of girls (Abdullah 1971). The other editor was Rohana Kudus, who pioneered private schools for girls in West Sumatra (Djaja 1980). The pages of *Sunting Melayu* were full of contributions from advocates of girls' schooling, apart from the occasional letter from someone raising concerns about its consequences, particularly for morals.

The engaging thing about *Sunting Melayu* is that almost all its contributions came directly from female readers, creating a feeling that the paper represented the thoughts of members of a club of young women who felt free to air their opinions and experiences among themselves. These were the first generation of Minangkabau women to have received a Western-style schooling; many contributors were still at school, mostly at coeducational state schools. What is very striking, as with the case of Kartini, is how only a few short years of schooling (almost none of these women received more than elementary education) could produce such a strong impression of breaking open a new world. It emphasises the fact that the impact of education on women is not so much dependent on the length of that schooling as on its context and timing: just three years of elementary education in the 1910s could change an Indonesian girl's outlook on life more than a secondary education in the 1990s. The reason is that the ideas conveyed by education at that time were new to Indonesian society, so that any recipient of an elementary education was on the cutting edge of change, was an intellectual purveying ideas which were frequently in tension if not outright conflict with her environment. And as we have seen, this was anticipated to some degree at higher levels: education was expected to lead to social change in all sorts of areas like marriage and child-rearing.

What also needs to be taken into account is the particular ethnic and regional environment in which girls' schooling occurred. It had entered

Minahasan society in the late nineteenth century with little overt commotion; perhaps, as Ratulangi and Mrs Kandou argued in The Hague in 1916, because women already held a strong position in Minahasan society. Certainly some of the earliest women to take advantage of higher education were Minahasans (e.g. the first Indonesian woman doctor was Minahasan). In the matrilineal society of Minangkabau, where women were by custom expected to play a prominent role in social matters at least, village women of relatively high rank benefited from schooling earlier than those in, say, patrilineal Batak circles. But the ideas of that schooling could give rise to friction with relatives when they conflicted with *adat* expectations of girls, particularly in relation to marriage and employment.

The pages of *Sunting Melayu* overflowed with poems and letters in praise of schooling for girls, from young women, mostly in rural areas, who signed their names, citing also their village and father. For instance, in the issue of 27 July 1912, Siti Ruhana, a pupil in class 5 at Payakumbuh, sent verses which, roughly translated, said: 'I have been to school for a long time· now I sit in class five. Four of us girl friends are together and I give their names here . . . Oh my three friends, we study with a strong faith; so that we advance into the garden of a pure heart and a pleasant fate.'

For such girls, schooling had an almost religiously revelatory impact and bonded them to the privileged few who shared the new experience. And it was that schooling that enabled them for the first time to read the views of their sisters and to express their own opinions in print, an experience which clearly elated many of them. They supported one another in newly held opinions which might earn the ire of their nearest and dearest.

For instance, in the issue of 9 November 1912, Zahara of Bukittinggi wrote an article entitled 'Bad customs of ours', attacking parents who married their young daughters to old men, and criticising polygamy, the incidence of which was higher in West Sumatra than in most other parts of the Indies (see Chapter 5). Polygamy was a frequent target in the pages of *Sunting Melayu*. On 3 April 1913, Marni, the daughter of Mas Ada of Padang, wrote in heartfelt tones to tell the story of how her relatives had prevented her from taking a job as a clerk in Padang: she was qualified for the position but her brother would not permit it. The tale flowed onto the page breathlessly and indignantly, calling on her sisters for sympathy.

The attitude of these young women to education was whole-hearted: they saw its uses in so many ways. For many of them it was instrumental: it gave access to income-earning work, either of a modern type as teachers or nurses, or via skills in weaving and embroidery; and it made them more efficient mothers. It also had moral and social significance by introducing them to a better life free from bad old customs and featuring happy, harmonious families, as well as opening up to them a wider world of knowledge that linked them with women not just in West Sumatra or the Indies more generally, but throughout the world. All of this was encapsulated in the word *kemajuan* (progress) to which education was the key. Reading *Sunting Melayu*, like reading Kartini's letters, impresses one with the full lived significance of this experience of access to a new kind of autonomy, with all its attendant joys and sorrows.

Nationalism and education of girls

Indonesian male nationalists had definite ideas about why girls should be educated. Women needed modern knowledge to understand and support the nationalist movement, and to raise healthy and loyal Indonesian citizens. Little of this rationale was framed with any reference to the interests of women themselves. Although their views were not generally addressed to the colonial state, from which they expected little, they indicated what they felt to be the obligations of governments in a future independent Indonesia.

By the 1920s most Indonesian women's organisations had begun to be influenced by these nationalist views. The first national congress of these organisations, held in Yogyakarta in December 1928, clearly signalled its nationalist orientation, which was a feature of the federation of women's organisations that emerged from the congress. The first resolution passed by the congress concerned girls' schools. It urged the government to increase the number of separate schools for girls because of the continuing difficulty in getting many parents to send their daughters to coeducational schools (Congres Perempoean 1929: 20). The need for education surfaced often in the speeches of leading women at this congress, as at those that followed. The congress marks a turning-point as nationalism began to dominate the women's movement. Views about education reflected efforts to combine a nationalist justification for education with a search for women's autonomy.

One of the most prominent speakers at the congress was the same Siti Sundari who had contributed to the 1914 Declining Welfare Commission and participated in the Colonial Education Congress of 1916. In her speech, entitled 'Responsibility and ideals of Indonesian women', she made a number of observations about education (Congres Perempoean 1929: 49–61). She argued very strongly against older traditions of educating children, whereby, she claimed, children were considered as the possessions of parents who could be treated according to their own wishes. According to new educational notions, she said, education was about developing the child's own gifts. This child-centred view of education naturally had important novel implications for girls in particular. She went on to make out a nationalist case for freedom in the education of girls. Women had important responsibilities in working to strengthen the Indonesian nation, and to do so they would need freedom: 'For a long time Indonesian women have depended on others, when small on their parents, when adult on their husbands . . . Young women now ask for education directed towards independence, and freedom in social intercourse. Our education must look after this, so that we do not become just marriage fodder' (Congres Perempoean 1929: 59–60). For Siti Sundari, women's role in building the nation was primarily as mothers, but this was interpreted in a broad sense to serve as a basis for arguing in favour of educating girls for autonomy.

Another influential speaker at the 1928 congress on the topic of education was Nyi Hajar Dewantara, the wife of Ki Hajar (formerly Suwardi Suryaningrat). With her husband, she was one of the leaders of the nationalist private school system, Taman Siswa (Garden of Pupils), founded in 1922. Significantly, her talk was entitled 'Women's refinement', and had to be translated into Malay from Javanese. In line with Taman Siswa ideology, she argued that a woman's nature (*kodrat*) was to bear children, and her behaviour should always be in keeping with that destiny. Women and men were complementary, made to live together so as to bear and raise the next generation. Women must be careful not to let their sexual attraction for men dominate their motherly qualities, for fear of earning the scorn of men rather than their respect. It was women's responsibility to infuse purity and refinement into life, to be a force for harmony and not a source of conflict among men.

Contemporaneously, these views were being expounded by Nyi Hajar's husband in Taman Siswa publications, where he developed the institution's guidelines for the education of girls. Building on the view that men and women had quite different natures, he argued that equality of rights and status with men could never mean that men and women should be treated the same. Women's destiny to be mothers meant that they had softer, more refined feelings. In Taman Siswa, he wrote, it was felt that 'Women's existence is needed everywhere, because they have a great influence on their surroundings in terms of purity, refinement and spirituality, which is beneficial for activity in the world of education.' Since he considered the presence of girls in school had a civilising influence on the behaviour of boys, Ki Hajar was in favour of coeducation. Yet in order to protect women's *kodrat*, girls must be educated differently in some things, such as sport. Western women playing sport exhibited too much of their bodies. 'In sport we must take care that our girls do not just copy

Western custom in this matter of sports clothing, so as not to ruin the feeling of purity, that is their feminine feeling.' From a nationalist perspective, he argued, due care must be paid to girl pupils holistically, so as to ensure good physical and spiritual inheritance for the race, since women are the mothers of the next generation. In discussing the philosophical basis for what was intended to be a national education system providing an alternative to the colonial one, Ki Hajar Dewantara never put forward an economic justification for the education of girls. Rather, the moral defence he used rested on an amalgam of *priyayi* values from his native Java and European educational thinking, imbibed when he was studying in Holland (Dewantara 1967: 240–48).

As more Indonesian parents, and those of immigrant ethnic minorities like Arabs and Chinese, came to accept mixed primary schools, the numbers of girls at government-funded schools rose dramatically in the colonial period. In 1939 about 62,000 Indonesian girls attended schools and higher education institutions (most of them state-funded). However, this constituted less than a quarter of the total number of Indonesians enrolled, at a time when the colony's population stood at 60 million (Bemmelen 1982: 185, 204).

Education since independence

Ever since the Declaration of Independence in August 1945, Indonesian governments have been strongly committed to equality in education, recognising it as a right of all citizens, a means of promoting national unity and a necessity for economic development. In line with the Constitution, which rejected the notion of an Islamic state, governments since 1945 have also chosen a secular state education system, although the state does extensively subsidise (and supervise) religious schools that conform to its criteria.

The fact that Indonesian governments have promoted secular education has caused little friction with devout Muslims, who have their own, largely state-subsidised schools. Within state schools, the prevalent notion of *kodrat* accords with Indonesian Islam, although there was conflict when the wearing of Islamic head-coverings by girls was forbidden in state schools in 1982. In this case opposition from Islamic organisations led to the withdrawal of that prohibition a decade later.

At the time of the Declaration of Independence, it was estimated that fewer than half the children of primary school age were enrolled (Oey-Gardiner 1997: 140). After the transfer of sovereignty in 1949, a rapid expansion of the schooling system occurred. The history of education since then has been one of increasing access to schooling and literacy more generally, for both sexes.

The emphasis at first was on universal primary schooling, which was only achieved in practice by the end of the 1980s after the bounty of the oil boom in the 1970s expanded government resources. Until then it had not been possible for schools to be built and staffed in the many remote rural areas of Indonesia. Foreign aid, readily available since the inception of the New Order, has also helped to expand educational spending. By the mid-1990s, when the population of Indonesia had reached 200 million, 95 per cent of children of primary school age were enrolled at school (UNDP 2001: 176). Although in 1990 the government adopted a policy of nine years' compulsory universal education by the year 2005, the timetable will not be achieved; even when the new goal was announced, about a third of children did not complete primary school. Retention rates decline still further at secondary level and rapidly thereafter. Only about 10 per cent of young people attended higher education in the early 1990s.

Apart from regular schooling, governments have attempted to encourage adult literacy by other means, including intensive campaigns and 'packages' of teaching materials for people who cannot or choose not to attend schools. By the end of the twentieth century adult literacy had reached 86 per cent (UNDP 2001: 143).

As far as gender difference in access in education are concerned, the point of divergence has been when primary school graduates have to transfer to junior secondary schools, which for rural families may require sending their children by bus into town or even finding accommodation at a distance from home. At this stage some parents still consider this undesirable for their daughters, and the expense of schooling, although low, is an obstacle in what remains a poor country. Given the need to choose, sons get priority. It should be remembered that formal education supplements, but may also conflict with, instruction within the home, where girls are still taught to take a greater share of household chores than boys. Moreover, even with the same level of education, men earn more than women. At secondary and tertiary levels of education, where the proportion of children at school drops considerably, girls lag behind boys. The proportion of girls to boys at primary level in the 1990s was around 93 per cent, dropping to 87 per cent at lower secondary and 85 per cent at higher secondary schools (Oey-Gardiner 1997). The drop-out rate is highest among the poor and in rural areas. Although around 93 per cent of girls are enrolled in primary school, still only 8 per cent of girls reached the tertiary level in the 1990s compared with 15 per cent of boys (UNDP 2001: 221).

Access to education has always been an important topic in Indonesia, including its gender aspects, particularly since the international attention fostered by the United Nations Decade for Women (1975–85). However, it has not since independence been a matter of controversy: governments have been committed to increased access and to equalising literacy rates between men and women: currently there is still a gap, with women lagging about ten points behind men (UNDP 2001: 212). Apart from quantity, however, there is the question of the quality of the education system, which has frequently been criticised. In part this has been the result of low per capita expenditure on education, but it was also a consequence of tight control exerted by the New Order regime, involving prescribed textbooks, rote-learning and centralised examinations, as well as centralised appointment of teaching staff. Although at higher levels of the system increasingly students were taught in private institutions because government-funded schools could not meet demand, most private schools were also subject to strict government supervision. As a result, there was increased uniformity in the content and pedagogy of Indonesian education. Although justified in the name of equality and national unity, this system was regressive in a number of ways. For instance, ethnic traditions were suppressed and the Chinese minority and regional groups were forced to comply with Jakarta's standards.

Until recently, the gendered content of educational policy was not subject to critical scrutiny, partly because of the priority given to making schooling more accessible for girls, partly because of the New Order Government's well-known suppression of criticism and partly because the gender bias built into the education system reflects conservative values endemic in Indonesian society. Gender bias had been built into the system first by the Dutch and subsequently by policy-makers like Ki Hajar Dewantara who was the first Minister of Education in the independent Republic of Indonesia and a long-standing educational advisor. Other prominent educationists had also taught or been educated in Taman Siswa schools. Like so many other aspects of education, the gender bias of the curriculum and pedagogy, already incorporated into the education system, was not challenged by the New Order regime. Hence textbooks tended to depict women and girls in stereotyped nurturing, child-rearing and domestic roles while boys and men dominated the public sphere. Continuing a practice started in the colonial era, some secondary schools were also designated to specialise in home economics; they were attended exclusively by girls, just as the technical schools that taught trades were the preserve of boys. (The vast majority of secondary school pupils, however, have always attended schools with a general curriculum.) Amongst teaching staff, women are concentrated at the lower levels.

Until very recently, only foreigners studied gender bias in the Indonesian education system, reflecting the priorities of Indonesian state funding of research. In their study of schooling in Bali in the late 1970s,

Jan Branson and Don Miller (1992) concluded that the national education system was a force for change in rural life, but not necessarily for the
better as far as the construction of gender was concerned. In their view,
schooling influenced pupils to disdain their parents' occupations and to
embrace a sexual division of labour which favoured boys over girls, a
departure from the greater equality between the sexes to be found in
older-style village life. This was the result of the Western values centring
on individualism embodied in modern education.

Branson and Miller's conclusions are supported by Lynette Parker's
work on schooling in Bali in the 1980s. She argued that 'through school
curricula and institutional routines, *the government assigns each of the gen-
ders one of these goals: girls get the job of moral responsibility and service,
principally within the family, and boys get the job of economic development*'
(her emphasis, Parker 1993: 9). As she goes on to show, class (and in the
Balinese context, caste) is intertwined with gender to undermine equality in the classroom. In school at least, a higher-class/caste Balinese girl
experiences a greater degree of freedom from gender restriction than that
felt by her lower-status sisters. From early this century onwards, it seems
education has had more to offer to upper- and middle-class girls.

In her analysis of gender roles in elementary school texts in the early
years of the New Order, Martha Logsdon noted a remarkable tendency to
portray gender roles similar to those promoted in the West, with women
restricted to home duties. So divergent did this seem from the real roles
played by most Indonesian women that it required explanation. In her
view it was linked to the government's desire to transform Indonesians
into a modern 'developed' country. 'The role which Indonesian children
seem to be prepared for by these books is a patrifocal, male-dominated
society, in which women can be prepared to serve as a "reserve labor
force" (they are, after all, encouraged to study hard) but in which their
primary role is reproduction' (Logsdon 1985: 260).

It is difficult to assess the actual effect on the lives of men and women of
the gender construction implicit in Indonesian schooling. For one thing,
it cannot be isolated from other similar influences reaching people though
other arms of the state apparatus, like the family planning programme.
We know, too, that most ordinary women continue to live very differently
from the middle-class and domesticated model purveyed by the state
education system. But such pervasive gender ideology must at the very
least be considered an obstacle to extending their autonomy.

The Asian financial crisis of 1998 caused great concern about access
to education in Indonesia, as government funding shrank and parents
took their children out of school to reduce costs and contribute to family
income. There is some evidence that girls were more affected than were

boys by these events, something that aroused the concern of a number of women's organisations. More positively, the democratisation of Indonesia since the end of the New Order in 1998 has enabled fresh approaches to thinking about education. The highly centralised, rote-learning system is being dismantled and more attention is being paid to the content of education. For instance, the National Human Rights Commission and women's organisations criticised sex-stereotyping in school texts and the tendency of girls to take up a limited range of subjects, particularly at higher levels, thus limiting their career options (Komnasham 2001). There is a clear connection between lower levels and kinds of education that girls receive and the fact that they are employed in less remunerative jobs (see Chapter 8).

As the heavy hand of New Order control on research was lifted, Indonesian scholars were free to investigate the issue of gender bias in the education system. One of the books on the subject was a recent publication by Muthali'in (2001), which studied primary schools in Java and Bali. He concluded that there was indeed pervasive gender bias, in subjects, textbooks and pedagogy, and strongly recommended changes to the education system. It remains to be seen whether regional autonomy legislation, which took effect in 2001 and has devolved some responsibility for education to the district level, will make it easier or harder to address these concerns. It is likely that the problems of implementing educational devolution will mean that gender concerns will be given a low priority.

Conclusion

There was a clear difference in the colonial and post-independence discourses about responsibility for ensuring girls' access to education. In the Dutch East Indies, few argued that schooling for girls had important economic benefits, for themselves let alone for the colonial economy. On the contrary, given the cost of training more female teachers and expanding school places, why should the colonial government invest in schools for girls or subsidise private ones, and why should parents undertake the expense, in school fees or opportunity costs, of sending their daughters to school? It was considered too soon to provide much education for the great mass of the female population who lived off agriculture or the informal sector: schooling for them must remain scarce and simple in nature, providing little economic benefit. Most of the debate revolved around what to do about education for daughters of the wealthier minority, most of whom would never be expected to earn their living, although some of them might go on to train for modern occupations like teaching, nursing, typing, etc. The defence of education for girls here rested on moral and social outcomes: the ability of educated women to raise the moral tone and thus the status of Indonesian society, especially by helping to combat social evils, and to become suitable mothers and wives for male leaders in the new age of progress. Such notions persisted into the New Order and came to be questioned only at the end of the century.

These arguments were put forward with varying degrees of emphasis by many advocates of the education of girls. Few protagonists couched their case in terms of the ability of education to increase female autonomy: that has not been a politically tactical argument in an Indonesian society where collective values prevail. Aspects of female autonomy nevertheless haunted the debate and were heard quite strongly from the young women who reflected on the significance of schooling for their lives. However conservative and even restrictive the content of schooling during the colonial period, those who received it felt themselves to be a privileged elite with direct and indirect access to a range of new ideas. For these people, their world was transformed. For some the experience led directly to nationalism; for many women it put them in conflict with their own families while opening up new opportunities and new networks in their own imagined community of educated sisters of the kind that *Sunting Melayu* represented for Minangkabau women. For later generations of Indonesian girls, a little knowledge was not such a dangerous thing: it would take a much deeper draught for them to overcome the restrictive aspects of the existing education system which had been captured first by the nationalist agenda and then, in the New Order, by a particular view of women's role in 'development'. As schooling for girls became more widespread it lost much of its transformative power and instead contributed to the domestication of women, something that is only now beginning to be recognised.

3   Early marriage

As the previous chapter on education showed, a prime concern of Indonesian women in pressing for schooling for girls was to prevent them from being forced into early marriage. Concentrating more directly on how the age of marriage became a political issue in twentieth-century Indonesia, this chapter investigates the changing intensity, focus and participation in debate over the issue. Compared with India, the incidence of very early marriage among Indonesian girls appears never to have been very high, yet among those trying to 'modernise' Indonesia it was considered to be a 'social evil' that parents married off their daughters at or before the onset of puberty. Social reformers differed as to the reasons for their concern and as to what action should be taken and by whom. In particular there were strong disagreements about whether government intervention was either desirable or effective in raising the age of marriage.

The age at which it is appropriate for girls to marry has been a contentious matter in many countries. In societies where marriage was considered to be the prerogative of families, the children themselves were rarely consulted and the age of marriage, or at least of betrothal, was likely to be quite young, before children could exert their own will. Although physical readiness for sexual intercourse and child-bearing was a consideration, this was a matter for the supervision of adult kin, and the timing of the wedding could if necessary be separated from the consummation of marriage. Apart from families, the only other institutions directly concerned with marriage were likely to be religious ones.

Indonesia in the twentieth century has seen the gradual and often disputed emergence of 'modern' ideas about marriageable age. Until recently, few Indonesians knew their precise chronological age because birth records were rarely kept, and marriages tended to occur early under the control of kin and religious (primarily Islamic) authorities. It was the presence of Dutch colonial rule which made the question of marriage age

This is an abridged and revised version of an article written with Sharon Bessell (Blackburn and Bessell 1997). My thanks to Dr Bessell and to *Indonesia* for their permission to publish in this form.

into a political issue, as Western education spread notions of individual rights and the state extended its influence over family life. After independence in 1945 the nature of the debate about early marriage changed: the Indonesian state had greater legitimacy in the realm of social reform, the arguments in favour of later marriage shifted somewhat, and new players entered the scene. Women's organisations now play a less prominent role.

The debate about 'child marriage' in the Netherlands Indies

During the colonial period, public debate about early marriage was framed in the context of 'child marriage'. In the lexicon of social reformers, child marriage is a term of opprobrium. Almost exclusively associated with girls, it carries overtones of child sexual abuse, of precipitating children too early into adulthood and at the very least of depriving them of the right to choose their spouse. Differing attitudes to child marriage formed part of the clash of cultures between 'modern' and 'backward' peoples which characterised many colonial situations, not only in the Netherlands Indies.

The best-documented case of the politics of child marriage is undoubtedly British India, where the problem of Hindu child brides was compounded by a stigma against divorce and widowhood and the tragedy of *sati*. Campaigns by Indian and British reformers led to legislation being passed by the colonial government against child marriage, notably the Child Marriage Restraint Act of 1929 (Forbes 1979).

Compared to British India, the politics of child marriage in the Netherlands Indies was more muted and did not result in legislation. It was, however, a cause close to the hearts of social reformers in different camps, including both women's organisations and state authorities. Although the actual incidence of child marriage in the Indies was unclear, it was felt by many people to be unacceptably high. Being Muslims, most Indonesians contracted marriages under Islamic law, which stipulated no minimum age. Girls need not personally agree to marriage: consent could be given on their behalf by their male guardian, a father or grandfather. Those who opposed child marriage did so on a number of grounds associated with 'modern' values: protection of children (especially from sexual abuse), championing of the rights of girls to determine their own futures and the need for a modern, respected nation to be based on strong, stable families. All these reformers can be seen as participating in a common project of refashioning the Indonesian family in line with 'modern' notions of childhood and motherhood.

A formidable array of factors confronted campaigners for change. Not only were there vested interests in the form of supporters of the rights of Islam and of parents and kin to control children, but also the practical obstacles were daunting. The only accurate age data for Indonesians related to a few Christian groups in the Outer Islands. In many cases, too, the formal wedding ceremony was not immediately followed by cohabitation or physical consummation, which might be postponed for months or years, thus confusing the issue of alleged physical damage to prepubescent wives. Conversely, in regions of Eastern Indonesia where bride-price was demanded, cohabitation might begin before the formalities of marriage were completed on payment of the final instalment of bride-price.

Early statements by Indonesian women

As we have seen, from early in the twentieth century Indonesian women who had received a Western education began to draw attention to the problem of child marriage. One of the earliest cries of outrage came from R. A. Kartini, a consistent opponent of customs she considered oppressive to women. Thus in 1901 she wrote to her Dutch friend Mrs Abendanon about the marriage of Mini, the thirteen-year-old daughter of the Regent of Ciamis:

I had tears of rage and regret and desperation in my eyes – and especially of sympathy for that poor child when I read the announcement of the proposed marriage. Mini, that dear, wonderful child, who had such a promising future – marrying – that young thing! – oh, I still cannot imagine it. It is outrageous! Oh, do not create illusions which must be destroyed – do not encourage dreams, when one knows beforehand that rude awakening must follow. It is *cruel – cruel*! (Kartini 1992: 121)

The letter shows how much Kartini had absorbed from her Dutch friends and teachers: to her Mini at thirteen was still a child, and she felt that the girl's dreams of a 'promising future' had been betrayed. As a young woman of the same *priyayi* class, Kartini found it easy to imagine that Mini entertained her own dreams, the result of exposure to a world beyond the narrow one of *priyayi* girls where early marriage like this was not unusual and was seen by many merely to mark a transition into adulthood. The first heads of Kartini schools, private elementary schools established for girls by the Dutch in Java from 1913 onwards, frequently reported that pupils of twelve to fourteen years were withdrawn from studies by their parents because they were to be married (Vereeniging Kartinifonds 1938: 46, 64; Kartinifonds 1939: 21).

Not only among Javanese *priyayi* families were girls in the early twentieth century beginning to protest against being married off by their
parents. As mentioned in the previous chapter, in the weekly newspaper for women *Sunting Melayu*, young women in West Sumatra were
also taking a stand against parental pressure to marry early. Correspondents to the paper argued strongly that a girl should be allowed to attain
the adult qualities required of a wife and mother, so that her marriage
could be stable; otherwise divorce would result with all its undesirable
consequences. Parents who ignored such considerations when arranging
their daughters' marriage were depicted as selfish. One daring contributor advocated that girls should not be married before the age of eighteen
(because otherwise 'her body will quickly deteriorate' and 'if she gives
birth to a child, she won't know how to look after it') and that it should
be left to the girl herself to find the husband ('Girls are human, aren't
they? They also have brains') (*Soenting Melajoe* 1914). This brought a
heated response from a male member of the old guard, arguing that the
age of eighteen might be suitable for a cold country but not for the Indies,
on the grounds that in hot climates children matured faster. Moreover,
he argued, it was ridiculous to say that until the age of eighteen girls did
not know how to look after children, since most had looked after younger
siblings. If the girl had menstruated and reached the age of fifteen, she
was old enough to marry.

It is right for parents to choose the husband. And among us [matrilineal]
Minangkabaus, the rights of male elders must be consulted. If you leave it to
a girl, she may be tricked into marriage by a womanizer or misled by men who
deceive girls as we read about in Europe (the story of Don Juan).

A daughter must respect her parents and their wishes so as not to cause them
sorrow. (Lelo 1914)

The rights of *adat* (local custom) were argued here against the foolish-
ness of Western custom. In Minangkabau novels, this battle of Western-
educated children against parental and *adat* claims dominated plots, and
often centred around choice of marriage partner (Stuers 1960; Postel-
Coster 1985).

The same year (1914) saw the publication of the volume dealing
with women from the report of the Commission Enquiring into Declining Native Welfare in Java and Madura. As mentioned in the previous
chapter, the volume contained submissions from nine Javanese women
commenting on what would be required to raise the status of women.
Seven of these correspondents, including the well-known educator Dewi
Sartika from Bandung, all mentioned the necessity of abolishing child
marriage and more broadly the need for women to be consulted about

marriage partners. Dewi Sartika labelled child marriage 'truly a cancer in the Native society, which must be rooted out'(Netherlands Indies Government, 1914: Bijdrage Sartika). All argued that sound marriages could be contracted only when the parties involved were adult and had fully consented, not been coerced by parents. Otherwise, warned Dewi Sartika, their children would suffer in turn and women might even be driven into prostitution by the break-up of marriage. The answer, they all agreed, was education: people who had been educated did not submit to 'barbaric' customs.

The views of civil servants

The 1914 volume of the Declining Welfare Report was also interesting for the first public official analysis of child marriage by Dutch and Indonesian civil servants. One of the members of the commission undertaking the enquiry was Raden Achmed Jayadiningrat, then the Regent of Serang (Banten), an area subsequently shown to have a high incidence of child marriage. In Serang, he reported, child marriage of girls of seven to ten years used to occur according to the custom referred to as *kawin gantung* (suspended marriage), whereby children were formally betrothed but actual consummation of marriage was delayed for four to six years. According to Jayadiningrat, however, in villages in the north of the district postponement of consummation belonged to the past, the main motive of parents being to marry off their children as quickly as possible. The Regent of Wonosobo also stated that the age of marriage was declining in his district: at the time of the report, girls were usually married off at the age of ten to fifteen and boys at the age of thirteen to fifteen. Some thirty years before, he claimed, average age was about five years older.

The two regents summed up the main reasons for early marriages in rural Java in similar terms. There were economic advantages to parents in gaining the help of a son-in-law, or through receiving the contributions which guests customarily made at a marriage feast. At the same time, parents saw early marriage as in the interest of their daughters: if marriage were postponed the child might 'go astray' and lessen her chances of marriage. After all, because children went to work early, they grew up quickly. The regents claimed that people were ignorant of the disadvantages of early marriage both for the couple and for their offspring. Finally, they said, the Javanese were conservative and early marriage was an established tradition (Netherlands Indies Government 1914: 6). Many of these reasons were also advanced in later years: they represent a mixture of parental desire for gain through marrying their daughters, a conviction that childhood was brief and a fear of the sexuality of girls.

The rest of the report's notes on child marriage summarised further evidence and commented on the phenomenon. As against the observations of the two regents and reports of a rise in the incidence of child marriage in twenty-six districts, it was noted that in twenty-seven other districts 'this abuse' was declining, either for economic reasons (e.g. coolies were easy to get, so the labour of a son-in-law was less necessary; or the cost of living had risen, meaning dowry or wedding feasts were less affordable) or because 'the European example' was spreading. In general, concluded the report, 'marriage was more a matter for parents than for the children involved, especially among the more well-to-do'. Although many child marriages were no more than betrothals, there was no doubt where the report stood on the matter: early marriage led to divorce, to polygamy and to the early physical decline of the wife.

The Dutch were most scandalised by early consummation of under-age marriage, the sexual violation of childhood, for it was on this point alone that they took legislative action. Article 288 of the Criminal Law Code of 1915 stipulated that 'A man who has sexual intercourse with a woman who he knows or may well suspect is not yet of marriageable age, and inflicts physical injury on her as a result, incurs a jail sentence of at most four years', with heavier penalties in case of more serious injury. On the other hand, this conflicted with another article of the code which, as we shall see in Chapter 8, ruled out the notion of marital rape. As was later admitted, the law was unenforceable and not policed.

The Declining Welfare Report set the scene for later statements by Dutch and Javanese officials on the question of child marriage, for instance in the People's Council (Volksraad) in the 1920s. In this advisory representative assembly, the subject of child marriage was raised on a few occasions. It was usually European members of the assembly who voiced concerns over child marriage. In 1922, for instance, Bergmeijer referred to reports from missionaries in Sulawesi and Central Java of the sufferings of very young girls at the hands of husbands who abused and abandoned them (Netherlands Indies Government 1922b: 418). His observations echoed the concern expressed in an earlier report of a Volksraad committee, where an unnamed member was reported as urging the government to pass a law forbidding child marriage (Netherlands Indies Government 1922a: Ond.1-Afd.II-Stuk 6). In response to this pressure, two Indonesian official members of the Volksraad, the Regents Jayadiningrat and Ariodinoto, argued that although there was room for concern about child marriage, they were certain that the custom would gradually decline with education and social change. Neither showed any sense of urgency about it. According to Jayadiningrat, little had changed in villages since he testified to the Declining Welfare Commission eight years before, although among *priyayi* families and others where Western influence was stronger, girls were being married older, not usually before the age of sixteen. Jayadiningrat was aware that 'voices have been raised for the government to take measures against child marriage', but he wished to show that the matter was not as simple as many thought. For one thing, he said, there was no real evidence that girls suffered from it. Many people practised *kawin gantung*, whereby parents delayed handing over the bride until she 'shows the first signs of being a woman', presumably a euphemism for menstruation. 'Also on the side of the husband generally great calm and caution is taken, as required by *adat*', and as supervised by the girl's guardian. 'For these reasons', he concludes, 'it is very rare that in such marriages a woman suffers physical damage.'

As evidenced by the 1915 legislation, Dutch officials did not always find these arguments against the harm inflicted on girls quite so compelling. They were more impressed by the next set of cautionary comments by Jayadiningrat.

According to Muslim law, a father has the right to marry his daughter off, even against her will, as soon as she is marriageable. This is probably the reason why Muslim Javanese, who commonly wish to retain the choice of their son-in-law, will not willingly give up rules sanctified by religion and marry their daughters off as early as possible. Therefore I do not think it necessary or desirable for the government to take special measures against such customs.

Just as among the higher ranks of Native society, so too in the village, tradition concerning marriage will gradually of itself change for the better. The signs are already present: thus in towns where the ordinary villager often comes into contact with the intellectual section of the population, child marriage has almost disappeared. (Netherlands Indies Government 1922b: 40)

In these views Jayadiningrat was backed by Ariodinoto. While admitting that child marriage had 'harmful results', he agreed that it could not be overcome by force: 'we can only override it by reason, by the use of education' (Netherlands Indies Government 1922b: 241). The Director of Justice, responding to the debate in the Volksraad, showed a similar unwillingness on the part of the government to take action on the matter (Netherlands Indies Government 1922b: 402).

Dutch colonial views, 1920s

Behind the scenes, however, Dutch officials were less confident in their approach. During the 1920s they debated among themselves whether there was any effective action they could or should take on child marriage. The debate began with concern expressed by the Resident of Lampung

over a 'social evil' in his district, the custom of wealthy Lampungers marrying young girls who were treated as slaves: in fact he saw the custom
of secondary wives in Lampung as a direct continuation of the taking
of house-slaves, a practice declared illegal in the previous century. The
problem was compounded by the recent trend for these girls to be bought
from the neighbouring province of Banten, where poor fathers sold their
daughters into what was virtual captivity, labouring for their husbands
in remote and unfamiliar locations. The fact that divorce was very rare
among the Lampungers meant a woman's chances of escape were slim
(Acting Adviser for Native Affairs 1921). Dutch official attitudes to the
ease and frequency of divorce in Java were contradictory: whereas some
saw it as mitigating the harm of child marriage, others saw the strong
association between early marriage and divorce as evidence of the evil
effects of the custom. While it is true that divorce meant that unhappy
child marriages could be dissolved (unlike, say, among the Hindus of
British India where divorce was unacceptable), it must also be remembered that under Islamic law women could initiate divorce only with the
greatest difficulty.

Although the problem of Banten girls in Lampung was addressed by
the government by appointing a 'protector of Bantenese' in Lampung and
spreading information on the Lampung situation in Banten (Adviser for
Native Affairs 1923), the discussion led immediately into a wider debate
about child marriage. The Adviser for Native Affairs, Kern, explained
at some length to the Director of Civil Service the customs of marriage
among Indonesian Muslims. 'As a rule', he began, 'it can be said that the
peoples of the Indonesian Archipelago marry as soon as they are adults.'
But parents who wished to control the choice of husband often married
daughters off while they were still children. Child marriage, he claimed,
'must be considered an Indonesian institution', and since it was 'a principle of Dutch colonial government policy to respect native institutions',
it was 'therefore appropriate that our laws do not make child marriage a
punishable offence'. Moreover, he believed that most marriages at very
young ages were not in fact consummated until adulthood (*kawin gantung*), to which there could be no objection (Adviser for Native Affairs
1922). Freedom of choice for girls obviously did not receive high priority
with Kern.

Kern then considered the feasibility of government intervention. Legislation was unworkable and undesirable. 'If one limits oneself to surveillance, then one would have to cover all non-adult girls who are unmarried,
to make a judgement about whether they are already fully-grown before
they marry, or whether they can have intercourse with their spouses,
and . . . also keep watch on whether the husband does not by oversight
sleep with the girl.'

In Bandung, according to Kern, the regent took strong action to prevent child marriage, which he interpreted as marriage under the age of
sixteen, by requiring local Javanese officials to prevent such marriages
being contracted. Kern noted that this action 'aroused discontent'.
'I honour his courage and high conviction, but I wonder whether he is not
taking on a heavier burden than is advisable. It is going against Muslim
marriage law.' It was one thing for a devout Muslim regent to interfere in
that way, but if it were done on the initiative of a 'heathen government'
it 'would become an assault on religion'. In Kern's view, the only answer
was to rely on the social evolution already under way in the Indies.

Increasingly world traffic has broken the isolation of the Muslim world, calling
forth comparisons of the position of women in Christian and Muslim countries
which are to the disadvantage of the latter. Thus we see attempts to make a rational
explanation of religious law, and more and more women raise their voices and
urge more just treatment . . . This movement of catching up with the world outside
Islam leads one to expect that early marriage will decline. Government can speed
that process by promoting development in general and of women in particular.

To go further seems to me decidedly inadvisable.

The Director of Justice felt rather more concerned. In 1923 he acknowledged that there was pressure from some regents and residents in Java
to take action against child marriage, and that there was evidence that
although 'people try to give child marriage the appearance of only a
betrothal (*kawin gantung*), nevertheless the bodily immature but already
married girl is misused, i.e. that what is called consummation or rather
violation is not infrequent in child marriage'. Article 288 of the Penal
Code against injuring an immature wife through sexual intercourse was a
dead letter, since it had never been publicised and 'it would be extremely
difficult to produce evidence of the crime' (Director of Justice 1923).

The question is: what can the legislator do about this? He can, through legislation,
as so many times has happened, exercise moral influence; he can unambiguously
let it be known that child marriage is an anti-social and thus objectionable deed; he
can through legislation lend support to the Regents, vice-regents and sympathetic
village chiefs to fight against the evil of child marriage.

This need not happen by threatening punishment, which would not work . . .
But . . . it can be made objectionable and impermissible.

Kern responded by reiterating that it was undesirable and unfeasible
to interfere in deeply rooted practices which were often defended by
Indonesians as supremely ethical. 'It is obvious that too early marriage
is harmful. It is desirable it should disappear. But Islamic law, as here
received, condones it and one cannot oppose it without coming into
conflict with the *syariah* [Islamic law]' (Adviser for Native Affairs 1923).

It seems that Kern did not win this argument – at least not immediately. In 1925 the government Secretary issued a circular about child marriage to governors (Government Secretary 1925). Although there could be little objection to *kawin gantung*, it said, where consummation was not postponed and physical harm was caused to the young woman, 'combating such marriages is urgent and is the serious duty of our government'. The government had decided that legislation on the matter was likely not to be as effective as 'the evolution of ideas of Native society itself', but it relied on the personal influence of Native officials. 'Various Javanese Regents have already given a good example by telling marriage officials to oppose marriages with not yet marriageable women', although 'much tact and care are needed so as not to give occasion for complaint'. The government would also publish information in local languages about the physical and moral damage wrought by child marriage. And finally, in order to monitor whether 'the evil of child marriage' was declining without legal prohibition, the government required officials to provide, on a six-monthly basis, statistics about the number of child marriages contracted in their areas. The emphasis in the colonial authorities' response was again on the need to protect children from harm.

In the event, neither of the surveillance measures proved feasible. Two years later another circular called off attempts to bring prospective brides before officials to ascertain whether they were marriageable. For many years, it noted, this had been done and if the bride was found to be too young, the parents were 'seriously advised not to go through with the wedding'; indeed in some places marriage contractors were instructed not to authorise such weddings. However, it had been decided that such actions were problematic. It was not practical to require parents to call off a wedding when all the preparations had been made, and 'there are widespread, understandable objections to interrogating young brides, because the questions asked are offensive to her feelings and those of her family members, besides the fact that such enquiries are conducted by men unknown to her'. As a result, the Governor-General now wished to advise against such action (Netherlands Indies Government 1927).

The debate peaks

By this time the interest in and concern about child marriage had grown considerably. Evidence of the views of Dutch feminists was to be found in *De Vrouw in Huis en Maatschappij: Propagandablad voor de Vrouwenbeweging in Indonesie* (The Women in the Home and in Society: Propaganda Paper for the Women's Movement in Indonesia), an unusual paper edited in 1926 by a Dutch feminist, Mrs Corporaal-van Achterburgh, and written in both Dutch and Malay by European and Indonesian women. It was clearly motivated by a desire to bring women of different races together, at a time when, with the decline of the Ethical Policy and rapid growth in the size of the European community, such efforts were largely doomed. A number of Dutch writers in this paper reflected on the problems of Indonesian married life. For instance, it was noted that 'child marriages still flourish': 'And with festivities the martyrdom of a child's soul is celebrated, tearing her from her childish games, forced into a whirlpool of passion which she doesn't understand, the victim of a man often three or four times older than her, sometimes grey-haired. Thus one sees in the villages, children with children at the breast . . . An end should be made to this' (Op de Uitkijk 1926). The campaign against child marriage was also growing amongst Western-educated Indonesians. The year 1928 represented something of a peak in their public activity on this issue. In December that year Indonesian women's organisations held their first congress in Yogyakarta. Child marriage featured prominently on the agenda of concerns expressed. A speaker named Mugarumah made a speech specifically on that topic, and that indefatigable campaigner against the oppression of women in marriage, Siti Sundari, also denounced it. The congress made a resolution to stop child marriage: every member was requested to make propaganda about the evil of child marriage and to ask civil servants to assist by giving information to the people about it (Congres Perempoean 1929).

Despite the strong stand on child marriage at the 1928 congress, it is notable that the issue rarely featured in conferences of the women's federation that was then formed. Along with other issues associated with marriage, it obviously proved too controversial for the Islamic women's organisations. To keep them in the federation meant avoiding divisive topics. After all, the largest Islamic women's organisation, Aisyiyah, would have had difficulty taking a stand against child marriage when it was named after one of the Prophet's wives who had been married to him at the age of nine.[1]

Outside the constraints of the federation, however, women continued to campaign against child marriage. It was precisely the refusal of the federation to deal with issues such as marriage laws that contributed to the formation in 1930 of the more radical women's organisation Istri

---

[1] Two Islamic women's organisation journals from the colonial period, *Isteri-Soesila Taman Moeslimah* (Solo, 1924–6) and *Soeara 'Aisjijah* (Published in Yogyakarta 1932 and 1941–2) contained no articles on child marriage.

Sedar (Aware Women). In the pages of its journal *Sedar*, practices of forced marriage and child marriage were denounced, and change was demanded not just in people's behaviour but also in Islamic marriage law, on the grounds that women must have the freedom to control their own lives and that child marriage was likely to damage the health of both the wife and her offspring.

Nationalist parties were also active in campaigning against child marriage. In 1928 the secular nationalist Dr Sutomo, leader of the Indonesische Studieclub (Indonesian Study Club) in Surabaya, produced a book entitled *Perkawinan dan Perkawinan Anak-Anak* (Marriage and Child Marriage), significantly published by the government-owned Balai Pustaka, dedicated to issuing improving and informative works in Malay. As the only book published by an Indonesian on the subject of child marriage, it is clearly a significant contribution to the debate.

Sutomo's book puts him squarely in the league of nationalist social reformers. A medical doctor by profession, Sutomo pronounced in his Introduction that his intention was to write a book to be read by 'civil servants, teachers, doctors and others who on account of their position and daily work have the opportunity to lead the People from a dark world into the light' (Soetomo 1928: 6), a phrase that immediately evokes the title of the selection of Kartini's letters published by J. H. Abendanon: *Door Duisternis tot Licht* (Through Darkness to Light). Sutomo forms a bridge from Ethical Policy attitudes to those of the nationalist movement, continuing thus: 'There are many conditions and rules in our Indonesian society which need to be examined if we intend to gain a respected place amongst other nations, which is what we very much desire' (Soetomo 1928: 7).

One of those conditions in need of scrutiny was clearly marriage customs. Sutomo took great pains in this book to convince his Indonesian readers that the spirit of Islamic ideas on marriage was perfectly compatible with modern Western notions. The book was liberally sprinkled with quotations from the Koran and *hadis* (sayings of the Prophet) side by side with J. S. Mill, Western sociologists and the new Dutch guide to modern marriage, Dr Th. van de Velde's *Over 't Volkomen Huwelijk* (Ideal Marriage), published in 1926. Sutomo started out confidently: 'It is certain that a marriage which is intended to last forever, regardless of circumstances, must be based on a firm love, mutual respect, giving oneself to the other' (p. 12), and cited van de Velde's four conditions of love and happiness: sound choice of spouse; health; agreement about children; and well-matched sexual desire (p. 21).

About half the text of the book and all its lengthy appendices (speeches and regulations) concerned child marriage. Sutomo's greatest objection to child marriage was that it represented a form of forced marriage, burdening children with responsibilities which they could not fully understand (p. 37). Moreover, child marriage frequently led to divorce, which 'hinders good family life and is also a bad influence on the upbringing of children' (p. 40). It was up to Islamic marriage officials, he claimed, to help stamp out the evil of child marriage. Religious organisations, both Islamic and Christian, were already making praiseworthy efforts in this respect. In fact, Sutomo went to considerable lengths to document numerous cases where Islamic organisations in recent times had criticised child marriage. As a secular nationalist with a dubious reputation among Islamic organisations, Sutomo sought to bolster the Islamic credibility of his cause.

Apart from what he identified as the necessary and growing support of Muslim organisations, Sutomo hailed the women's movement as an ally, and urged Muslim women's organisations to join with others in a united front. Women's equality, he argued, would not harm society, and he pointed to Scandinavian countries as examples of the way in which women's movement towards equality had led to increased protection of children. He referred to the work of Kartini ('She convinced men of our nation about the oppression of men towards women') and to the female contributors to the Declining Welfare Commission (p. 47).

In conclusion Sutomo called on every right-thinking Indonesian to make child marriage a national issue. The government could do much through schooling where children were taught to postpone marriage and respect women, and civil servants and local officials also had a role to play. Pointing to the success of the government's campaign against opium-smoking, he hoped that the same kind of attitude change could occur in relation to child marriage (pp. 48–9).

Sutomo's book judiciously blended the arguments against child marriage which every interested party – Dutch, nationalist, Muslim and feminist – would wish to see expressed. As far as action was concerned, he called not for government legislation but for awareness-raising which would lead to a change in values. It is very much what one might expect of a reforming type of Indonesian nationalist who through his work as a doctor saw social problems at first-hand. It might not be going too far, either, to discern in his thinking on this issue the influence of his wife, a Dutch nurse whom he held in high regard.[2] It was certainly the most outspokenly 'pro-woman' of his writings and distinguished him as possibly the sole male nationalist to take up what were usually regarded as 'women's issues', as against just trying to recruit women into the

---

[2] See Sutomo's memoirs for his touching tribute to his late wife (Soetomo 1934: 127–8).

nationalist movement. The distinction here is, however, a fine one: for Sutomo, child marriage was a nationalist issue, because it affected the strength and reputation of the Indonesian nation.

Colonial government measures in the 1930s

Meanwhile, the Adviser for Native Affairs was saddled with the task of interpreting the six-monthly statistics on child marriage requested by the government in 1925 (Adviser for Native Affairs 1930 and 1932). For some years he wrestled with the motley collection of figures and comments provided to him by local officials (mostly local level Islamic marriage officials), becoming more and more frustrated in the process. The whole exercise faced insuperable problems.

First of all, there was no agreement amongst informants as to what constituted child marriage. In most cases, officials reported it to be either marriage of a girl below a certain age (anywhere from under nine to under sixteen years) *or* marriage before menstruation occurred. There was no way of establishing exact age for most girls without proper birth registration. In many cases it was obvious that the 1927 circular against requiring girls to appear before officials to establish age was not being followed. Witnesses were often called in to give evidence about age or an estimate was made by judging whether the outward appearance of the girl showed she had reached puberty. If 'marriageable age' were based on evidence of menstruation, no tactful and reliable way could be found to determine this, although in many cases again witnesses were questioned. Sometimes officials responsible for compiling the reports simply evaded the issue of definition, perhaps revealing how unfamiliar and incomprehensible the whole notion of child marriage was, or alternatively that they could not be bothered investigating it. In the western district of Borneo, for instance, child marriage was defined in circular terms as marriage where the girl was not yet marriageable, and in Benkulen and Aceh the bland statement was proffered that 'Only marriages between marriageable persons are known.'

The six-monthly reports contained a number of fascinating local variations in the monitoring of child marriage. In some districts (Krawang, Pamekasan and Temanggung) a girl was held to be of marrigeable age when she 'has a dream of orgasm', presumably demonstrating that she was ready for sex. In Blitar, 'to determine age, the circumference of the girl's head is measured with a thread, which is then laid on the girl's neck, and if the ends do not reach her nipples, the girl is marriageable'. In many cases the girl had to run the gauntlet of so many interrogators that she (and her relatives) must have found it a humiliating (or farcical) experience, particularly considering that by this stage the wedding arrangements had mostly been completed.

Secondly, there was the vexed question of *kawin gantung*, a practice which existed under other names in many places. The report sheets required officials to specify whether the so-called child marriage was in fact a case of postponed consummation. Understandably, it was impossible to ascertain whether such postponement actually occurred. In some areas, officials insisted that only *kawin gantung* marriages were permitted for child brides, whereupon all early marriages were recorded as *kawin gantung*.

Finally, the statistics were often unbelievable. Even statistics provided for the one district, where presumably the criteria were constant, fluctuated in illogical ways, undermining their credibility and making it impossible to establish clear trends. Alternatively, credibility was weakened when the local regent or resident was known to be strongly against child marriage, leading lower officials to cease registering any cases for fear of disapproval.

Despite the chaotic nature of the reports, the Adviser for Native Affairs found some value in them if only because the requirement to collect them illustrated the government's concern about child marriage. This put pressure on local officials and fuelled the efforts of non-government organisations, principally in the women's movement. Moreover, it was possible to draw a number of tentative conclusions from the collected data.

Firstly, it seemed to the Adviser that overall, the combined statistics and official comments which accompanied them showed that the incidence of child marriage was declining. The reasons advanced for this decline were many and varied. More predictable explanations were that people were becoming more educated and/or susceptible to pressure from their leaders, those in nationalist parties or in official positions, who opposed child marriage. Less obvious explanations included a report from Grobongan regency that people had noted the bad consequences of child marriage, including that 'often there were love affairs here between the mother-in-law and the son-in-law because the wife was still too young [for sexual intercourse], which resulted in violence', and because mishandling of young brides was also not uncommon. Similar observations came from Grissee, where according to the regent, 'fights often occur as a result of liaisons between mother-in-law and son-in-law', leading to parents-in-law 'mostly trying to urge the son-in-law to resort to public women while he may not still sleep with his young bride'.

Secondly, there was of course considerable regional variation in the apparent incidence of child marriage. In a few regions like West and Central Java and Solo, it appeared to be relatively high. In Serang Regency, for instance, in the period 1928–31 more than one thousand cases of child marriage were recorded every year. In the Outer Islands the only place registering significant numbers of child marriages was West Sumatra. As noted, however, reporting was dubious at best. At one point the Adviser for Native Affairs had queried the Aceh report that there was no child marriage in the region, calling the Governor's attention to Snouck Hurgronje's earlier writing on the Acehnese, which documented cases of child marriage. After that hint, the Governor obligingly came up with some figures of child marriage, presumably gained by twisting the arms of the local chiefs who were responsible for providing them.

By about this time, the results of the 1930 census were becoming available. The census collectors reported the familiar problems of establishing age and incidence of child marriage. No exact ages were listed; instead, collectors were required to list every individual as belonging to one of three age groups. The first of these, infancy, was relatively easy since it covered infants who were not yet walking, but it proved extremely difficult to distinguish the boundary between the next two categories, non-adult and adult, especially since married girls were likely to be automatically classed as adult: as in the English language, it seemed virtually impossible to view a wife as a child rather than a woman, as though marriage were a rite of passage. Assuming that the understatement of the level of child marriage was relatively uniform, however, one could still conclude from the census that the provinces with the highest rate were West and Central Java, followed by East Java, with some areas of Sumatra (Aceh, the northeast and the west) also showing as relatively high. In no district, however, were more than a few percentage of girls in the second age group listed as being married, leading the census compilers to conclude defensively that although there were undeniably 'many married children', the problem in the Indies was less serious than in India; and in any case, they added, 'such alliances are . . . not always of long duration'(Netherlands Indies Government 1930: vol. VIII, 51).[3]

Even before the census results had been published, the government had decided that attempts to collect statistics specifically on child marriage no longer served a useful purpose. In June 1932 another circular was sent to officials requesting them to cease providing their six-monthly reports. The statistics had been unreliable, and in any case it seemed that as a

---

[3] In British India in 1929 research on age of marriage estimated that 42 per cent of the female population were married before age fifteen (Forbes 1979: 413).

result of 'intensive combating' in many places, the incidence of child marriage was declining. 'Rejection of this practice can be left to public opinion. In the first place it rests with women's organisations to concern themselves with this matter' (Netherlands Indies Government 1932).

The colonial government made one last and abortive bid to tackle the issue of child marriage head on. In 1937 it launched a draft of an ordinance for optional monogamous marriage for Muslims. As will be discussed further in Chapter 5, the main thrust of the proposal was to offer Muslim couples the option of registering monogamous marriages. However, it also stipulated a minimum age for such marriages: eighteen for men and fifteen for women (Netherlands Indies Government 1937). When it proved unacceptable both to Muslim organisations and to nationalist parties, which resented colonial efforts to interfere in personal affairs, the government withdrew the ordinance after only a few months' informal discussion. That was the end of its efforts at social reform in the area of Indonesian marriage practice.

Indonesian women's intiatives, 1930s

The Indonesian women's movement, however, pressed on with the campaign against child marriage. Women in Muslim organisations began to be more vocal on marriage issues, partly in response to the government's marriage ordinance project of 1937. At its 1938 congress, for instance, the women's wing of the Islamic Union of Indonesia Party (Partai Sarekat Islam Indonesia – PSII), which had never before made political statements, included some outspoken comments on the need to abolish child marriage. S. Sumadhi denounced the marriage of young girls as caused by parental greed and likely to damage the health of mothers and offspring. A statement by the executive claimed it had received many requests to consider the matter of child marriage. Although it acknowledged that according to Islam child marriage was lawful, nevertheless the practice should be opposed. Young girls were not capable of taking responsibility as housewives and mothers (Pergerakan Isteri PSII 1940). Nevertheless, the organisation still refused to set an appropriate chronological age for marriage, preferring the assessment to be left to individuals and, no doubt, wishing to avoid a confrontation with religious leaders on the matter.[4]

One woman who kept the issue in the forefront was Chairul Syamsu Datu Tumenggung, a Minang married to a colonial civil servant living

---

[4] A contemporary publication by Aisyiyah, the modernist Islamic women's organisation, makes no mention of child marriage (Aisjijah 1939).

in Batavia and active in the Assocation of the Wives of Indonesian Civil Servants (Persatuan Isteri Pegawai Bestuur), for whom she edited the monthly journal *Pedoman Isteri* (Woman's Bulletin) in the 1930s. The pages of the journal occasionally carried articles opposing child marriage, principally arguing that the practice weakened the family. Mrs Datu Tumenggung also contributed a chapter entitled 'Combating child marriage' to the *Indisch Vrouwen Jaarboek 1936* (Indies Women's Yearbook 1936), a compilation of papers on women in the Indies by women of all races (Schreven and Boomkamp 1936). After sketching the incidence and causes of child marriage along familiar lines, she condemned parents for 'committing a crime against young children which can haunt them for their whole life'. Better-educated people, she claimed, were well aware of 'the evil' and their efforts against it, combined with those of the government and of civil servants, had led to a decline in the practice in recent years. How she could be so sure of this is unclear, since she admits to the many obstacles facing the campaign such as Muslim opposition based on the lack of a prohibition against child marriage in Islam, and the difficulty of ascertaining the age of girls. It is likely that the decline she observed was in urban society. Mrs Tumenggung acknowledged the value of Sutomo's book 'in arousing concern in many circles' and praised women's organisations for doing likewise. As a result, she claimed, 'people are slowly realising that indeed child marriage is a cancer in our world which must be strongly opposed'. Ever aware of the responsibilities of leadership, she concluded that 'This task, i.e. of bringing this understanding to their uneducated sisters, rests on the shoulders of those women who are called to it by their education and development.' In short, Mrs Tumenggung's stance accorded with that of Sutomo, crusading for a social reform by means of education and leadership.

Finally, at the end of the colonial period, the women's movement began to take practical if small-scale action on marriage problems, by setting up in 1939 the Marriage Consultation Bureau. By the time the women were married it was of course too late to prevent child marriage, but the bureau began to document cases of abuse and abandonment which it considered often resulted from forced or child marriage. The aim of the bureau was to offer assistance and advice to women in such difficulties. Their evidence is particularly interesting in the light it sheds on cases of arranged marriage which never 'took' because one partner refused to accept the other. Where this led to the wife being deserted without divorce, she was often in trouble, since under Islamic law it was very difficult for a wife to initiate divorce proceedings or to claim support. The bureau helped some women work through these legal and financial tangles (BBPIP 1939).

'Early marriage' discourse since 1945

Once Indonesian nationalists gained control of the state in 1945, women's organisations expected governments to take stronger measures than in colonial times to improve the situation of women. In 1946, shortly after the Declaration of Independence, the Ministry of Religion, which was given responsibility for registration of marriage, divorce and repudiation, issued a law on the matter (No. 22 1946), followed in 1947 by an instruction to marriage officials to discourage and avoid registering forced and child marriages (Suwondo 1981: 79). Maria Ullfah Santoso (later Subadio), an active campaigner on women's issues and Minister for Social Welfare between 1945 and 1947, observed that in practice the instruction was not fully implemented, suggesting that this could possibly be attributed to its relatively inferior status as an instruction (Soebadio 1981: 15). It far from fulfilled the demands of women's organisations, which continued to lobby for more substantive reform, despite some disagreement as to precisely what form any legislation should take.

Following the transfer of sovereignty in 1949, the struggle to raise the age of marriage was inextricably intertwined with the efforts of the women's movement to reform the marriage law, a matter that will be considered in greater detail in Chapter 5 of this book. Although Kowani, the women's federation, included organisations that differed on religious and political grounds, there was widespread consensus on the need for a national marriage law that would ensure women's rights in marriage, with particular concern over polygamy, child marriage and women's lack of rights within divorce. For more than two decades after independence, the agendas of women's organisations were dominated by the issue of marriage law and efforts to have such legislation adopted.

In August 1950, in response to concerted lobbying by both women's organisations and female members of the Provisional Parliament, the government formed the Panitia Penyelidik Peraturan Hukum Perkawinan, Talak, dan Rujuk (Panitia NTR or Committee for Marriage, Divorce and Reconciliation) to examine the prospects for a new marriage law. In addition to investigating possible legislative approaches to marriage and divorce, the committee considered the question of whether Indonesia should have one law for all citizens, regardless of religion, or whether laws should be specific to particular religions. This issue continued to create division until the introduction of the 1974 Marriage Law.

In December 1952, Panitia NTR produced a draft law on marriage, presented to the Ministry of Religion in 1954, which advocated a minimum marriage age of fifteen for girls and eighteen for boys. This initiated an on-going struggle between religious organisations and women's organisations, on the one hand, and between women's organisations and the parliament, on the other (Soebadio 1981). For Muslim women's organisations the matter of child marriage, like the associated issues raised by the marriage law debates, was fraught with difficulties, since male Islamic leaders resisted state interference in their religion.

While the ensuing debates, and the on-going concerns of women's organisations, included opposition to child marriage, the dominant issues were polygamy and discrimination against women in divorce and inheritance, regarded as being most detrimental to the status of women within marriage. Moreover, they posed the most direct threats to the interests of the women engaged in organisations and campaigns in favour of protective legislation. Although women's groups continued to lobby for reform of early marriage, it was overshadowed by these other concerns. One explanation for this prioritisation of grievances is the fact that marriage itself is a rite of passage by which girls become women.[5] In a society like Indonesia where very few women did not marry, those involved in organisations had already undergone that rite of passage and were confronted with more immediate concerns within the institution of marriage. While the rights of women were of primary importance, and some mention was made at various junctures of the rights and needs of children, child wives, often not in a position to speak on behalf of themselves, fell between these two categories. Moreover, the association of child marriage with life in rural areas tended to remove the issue to the periphery of the agendas of groups with a largely urban, and relatively educated, membership. In the 1950s, however, girls continued to marry very young, with signs of a gradual change in the following decade.

Opposition to child marriage was based on concerns about the implications for girls' health and education, and women's organisations spoke on behalf of those who were married off, or likely to be married off, at an early age. As in the colonial period, child marriage was also often associated with forced marriage, where consent was absent and the girl might not have met her husband prior to the marriage, a state of affairs strongly opposed by a range of women's organisations and by (often female) representatives of political parties including Partai Komunis Indonesia (PKI – the Indonesian Communist Party) and Partai Nasional Indonesia (PNI – the Indonesian Nationalist Party) (Nasution 1992: 220–3).

---

[5] That marriage is considered to be a rite of passage into adulthood is reflected in the 1979 law on Child Welfare, which defines a child as any person under the age of twenty-one unless already married.

After 1965, the New Order Government of President Suharto had new priorities for women. In particular, in 1968, it began to promote family planning in an attempt to reduce Indonesia's high growth rate. This offered a new reason for the state to support a higher age of marriage of girls, in an attempt to reduce the number of years of child-bearing. At the same time, the women's movement maintained its pressure on the government. In 1973, a report entitled 'The status of women and family planning in Indonesia' was published, based on the work of a research team comprised of a number of individuals (notably Nani Suwondo) who had been active in the women's movement and in the campaigns to reform marriage laws. It observed that although minimum age at marriage was rising, child marriages still occurred, particularly in the villages and especially in West Java. The need for comprehensive marriage legislation applicable to all Indonesia was emphasised (Ihromi 1973).

The 1974 Marriage Law

In 1973, a new marriage bill, applicable to all Indonesian citizens, was finally introduced by the government. During 1973–4, the bill became a source of considerable tension between various interest groups. In its final form, the legislation was a result of considerable compromise on a range of matters (including polygamy, as will be discussed in Chapter 5), and the minimum ages that were ultimately adopted were lower than those identified in the initial draft and advocated by a number of women's organisations and the official family-planning policy. These compromises were concessions to Muslim lobby groups, both within and outside parliament. The amended act was promulgated in 1974. Thus the New Order Government became the first in Indonesian history to succeed in passing national marriage legislation, but even such a strong and authoritarian regime was obliged to make concessions to Islamic opposition, including in the area of minimum marriage age.

In February 1973, a consultation between members of parliament and members of the women's federation, Kowani, concluded that the appropriate minimum age for marriage was eighteen years for females and twenty-one years for males. In July of that year, the draft marriage legislation advocated these ages (Soebadio 1981: 17). Ultimately, the 1974 legislation adopted minimum ages of sixteen and nineteen years for females and males respectively. Significantly, the legislation also states that dispensation may be granted to allow the marriage of individuals who have not yet attained the minimum specified age. It does not, however, identify the circumstances that justify underage marriage.

It is difficult to assess the impact of the 1974 law on marriage age. The population censuses of 1971, 1980 and 1990 indicated an upward trend in marriage age, in both urban and rural areas and among both males and females. Census results also confirmed earlier evidence that a far greater percentage of girls than boys marry before the age of twenty. There was variation between provinces with some, such as West Java, continuing to show a higher incidence of early marriage. Trends towards later marriage were more pronounced in urban than in rural areas, and studies in Java showed that the move to later marriage was strongest among the urban middle class (Taj 1990). Nevertheless, in rural areas there was also an identifiable trend towards later marriage. While child marriage (referring to girls under the age of fourteen) was, according to official figures, becoming relatively infrequent, marriage remained widespread among girls below the age of twenty, and the term 'early marriage' usually related to the fifteen to nineteen age group, amongst whom more than one-third were already married in 1980. It was, however, impossible to ascertain from census figures the percentage of girls who married under the legal age of sixteen, as the age cohorts used were under fourteen and fifteen to nineteen.

A central question is the extent to which the introduction of the 1974 Marriage Law was responsible for the upward trend in marriage age. As indicated above, there were signs that the practice of marrying off very young girls, in many cases before puberty, was declining before the introduction of age restrictions. The demographer Gavin Jones has argued that the 1970s witnessed a 'revolution in marriage patterns after at least half a century, and probably much longer, of near stability', whereby the marriage of girls under the age of sixteen became less frequent (Jones 1994: 76). The origins of this transition predate the 1974 law.

On the other hand, research carried out in the Bangkalan Regency of Madura in 1977, suggests that the marriage of girls under the age of sixteen remained commonplace and was widely accepted within the community. The study found that, of the 130 village heads interviewed, only approximately one in four knew the legal minimum age for marriage (Adfdol 1979). That few people in rural areas, including community leaders and local officials, were conversant with the new law indicates that both the debate about the appropriate regulation of marriage, including minimum age, and the impact of the law itself was, initially at least, confined to a relatively small and elite group of political, religious and social organisations. Later research has confirmed that in Madura the age of marriage remains low, explained by the conviction of the Madurese that the important thing is to follow their own version of Islamic law (Jones 2001). Moreover, because marriages below the age of sixteen are not permitted without special dispensation, it is likely that they are vastly understated in the statistics. Anecdotal evidence shows that some local officials collude with parents in disguising child marriage: false certificates of age are issued or age is incorrectly recorded at marriage. Corruption makes this possible, especially if a pregnant girl needs to be married off quickly, but cultural attitudes are also still important: particularly in strongly Islamic rural areas many people still consider it desirable that girls be married as early as possible.[6]

Over time, legislation is likely to be one factor contributing to the rising age of marriage, particularly in urban centres and places where people hear and respond to government information. In rural and remote areas, the impact of the legislation is likely to have been limited, as indicated by research in Madura. Other factors, including the strength of Islamic practice, and increasing the participation of girls in primary school, have probably been significant. Changes in the nature of marriage, particularly greater spousal choice and a move towards the convergence of marriage ceremony, consummation and cohabitation as opposed to *kawin gantung*, are also conducive to later marriage (Hull and Hull 1987; Taj 1990). Further, greater employment opportunities for girls in some areas, resulting from the expansion of the industrial sector from the mid-1980s and the feminisation of the industrial labour force have helped increase marriage age and spousal choice among teenage girls by giving them a somewhat greater degree of control over their lives (Wolf 1992).

As discussed earlier, a primary motivation for official efforts to introduce a minimum age for marriage was its perceived role in family planning. In the late 1970s and early 1980s, the government launched a campaign aimed at reinforcing the delay of first marriage for girls until the age of sixteen, that is the minimum age for marriage under the 1974 legislation. By the 1990s the government was encouraging a longer delay of marriage, with twenty identified as the preferred minimum age for females and twenty-five for males (UNICEF 1994: 76). After the collapse of the New Order, voices within the women's movement again took up the call for higher marriage ages (*Jakarta Post* 27 August 2003; *Kompas* 8 January 2001).

By this time, the state had taken up international rhetoric on reproductive health which had become a part of official rhetoric, calling attention to the high maternal mortality associated with teenage pregnancies (see below and Chapter 6). The health and education interests of young people have continued to be reasons proffered by the state and women's

[6] For other accounts of the continued practice of child marriage since 1974, see Siwidana (1981) and *Suara Merdeka* 16 October 1982.

organisations for encouraging a higher marriage age. Efforts to extend basic education to both boys and girls, a cornerstone of New Order policy, have been an important factor in delaying marriage, at least into the early teen years. Keeping children in the formal education system for a specified number of years has also contributed to a changing notion within society of appropriate activities and roles for children by promoting childhood as a prolonged phase that should be characterised by activities that are distinct from the adult world. This notion is not easily reconciled with marriage or the role and image of mother or wife.

Child-focussed organisations enter the scene

Since 1974, the issue of early marriage has not featured prominently in the agendas of women's organisations. While the issue has become of marginal concern to women's groups who were, in the past, the main advocates of later marriage, it has been taken up by groups focussing on children's issues and rights.

The 1990s witnessed a proliferation of child-focussed organisations that have a broader agenda than the promotion of child welfare, instead adopting an empowerment- and rights-oriented approach to children's issues. In recent years, opposition to early marriage has been endorsed by a small number of these groups which emphasise children's rights, particularly to education and to 'childhood' as a time not only of learning but also of play and development. Early marriage is seen as contrary to the fulfilment of these rights.[7]

In 1992, one such organisation, KOMPAK (Komite Pendidikan Anak Kreatif – Committee for the Education of Creative Children), published an illustrated booklet entitled *Pengantin* (*The Bride*) to illustrate the detrimental effect of early marriage on girls. It described the marriage of a young girl, Riani, to a man almost twenty years her senior as follows: 'All that remains is Riani with a broken heart, because of the loss of her childhood which should be a time of learning, laughter and play with other children her age. At the time she was not yet 12 years old.' *The Bride* described the health risks associated with early marriage, discussing the plight of Riani's sister who, after being forced to marry at a young age, gave birth to a child who died and suffered severe health problems herself. While the physical risks of early marriage were identified as a prime

---

[7] According to the 1990 census, fewer than 1 per cent of girls aged between ten and fourteen were married; 0.41 per cent in rural areas and 0.16 per cent in urban areas. For the fifteen to nineteen age cohort, however, the figure jumps to 18.19 per cent for all females in Indonesia: 23.5 per cent in rural areas and 9.06 per cent in urban areas.

reason against the practice, the notion of a child's right to childhood was central. Here, KOMPAK drew a close connection between early marriage and premature entry to the workforce, noting that both are situations that rob children of their rights. KOMPAK worked primarily with young girls employed in the industrial complexes on the periphery of Jakarta but identified a similar set of factors, including poverty, the view that girls are and should be submissive and docile, and the neglect of children's rights, as operating to push young girls into the workforce prematurely and into early marriage.

Another child-focussed organisation, SAMIN (Sekretariat Anak Merdeka Indonesia – Secretariat for Independent Indonesian Children), has raised concerns about the connection between early marriage and child prostitution. This NGO initiated research into the extent and nature of child prostitution in Indonesian, which included an examination of the marriage law, particularly minimum age regulations, and the consequences of early marriage. The high divorce rate among couples who marry when the girl is very young has, in some circles, been mooted as being one factor that may lead young divorced girls towards prostitution.[8] Research on prostitution in Indonesia has also identified a link between early marriage and prostitution. In the case of Indramayu, a province in West Java known to be a major source of prostitutes, early marriage together with low levels of education and high levels of divorce have been identified as reasons for the high number of sex workers (Jones, Sulistyaningsih and Hull 1995: 39–41).

That the issue of early marriage is receiving attention from some of these organisations indicates greater recognition of childhood as an extended period, during which rights as well as welfare should be acknowledged and advanced. Linking early marriage to notions of children's rights is, however, new and remains tentative.

The international arena is a source of pressure on the Indonesian government in relation to age of marriage. The United Nations body most concerned with children's affairs, UNICEF, has expressed concern at the continuing incidence of early marriage in Indonesia, and has periodically in annual publications noted the significant number of women who marry at or before sixteen years of age. For instance, its *Situation Analysis of Women and Children in Indonesia* in 1994 described the issue of early marriage as 'complex because it is rooted in the beliefs and traditional social attitudes of people and is often exacerbated by poverty. Parents are

---

[8] Based on interviews conducted by Sharon Bessell in Indonesia in 1994 and 1995, and personal correspondence.

often eager to marry off their daughters as soon as they reach puberty to avoid the stigma of remaining unmarried as well as being an economic liability in poorer households' (UNICEF 1994: 85).

Echoing the concerns of earlier proponents of later marriage, UNICEF draws links between early marriage and low levels of education on the one hand and high levels of maternal mortality on the other. The health risks associated with early marriage and early childbirth are underscored by statistics that indicate maternal mortality among women under the age of twenty is over 160 per cent higher than that of women in the twenty to twenty-nine age bracket (UNICEF 1994: 95).

Conclusion

In the course of the twentieth century the debate about marriageable age in Indonesia has waxed and waned in intensity, and the debaters and their arguments have shifted over time. Launched in the period of the Ethical Policy in the Netherlands Indies, a period when 'social evils' in Indonesian society began to be identified and addressed, the debate reached a peak in the 1920s when women's organisations, secular nationalists and the colonial state agreed on the need for social change. The possibility of government intervention was explored but largely rejected, both because of the practical difficulties involved and because the notion of minimum marriage age was too intimately interwoven with broader marriage law reform. The latter subject aroused too much opposition in strongly Islamic circles for any government to engage with it in a serious way until the New Order regime implemented the 1974 Marriage Law. In the meantime, as a result of other social and economic trends in Indonesian society, the age of marriage began to rise of its own accord, reducing the urgency of the debate.

In the long run, it is doubtful how important legislation or government efforts have been in raising the age of marriage, particularly since it seems many Indonesians are quite unaware of the legal minimum age. Change in attitudes has been the most important contributor to girls marrying later, and this is the result of many factors, including indirectly related social and economic changes (such as increased literacy and new employment opportunities for women) and also, more directly, the efforts of organisations and leaders of the kind referred to in this chapter.

The forces of resistance to change have consistently been those who felt most threatened by change: families (particularly parents) who considered they were acting in the best interests of the group and the individual in marrying off young daughters, and devoutly Islamic groups who felt that an attack on early marriage was indirectly an attack on Islamic law, which had no concept of mimimum age and permitted girls to be married off without being consulted. Over time it seems that both these sources of resistance have come to accept the desirability of later marriage for girls, in the belief that in a 'modern' society longer schooling is required for girls and that adults make better mothers and wives.

4   Citizenship

The role of Indonesian women as members of a polity has been a contested one. The first issue to arise during the colonial period was whether women should have the right to vote; later during independence the right of some Indonesian women to citizenship was disputed; and at the end of the twentieth century, quite unexpectedly, there was a vigorous debate about whether a woman had the right to lead the country. This chapter draws together these debates under the rubric of citizenship, since they all relate to the equality of women with men as citizens of the Indonesian polity.

Consideration of citizenship brings into focus the relationships between the individual, the collectivity and the state, in a way that highlights important political concepts such as identity, freedom, equality, justice, care, participation and power, all central concerns of feminist politics. In the context of twentieth-century Indonesian history, these have all been contested matters as far as women are concerned, and they have particular resonance now with the return of democracy to Indonesia.

Taken as a whole, literature on citizenship canvasses three related issues: membership of a political community, the rights and obligations associated with that membership, and participation by those members in the life of that polity. This chapter investigates Indonesian women's experience of each of these aspects of citizenship. As the largest Islamic country in the world, Indonesia's case carries weight since Islamic women are frequently perceived as political victims rather than active, full political citizens.

Membership

Citizenship highlights the individual's legal identity as a member of a polity. Western political theory is divided in its representation of the

This chapter incorporates excerpts from one of my published articles (Blackburn 1999c). I thank *Australian Journal of Political Science* for permission to use it.

citizen: whereas organicists or communitarians see citizens as integral components of their communities, liberals envisage them as independent individuals relating directly to the state. It is the former notion that has had most resonance in twentieth-century Indonesia. In modern states, all citizens are legally equal in their relationship to the state. Inevitably, this creates conflicts with other kinds of membership which citizens experience, and which prevent that equality from being realised (Yuval-Davis 1997).

Before Indonesia became independent, the question of who was a citizen hardly existed, since inhabitants of the archipelago were colonial subjects. In this period, however, the foundations of later citizenship were laid. The Dutch colonial authorities divided the Indies population into three main categories: Europeans (less than half a million in 1930), Foreign Orientals (mainly Chinese and Arabs – about 1.2 million) and Natives (more than 59 million). Strictly speaking, Europeans were the only real citizens, and as such they enjoyed the greatest privileges. Religion provided another layer of difference in this society: while the vast majority were Muslim, there were Christian, Hindu, Buddhist, Confucian and animist minorities. Dutch colonialism established a legal system that acknowledged the many identities of its subjects, at least as far as personal law was concerned: matters such as marriage and inheritance were left to customary and religious law. Whether or not women were treated as equal then depended on the ethnic and religious group to which they belonged.

Among Indonesian nationalists in the early part of this century, membership of the putative nation began to be imagined: since the country had never previously existed, the content of 'Indonesian-ness' needed to be invented. Most nationalists were reluctant to accept non-indigenous peoples within their own organisations, foreshadowing their exclusion from the nation-to-be. The role of women as boundary-markers and as educators of children who would identify as Indonesians became increasingly important. Women who had sexual relations with men regarded as non-Indonesian, such as Europeans or Chinese, could be reviled by nationalists, and in turn those 'alien' groups also became more exclusive in their behaviour. The underlying assumption that women should always 'follow' men and that their children should belong to their father's group led women who associated with 'outsiders' to be considered as traitors to their nation.

After the Declaration of Independence in 1945, the new Constitution of 1945 stated (Chapter X Article 27): 'Without any exception, all citizens shall have equal position in Law and Government.' The break with the hierarchical and racist colonial past was clearly made. The legal identity of various groups as Indonesian citizens or otherwise took some time to sort out, decades in the case of many people of Chinese ethnicity. Even now, ethnic Chinese with citizenship papers are still regarded by many fellow-Indonesians as outsiders. Equal membership of the Indonesian polity is obviously more than a legal matter, as Chinese Indonesians have suffered discrimination on a number of counts, having to do with the practice of their religion, use of language and access to state schools and universities. Being marked as 'non-Indonesian' can be a matter of life and death when there is a breakdown in law and order and resentful mobs turn on Chinese Indonesians. In the May 1998 riots in Indonesia leading up to the replacement of Suharto as president, gangs singled out ethnic Chinese women for special treatment: they were raped and sexually assaulted in a disturbingly vicious way (see Chapter 8 on violence).

Another issue in the identification of women in particular as Indonesian citizens related to the legal identity of women who married foreigners. According to law since the colonial period, women take on the citizenship of their husband. From time to time this has been a matter of dispute by women who feel aggrieved at the way in which they are treated as subordinates of men. After all, Indonesian men who marry foreigners do not thus lose their citizenship – and their children in the case of divorce, since the children follow the citizenship of their father. This inequity only began to be addressed in new legislation before the parliament in 2003 (*Jakarta Post* 9 February 2003).

As these cases illustrate, the most pervasive problems for women relating to their identity as members of the polity arise from the fact that citizenship is only one form of membership in their lives, and not always the dominant one. From colonial days onwards, governments have not wished to override women's membership of subordinate communities that limit their rights. When it comes to the point, women's membership of families and religious and ethnic groups has been considered more important than their membership of the polity. The state has been reluctant to deal with women on an individual basis; it prefers to see them as part of communities. There are good reasons for this, since the state has not been willing or able to devote resources to deal with the consequences of treating women as equal individuals. The support of widows, divorced and elderly women, single mothers and so on is left to the care of local communities. The price to be paid is that women must also, on occasion, suffer subordination within those communities.

Community does not here refer to a private domain as distinct from a public one, related to that female=private/male=public dichotomy, well known in liberal discourse and attacked by many feminists. As Maila Stivens (1990) has noted, that distinction has been largely meaningless in

Indonesian society, where notions of the private scarcely exist and women have always moved and worked freely in public places like markets and fields. Longstanding communities have, however, had differing traditions of gender, from the matrilineal society of the Minangkabau to the more patriarchal style of the Balinese. Some of these communities offer great freedom to their women; the problems arise in relation to the restrictions that many of them impose.

Examples abound of women's subordination in such communities, and of the state's reluctance to combat such discrimination. As shown in the previous chapter, during the colonial period, the government was aware and disapproved of the practice of parents marrying their daughters off at very young ages, sometimes before adolescence. When it was clear that the difficulties involved in trying to intervene on behalf of girls were too great, the government gave up the attempt, leaving girls at the mercy of their families on the grounds that they could not interfere with religion and custom, and trusting to social change to solve the problem. Even the Marriage Law that was finally passed in 1974 failed to eradicate discrimination against women in marriage, leaving them subject to religious codes that, for instance, oblige Muslim women to accept co-wives and make divorce easier for husbands to initiate than wives.

The state has disregarded Islamic law in areas it regards as 'public' such as criminal law. Thus the notion contained in *syariah* law that women's witness is worth less than men's has been ignored in Indonesia's criminal code, inherited from the colonial period: in criminal matters there is no distinction between men and women. In contrast, personal and family laws have been left to religious and *adat* (customary law) courts, involving varying degrees of discrimination against women in relation to inheritance, custody of children and so on. (As we shall see, however, the state has not been averse to interfering in the operations of Islamic courts.)

The notion of Indonesian women as equal citizens with men is undercut, therefore, by governments' recognition that their membership of subordinate groups in society actually overrides their 'equal' membership of the polity in a number of respects. For most women, in fact, their membership of family, kinship group, village, ethnic or religious group determines the subordination that faces them in their daily lives, contradicting the fine rhetoric of equality of individuals embodied in the constitutional statements about citizenship (von Benda-Beckmann 1994; Bowen 2003).

While Indonesian ethnic groups are patriarchal to varying degrees, in all there is some kind of discrimination against women. More-over, as Kathryn Robinson has remarked (1994: 72), 'In contemporary

Indonesia, modes of fashioning ethnic difference are tied up in the constitution of gender difference and gender relations.' As ethnic groups seek to maintain themselves in the face of forces like schooling that push for national homogenisation, and the current trend to decentralisation, there is resistance to changing relations between the sexes.

Where the state can relate directly to individual citizens in pursuit of its own interests, it has done so, and not always in the interests of women. The New Order Government's supervision of civil servants' marriages is a case in point, of particular interest because in some ways it was intended to benefit women. As will be discussed in more detail in the next chapter, the New Order wished to reform marriage along 'modern' monogamous lines as part of its developmentalist project. Although it failed to achieve these ends through the 1974 Marriage Law, the government had more control over its large bureaucracy. It proceeded to introduce regulations in 1983 whereby civil servants had to submit their marriages to scrutiny by their superiors who were instructed to make it impossible for them to enter polygynous marriages and very difficult to obtain a divorce. Although intended to protect wives as well as to create a more harmonious state, the move went along with other measures that made civil servants' wives uncomfortably dependent on their husbands (Suryakusuma 1996). Women were in effect moving from a small community of subordination to a larger one.

The membership aspect of citizenship is thus an ambivalent one for Indonesian women. As members of ethnic, religious and other groups there are certain restrictions on them, but also, as in most Southeast Asian societies, they have enjoyed considerable freedoms, varying of course according to class and age: examples include considerable physical and social mobility and control of their own property. The challenge for women is to defend the freedoms conferred on them by tradition against encroaching repression by the state, and to try to use state pressure to erode undesirable features of local gender traditions. In other words, they try to incorporate into Indonesian identity the aspects of the country's constituent communities which best suit them, and to use their relationship as citizens with the state to enlarge their freedom. This is likely to be a difficult task, but it is becoming ever more pressing in the current era of decentralisation in Indonesia, when the Autonomy Law of 1999 has conferred far more power on districts to impose their own conceptions of customs and even of Islamic law.

The Indonesian state has been too weak or reluctant to try to displace subordinate groups as they exert control over women. When it does claim the citizenly obedience of women, it is not always to their advantage. As we will see in the next section, it is more likely to demand new duties from them than to confer new freedoms.

Rights and responsibilities

In Western political tradition a long debate has been waged between the liberal view of citizenship which champions the rights of individual citizens against the state, and the communitarian view, which sees the citizen as part of a collective to which he or she owes responsibilities. There are difficult issues here relating to justice, liberty and care that affect women in particular ways. Indonesia has a history of prioritising the communitarian tradition of citizenship: rights are conceived as pertaining to communities rather than to individuals, often to the disadvantage of women who are expected to fulfil numerous obligations but to have few rights.

Although Indonesian women have been reluctant to use the language of rights, they have in fact successfully deployed this terminology in their struggle for justice. As we have seen in Chapter 2, women's right to an education was fought fiercely by women like Kartini and largely won in subsequent decades. This formed a foundation for other rights demanded by them, such as the right to choose one's marriage partner and the timing of marriage.

Interestingly, devout Muslim women appealed to the Koran as an authority for educating girls, arguing that the Prophet said that both men and women had a *duty* to acquire knowledge. This represents an appeal to a different kind of discourse, and a powerful one at that in a religiously oriented society. Unlike rights discourse, it does not posit a claim by the individual or group against the state in the name of equality or justice, nor is it an obligation imposed on citizens by the state. Rather, Muslim groups implied that it was the individual's duty (and presumably that of parents in the case of a child), decreed by Allah, to gain an education by his/her own efforts. Within the modernist Islamic movement in particular, a tradition persists of not relying on the state but rather of mobilising the religious community to meet its own goals.

With the rise of the nationalist movement, male leaders like Sukarno argued that women should postpone all talk of their rights until after independence was gained, since the only relevant right was that to national self-determination – a clear case of communitarianism (Brown 1981). That the male-dominated nationalist movement disapproved of women making any claims for equality against the colonial state is showed by their almost total opposition to the notion that the Dutch administration might legislate for more equal marriage laws, as discussed in the next chapter.

However, rights did feature on the agendas of secular Indonesian nationalist organisations, even the most nationalist of them. One gendered case of citizenship rights relates to the right to vote, an issue of enormous importance for women's participation in the polity.

The right to vote

The movement for women's suffrage in Indonesia originated with Dutch-women seeking the vote for themselves, since women did not gain the vote in the Netherlands until 1919. In the Indies the movement broad-ened its scope when the Dutch began establishing representative coun-cils in the Indies, first at municipal level and, in 1918, at the national level with the opening of the People's Council or Volksraad. Although the latter was largely an advisory body with very little power, it was hoped it might develop into something more resembling a parliament. In 1908 a branch of the Dutch Women's Suffrage Association (Vereenig-ing voor Vrouwenkiesrecht or VVV) was founded in the Dutch East Indies, as an extension of the movement in the Netherlands. At first con-cerned purely to support the Dutch campaign, the VVV became inter-ested in women's suffrage in the Indies when restricted male suffrage (based on income and literacy) was introduced there for municipal coun-cils in Batavia, Semarang and Surabaya. In 1915 the Indies VVV sent a request to the Queen supporting equality of voting for the municipal councils. The request was rejected in the Netherlands (Jaarverslag 1915). In 1918 the Indies branches of the VVV lobbied the new People's Coun-cil members about their support for women's suffrage and requested that the Governor-General open elections for municipal councils to women (Jaarverslag 1918). Voting at this level was critical because elected (as opposed to appointed) members of the national People's Council were indirectly chosen by the municipal councils.[1]

When women gained the vote in the Netherlands in 1919, the Indies branches decided to continue the campaign for suffrage in the colony and renamed themselves Vereeniging Voor Vrouwenkiesrecht in Nederlands Indie (Association for Women's Suffrage in the Dutch East Indies).[2] They found support for women's suffrage in the Batavia municipal council and attended the 1919 meeting of the People's Council that voted in favour of women's suffrage. The VVV followed this up with a deputation to the Governor-General on the matter (Jaarverslag 1919).

---

[1] Only a minority of People's Council members were thus indirectly elected, the rest being appointed by the Governor-General, and the Council's powers were almost non-existent. Representation was skewed towards the Europeans. Not until 1931 did Indonesians make up half of the People's Council. After various reforms to establish other local councils and expand the electorate, in the late 1930s elections were held for thirty-two municipal councils (mostly in Java) and seventy-six regency councils in Java which in turn elected members of the People's Council. The eligible electorate was small: for instance in the two largest municipalities of Batavia and Surabaya, the combined number of voters in 1938 was about 16,000 European citizens, 8,000 Indonesians and 3,000 'Foreign Orientals' (Netherlands Indies Government 1940: I, 144).

[2] For the sake of simplicity, I will continue to refer to this organisation as VVV, although it changed its name several times during the colonial period (see Blackburn 1997).

At this stage the hopes of the VVV to achieve the vote in the colony as well as the mother country appeared well founded. In 1925 the Netherlands Parliament, now augmented with female members, removed from the Indies Administration Law the words that made suffrage exclusively male. From then onwards, it was up to the Indies authorities to open up suffrage for women. Subsequently, however, progress towards reform was stymied in the Indies. As Indonesian nationalist politics became more radical in the 1920s, opinion in government circles and among European-based parties hardened against any kind of change deemed likely to destabilise Indonesian society and colonial power relations. Membership of the People's Council, dominated by Europeans and appointees, also became more conservative. Colonial governments rebuffed VVV requests for the vote with the statement that it would not be possible to give the vote to European women while withholding it from Indonesians, and that in Indonesian society there was no desire to give women suffrage (Locher-Scholten 2000).

Their failure at first immobilised the VVV in the Indies. Later in the 1920s, however, they attempted to take up the challenge to prove that Indonesian women, at least in the educated classes, did indeed want the vote. The VVV recruited Indonesian members and tried to contact Indonesian women's organisations to raise awareness of political rights for women. This association between Dutch and Indonesian women was a strained one, particularly as the Indonesian women's organisations became identified with the nationalist movement. Leaders of the VVV had no sympathy with aspirations for independence in the colony: they wished only to gain voting rights for educated women, including the small minority of Indonesian women who had received a Western education. The attitude of many in the VVV was condescending towards its less-enlightened native sisters and their increasingly conservative stance mirrored that of the European community in the Indies in the late 1920s and 1930s (Blackburn 2000; Locher-Scholten 2000).

In the 1920s a small number of Indonesian women nevertheless joined the VVV, attracted by the opportunity to participate in seeking political rights for women at a time when very few Indonesian women's organisations showed any interest in such matters. Two of these determined women who were briefly members of the executive of the VVV were Rukmini Santoso, one of the sisters of the famous pioneering Indonesian feminist Kartini, and Rangkayo Chailan Syamsu Datu Tumenggung, who featured in the previous chapter as a campaigner against child marriage.[3] Another well-known Indonesian woman supporter of the suffrage

---

[3] She appears to have joined the VVV in 1931. In 1938 she stood, unsuccessfully, as candidate for the Batavia municipal elections.

movement was Mrs Abdul Rachman, the wife a highly-placed Javanese civil servant (Stuers 1960). These last two women formed a link between Dutch suffragists and the burgeoning Indonesian women's organisations of the 1920s (Blackburn 2000). The early Indonesian women's organisations, established in the 1910s, sought mainly to advance the social welfare and education of women. Those organisations that entered the political arena in the late 1920s at first identified with the nationalist aspirations of the male-dominated nationalist parties and did not focus on seeking political rights for women under colonial rule.

The VVV resented their failure to control their Indonesian sisters. When the Indonesian women's movement held its first national conference in 1928, the VVV expected to be invited to advise on political strategy; instead they were ignored. Sophie van Overveldt-Biekart, the VVV president at the time, commented that she doubted 'whether it is in the interests of Indonesian women to exclude us, when our and their interests meet at so many points and when we, European women, are better prepared for the struggle, and can in many respects provide them with information and support' (Overveldt-Biekart 1928: 3).

Mrs van Overveldt-Biekart typified the increasingly dominant conservative section of the VVV, which showed no understanding for the rising Indonesian women's movement. Indeed, at a low point in the organisation's morale, in 1934 the VVV was about to decide to abandon its usual request to the government to nominate both European and Indonesian women to the People's Council in favour of pressing for a European appointment only. The move was foiled by Mrs Datu Tumenggung, who turned up at the annual general meeting with a group of friends to vote against it (Algemeene Jaarvergadering 1934). In the following year, as a gesture in recognition of the need for a 'woman's voice', the Governor-General appointed a Dutchwoman to the People's Council.

Despite racism in the VVV, at critical times two European VVV members remained true to their pursuit of women's suffrage regardless of race. They were the Dutchwomen appointed by the colonial government to the People's Council: Mrs Razoux Schultz-Metzer,[4] appointed in 1935 and her replacement in 1940, Mrs J. Ch. Neuyen-Hakker. Although these women were, or had been, members of the VVV, they showed few signs of feminist convictions except on suffrage matters, when they supported women's rights regardless of race. In 1937 Mrs Razoux Schultz-Metzer introduced a motion, subsequently passed by the People's Council, urging the government to introduce women's suffrage for all racial groups

---

[4] Trained in the Netherlands as a teacher, Mrs Razoux Schultz-Metzer had married a Eurasian and founded the women's wing of the Indo-Europeesche Vereeniging (Eurasian League), concerned mainly with social welfare activities.

(Locher-Scholten 2000: 169). In 1937 the government made another reluctant reform, granting 'passive suffrage' to women by allowing women of any race to be elected to municipal councils. This resulted in the election of four Indonesian women to those councils from 1938 onwards. When the government finally proposed granting suffrage to European women but withholding it from non-European women, Mrs Neuyen-Hakker led the resistance which finally caused official capitulation. In a rousing speech she asked: 'Do women here, just as in the most civilised countries in the world, have the right to participate in determining by whom the laws, to which they will be subject, will be made. . .? No? Then it should also not be granted to Dutch women. Yes? Then it applies for all women who have sufficient education' (Netherlands Indies Government 1941: 1215). It was an amendment moved by Neuyen-Hakker that won People's Council support, and finally government agreement in November 1941, for active suffrage (the right to vote as well as to be elected) for educated women in the Indies. The fact that the amendment made it a matter of choice whether eligible women registered themselves as voters also took the sting out of two objections raised by the government: that women did not really want suffrage and that it would be too difficult to identify eligible women voters for registration.

So much for the role of outsiders in pressing the cause of women's right to vote in the Netherlands Indies. What part did Indonesian women's organisations play in demanding suffrage? As noted, they were slow to take up the suffrage issue, although none openly opposed women's right to vote.

There were a number of reasons for this reluctance. More conservative organisations, particularly those based on religion, implied that women were not yet ready for a role in public political life. Indonesian women were not accustomed to play a part in politics, and had never been encouraged to do so. Politics appeared, by default, to be a man's world in which women did not feel at ease and for which they had no training. There was no objection to women being consulted: in a number of places women landholders, for instance, actually participated in village council elections. But there was no strong tradition of women appearing in public political roles. Ironically, given the sequencing of suffrage expansion followed by the colonial rulers, it was active suffrage rather than passive suffrage that found more acceptance in conservative Indonesian circles: what was new was women taking seats in public councils.

Another quite different reason for some Indonesian women not supporting the suffrage campaign was nationalism. Those who espoused nationalist views most strongly often regarded suffrage as a diversion. What was the point, they implied, in seeking to vote for or be elected to municipal or higher councils when those bodies had little power in a colonial setting, and when the most important goal was national independence? Those who followed the so-called 'non-cooperating' path of Indonesian nationalism by rejecting involvement in colonial institutions, took no part in the suffrage debate. Strikingly, the most outspoken Indonesian feminist in the Indies, Suwarni Pringgodigdo, spurned the suffrage movement because she identified with Sukarno's Indonesian Nationalist Party (PNI) which was outlawed by the Dutch in the 1930s for its radical anti-colonial stance.[5]

During the 1930s, as the Indonesian women's movement grew in sophistication and experience, more members began to campaign for women's political rights. Towards the end of the decade national conferences of the movement were for the first time demanding women's right to vote. Rivalry with the Europeans served to prod nationalists forward at this stage: it was galling for a European woman, and not an Indonesian, to be appointed to the People's Council in 1935, and even more for the government to contemplate giving the vote to European but not Indonesian women in 1941. After the appointment of Mrs Razoux Schultz-Metzer in 1935, a number of women's organisations and Indonesian newspapers proceeded to propose to the government names of suitable Indonesian women who should be appointed in future: these names included Mrs Datu Tumenggung and the lawyer Maria Ullfah Santoso (Blackburn 1999a). In 1938, for the first time, the national conference of Indonesian women's organisations passed a motion on women's suffrage: after a speech by Mrs Datu Tumenggung on the matter, the conference cautiously recommended that member organisations 'carry on work and education concerning suffrage as freely as possible' if their organisations permitted political activities (Buku Peringatan 1958: 31–3).

Four Indonesian women, all prominent in the women's movement, were elected to municipal councils in and after 1938 under the new system of passive suffrage for women.[6] In August 1939, when the government failed to respond to requests to appoint an Indonesian woman to the People's Council, forty-five women's organisations took the unprecedented step of holding a public protest meeting after being refused permission to hold a demonstration on the matter. Stressing the injustice

---

[5] Born in 1910, Suwarni Pringgodigdo-Joyoseputro founded at the age of only twenty the radical women's organisation Istri Sedar. In the 1950s she was a member of parliament. For biographical notes see Stuers (1960: 181). It is noteworthy that Istri Sedar voted against the 1939 resolution of the Indonesian women's protest meeting (mentioned below) for women to be appointed to the People's Council (*Isteri Indonesia* 1939).

[6] They were Mrs Sudirman in Surabaya, Mrs Sunario Mangunpuspito in Semarang, Emma Puradireja in Bandung, and Sri Umiati in Ceribon.

of European but not Indonesian women having a voice in the People's Council, the meeting concluded with a resolution urging the government to nominate an Indonesian woman for the next People's Council term (*Isteri Indonesia* 1939).

In the end, the nationalist movement, the Indonesian women's movement and the VVV converged in pressuring the colonial government to grant female suffrage. The nationalist movement in 1939 embarked upon a campaign for an Indonesian parliament, a democratically elected body to replace the People's Council. This was the price they demanded for cooperating with the colonial government in the face of what they argued was the approaching threat of war. Gapi (acronym for Gabungan Politik Indonesia or Indonesian Political Coalition), the alliance of Indonesian organisations formed to press for democratic reforms, committed itself to universal suffrage as part of its campaign, which was supported by a large number of Indonesian women's organisations (Blackburn 1999a). In July 1941 the national conference of women's organisations supported in principle Gapi's action for a parliament (*Isteri Indonesia* 1941).

Up until the formation of Gapi, male nationalists had not mounted a concerted campaign for women's suffrage, and even within the coalition the demand was incorporated in a more general one for universal suffrage: after all, most Indonesian men were also deprived of the vote in the Indies. At the public meeting held to launch Gapi in 1939, it is significant that despite the presence of women in the audience, there were no female speakers and no mention of votes for women, merely the need for a parliament elected by 'the people' (Gaboengan Politik Indonesia 1939).

Nothing changed until the outbreak of war in Europe. The Indies was on a war footing with Germany even before it was invaded by Japan in January 1942. The colonial authorities began to respond more sympathetically although still very cautiously to demands for political reform in the colonies, leading to their final capitulation to demands for active suffrage for a small group of educated women, that is suffrage for women on the same limited basis as for men.

Although the right was an empty one, since no elections were held before the Japanese Occupation, it broke the ground for universal suffrage. The significant fact was that by this time there was virtually no opposition left to women's right to vote. Only three members of the People's Council voted against it – a Dutch Catholic who had consistently opposed women of any race being permitted to vote, and a Chinese representative and a conservative Sumatran who considered the right conflicted with the customs of their ethnic groups. They were harmless remnants of conservatism: the tide had turned in favour of women's political rights.

Amongst the Indonesians, it is interesting to consider the significance of regional differences among the suffrage protagonists and opponents. In the few areas where educational levels were relatively high, especially among women, support for women's rights tended to be greater. The prime example is the Minahasa, in northern Sulawesi, where Christian missions had spread Western education very effectively. Male Minahasans like Sam Ratulangi were outspoken in their defence of women's suffrage. Conversely, in regions where there was less contact with Western ideas and a more patriarchal culture, such as Bali, women's suffrage was either ignored or was opposed. In such regions, too, there were no local councils for which election was an issue: most such councils were found in Java, where the bulk of the population was concentrated.

Part of the colonial government's argument against women's suffrage was that it was contrary to Indonesian custom and religion in some regions. An example proffered was Minangkabau in West Sumatra, where the regional council rejected a proposal in 1940 by three of its members to allow passive suffrage for women. Those who narrowly defeated the motion claimed that the presence of women in a public council violated Islamic principles and customary practice. Islamic attitudes will be discussed further below. The fact that the government appointed most of the (very conservative) members of the council obviously influenced the outcome of the vote. A number of prominent Minangkabau men and women immediately rejected the notion that their region prohibited women from taking a public role (Boerhan 1941). It is indeed ironic that Minangkabau, well known for its matrilineal inheritance system, for its strong women's organisations and for its outspoken women like Mrs Datu Tumenggung, should be represented as an impediment to women's suffrage, although it is true that women had no formal role in customary public institutions. Again, it seems that voting by women is sometimes more easily accepted than their representation.

Some of the strongest opponents of women's suffrage were to be found amongst the minority Arab and Chinese groups in the Indies. Their organisations never displayed any support for the movement, which was roundly criticised by some leaders of these groups within the People's Council. It was rare for any Chinese, especially a woman, to defend the notion of votes for women.[7] By the time of the last debates of 1941, however, the Arab and Chinese representatives were divided on the issue. Rivalry between the racial groups meant it was difficult for any group to reject suffrage once other groups had accepted it for their women.

---

[7] An exception was the Chinese woman doctor, Thung Sin Nio, who had been educated in the Netherlands (Chan 1995).

Among the antagonists of women's suffrage in the Indies it is remarkable how few opposed it as a matter of principle. Once women had won the vote in the Netherlands, only a few die-hards maintained the old arguments about women's inferiority or unsuitability for public political life. Those who rejected moves to extend the vote to women mainly did so on the grounds of expediency. As we have seen, the Dutch colonial authorities often stated that they had no objection to giving European women the vote but refrained from doing so merely because it would appear inequitable towards Indonesian women, whom they deemed not yet 'ready' for suffrage. They were wary after the rise of radical nationalism and (as shown in the next chapter) the fierce Islamic hostility they encountered when they proposed a cautious reform of marriage laws in 1937 (Locher-Scholten 2000: 175–6). This refrain about 'readiness' was taken up by a number of People's Council members too: thus it was just a matter of time before the reform would finally be granted.

Rights and responsibilities of citizens, 1945–1998

While the Dutch had conferred very limited suffrage on Indonesian men and women, the new Republic proclaimed in 1945 enshrined universal suffrage in the election law drafted in 1948. At the time of independence and until the late 1950s, it was possible for Indonesian men and women to demand and exercise their rights as citizens. As Jean Gelman Taylor has argued (Taylor 1996), this was a surprising period given the lack of any dominant tradition of liberal democracy in Indonesia. Only by reference to events at the time can one explain how a small group within the Indonesian elite managed to make its mark in favour of the equality of the sexes, overcoming the opposition of Islamic groups and of nationalists like Sukarno who had little time for individualistic or liberal notions that threatened national unity. In a famous speech in 1945 during the drafting of the Constitution, the Javanese lawyer Supomo voiced what was felt by many nationalists who adhered to the integralistic view of the state:

We want a spirit of the family principle which must include all the fields of human activity, not just in the economic, the social, but also in the political field, the governmental field, that means that all of the relationships between the government and its citizens must be included in the family principle way of thinking... In that system the attitude of the citizen is not 'what is my right?' but 'what is my duty as a member of this large family?' (cited in Milner 1996: 234)

This way of thinking was encapsulated in the notion of *azas kekeluargaan* (family principle) built into the state ideology, Pancasila, as developed by

Sukarno. During the decade after the Declaration of Independence, however, notions of liberal democracy were at their peak in Indonesia, fuelled initially by the need for the new nation to get international recognition at a time when democracy was the fashion even in the most unlikely places. The provisional constitution of 1950 contained a very extensive list of the rights to which citizens were entitled (Supomo 1960).

During the late 1940s and in the 1950s, many Indonesians became accustomed to exercising and demanding their rights as citizens, and the Constitutional Assembly in the late 1950s witnessed many passionate speeches on the subject (Nasution 1992). Women also took the opportunity to negotiate inside and outside parliament and lower level representative councils for extended rights, with varying degrees of success. The new nation, being so poor and fragile, called heavily on the voluntary service of women, who devoted enormous energy to activities such as literacy campaigns and care of orphans. Citizenship was seen very much in terms of the nationalist project of integration, but the state itself played a relatively small role in exploiting women's responsibilities as citizens: they voluntarily organised themselves to perform duties which they largely interpreted for themselves. While their awareness of their rights as citizens was just beginning to develop, their feelings of civic pride and duty ran high in the wake of nationalist victory. Much of that feeling of responsibility, it must be said, was probably directed as much to the local community as to the nation, about which many rural illiterate people still had only the haziest notion. The hardship of the times brought out the spirit of mutual aid in much of the population.

By the end of the 1950s, however, the period of liberal democracy was over. Sukarno abrogated the 1950 constitution, returned to the 1945 version with its greater scope for authoritarianism, and restructured the party system and the parliament to prevent them from challenging him. The period of Guided Democracy had begun, and with it almost all notions of the rights of citizens came to an end. The pendulum swung heavily in favour of citizens' obligations, which were called upon continually in the subsequent decades, as Guided Democracy turned into New Order in the late 1960s.

As far as women as citizens were concerned, the regimes of Sukarno and Suharto made distinctly different demands on them as citizens, but equally disdained notions of their rights. Both regimes mobilised women for their own purposes. With more radically nationalist expectations, Sukarno dragooned even Muslim women's organisations into military-style drills as women were called upon to prepare to defend the state against the machinations of neo-colonial oppressors, particularly connected with the struggle for Irian Jaya and against the formation of

Malaysia. Sukarno harked back to the notion of the state as a family, but since in his view the nation was in a state of revolution, all members of the family, including women, had to respond in heroic terms.

Under the New Order, women were defined in particular ways as citizens with gendered responsibilities. The nationalist project was now seen as developmentalist, a far cry from the revolutionary days of Sukarno. Gender roles could return to 'normal', where normality meant an amalgam of Javanese *priyayi* and Western bourgeois models of the nuclear family, in which people could contribute to both the material and the moral betterment of themselves and the nation. The reality of pluralism in Indonesia was largely ignored, as more restrictive gender roles were imposed on women (Robinson 1994). Ordinary women were expected to fulfil their duties as citizens through the state organisation known as PKK (Family Guidance Movement). From the 1970s onward, the most important contribution that women could make towards development, in the eyes of the New Order, was as 'responsible mothers', which entailed limiting the numbers of their offspring. This will be further discussed in Chapter 6.

Under both Sukarno and Suharto, talk of 'rights' smacked of Western liberalism, which was declared un-Indonesian. Although the 1945 Constitution does mention the equal rights of citizens, it is careful to stipulate that rights are subject to laws, and Indonesia's laws severely restricted such civil rights as freedom of assembly and expression. The New Order regime spoke of social and economic rights in a communitarian fashion, legitimising its rule by reference to national development, where it considered it had a proud record in fulfilling its citizens' rights to income, health and education. Among Indonesian women's organisations talk of rights was very subdued, although officially the country played its part in international arenas promoting women's rights.

Towards the end of the New Order regime, state views and indoctrination began to be challenged by its citizens, in line with growing awareness in Indonesia generally about rights. With the rise of an educated middle class, improved communications with the rest of the world and pressure from aid donors, the legitimacy of rights discourse grew in Indonesia. A major sign of this was the government's establishment in 1993 of the National Commission on Human Rights, a body which to the surprise of many proceeded to act with a high degree of independence.

Women articulated concerns about the gap between their ostensible rights as citizens and the reality of their lives. For instance, they were discriminated against in employment, despite laws to the contrary, a matter further explored in Chapter 7 on economic exploitation. The non-government Institute for Legal Aid regularly reported on the state's failure to correct the oppression of women (e.g. Andriyani 1994). This brings us to the final point about citizenship – the agency of citizens in shaping the polity – but before doing so I want to note a difficulty relating to rights which connects with the previous section on citizenship as membership.

Ethnic and religious groups have their own gendered traditions of rights and responsibilities, posing the kinds of problems for the Indonesian state which have already been noted. As Tony Reid has argued (Reid 1998b), there are many sources for a pluralist tradition in Indonesia to balance the integralist strand on which most Indonesian governments have drawn since independence. Although with regard to prospects for democracy it is heartening to remember this point, it also means that notions of rights have to be very carefully negotiated between different groups jealous of preserving their own cultural traditions. The rights for women for which groups campaign may have more to do with group identity than with feminist ideas of emancipation. As an example we might note the furore over the government's attempt to prevent girl pupils in state schools from wearing the Muslim headcovering, the *jilbab*, in the 1980s (Brenner 1996). It took a sustained campaign by Islamic organisations for women's right to wear the *jilbab* for the decree to be reversed. For women, the importance of gender rules within communities means that struggles for individual rights frequently have to be conducted within their own ethnic and religious groups if they are to be effective on the wider stage of the Indonesian polity.

Nevertheless, as we have seen, there is a tradition in Indonesia of women fighting for their rights. In the current period of democratisation in Indonesia, this tradition is being renewed. Some of these struggles have to be fought on the relatively unfamiliar ground of personal rights. Evidence for this seems to be provided by the recent surge of opposition to gender violence in Indonesia, as discussed in Chapter 8. Where the state has been objectionably intrusive, even coercive, in the lives of women, women will need to look beyond communitarian approaches to assert their rights to protect their personal lives from the state. These are cases not of the right to the provision of goods and services, but of the right to be free of oppression, to make one's own choices. It seems that for many poor women, it is particularly difficult to make such assertions: this kind of 'rights' discourse has largely been the domain of better-educated women.

Political participation

Theorists of citizenship are divided on the matter of political participation. The debate is framed in terms of what kind of democracy is desired:

one in which citizens are mainly passive, giving the state a fairly free hand on the condition that it does not infringe their rights, or a 'strong democracy' in which citizens are highly active in politics, exercising their right to shape government policy (Barber 1984). What is at stake here is the amount of power exercised by citizens vis-à-vis the state.

Since most governments in Indonesia this century have been authoritarian, this debate has had little resonance. Citizens have had little scope to participate in politics. The Dutch discouraged it, the Japanese forbade all but a tiny elite to try to play a role in politics, Sukarno limited severely the range of political organisations and their expression of ideas under Guided Democracy, and Suharto went a step further by banning more organisations and imposing what was called the policy of 'floating mass', whereby political parties were not permitted to operate in villages. Under both Sukarno and Suharto only a limited range of political activities were permitted and they were carefully controlled and orchestrated, like Sukarno's 'Crush Malaysia' demonstrations and Suharto's elections, where a prescribed majority of votes was regularly won by the electoral machine, Golkar (Sekretariat Bersama Golongan Karya – Joint Secretariat of Functional Groups).

As far as women are concerned, these government-imposed restrictions have been yet another layer of obstacles to empowerment, on top of the problems posed by poverty, shortage of time, inexperience and societal disapproval. Although Indonesian women undoubtedly exercise some kinds of power, even affluent women have traditionally lacked experience and legitimacy in taking public roles in decision-making, at either local or national levels.

Nevertheless, as this book shows, some Indonesian women have always been politically active in attempting to influence government policy. During the colonial period their organisations were many and varied, some of them overtly political and others more covert, as befitted a time when political activity could easily attract a repressive response from the authorities. Compared with women in nationalist organisations, those in organisations established purely for women were less overtly political. However, even the latter could sometimes address the government in an attempt to influence policy, such as in supporting the right to vote.

During the Japanese Occupation, participation in politics was virtually impossible for women. The struggle for national independence after the war offered them many more opportunities: the first woman ministers entered Republican Cabinets, and many women flocked to join the newly formed parties and organisations preparing for the first elections in 1955 (Lucas 1996). During the period of parliamentary democracy in the 1950s, a diversity of political views, from Communist to Islamic, was reflected in organisations in which women participated.

In 1955 Indonesian women had their first opportunity to use the right to vote at the national level. What did it yield for them? Firstly, they were keen to take advantage of suffrage. Although it was not compulsory to vote, most women, like men, did so. Secondly, as pointed out in Chapter 1, few women were elected. A women's party was founded on the basis that women had a distinct political voice, but none of its candidates were successful and most parties and voters apparently did not accept that parliament needed a large number of women to represent their interests. In addition, of course, there were practical problems such as women's inexperience with party politics and the reluctance of men to yield power to them. The new parliament after 1955 contained few women and Cabinets included none. In a global perspective this was not surprising: women had difficulty getting elected anywhere in the democratic world at that time, especially in new democracies. But women's organisations were active lobbyists and hoped to gain reforms for which they had campaigned for years.

Unfortunately the cabinet instability that plagued Indonesia meant that controversial reforms desired by women's organisations had little hope of being enacted. Governments consisted of coalitions that made trade-offs to survive. As will be further discussed in the next chapter, one of these trade-offs was the matter of marriage law reform that was dear to the hearts of Indonesian women. It never got off the ground during the years of parliamentary democracy in Indonesia in the 1950s. However, other reforms in favour of gender equality were passed, such as equal pay for men and women civil servants, and governments fulfilled promises to raise women's levels of literacy.

Under Guided Democracy, the scope for women's political participation began to be limited when certain parties and organisations deemed inimical to national unity were banned, and the parliament was stripped of its power. No further elections were held, since according to Sukarno the '50 per cent plus 1' tradition of Western liberal democracy was divisive and unsuitable for Indonesia.

After 1966 the New Order Government 'restructured' the women's movement to eliminate any critical elements. Those women permitted to take a prominent role in political life under the New Order were members of elite families, usually the wives or daughters of men closely associated with the regime. For those few women, gender proved less of an obstacle than in the past: the President's daughter, Siti Hardiyanti Rukmana (commonly known as Tutut), briefly played a prominent role as a Cabinet minister and vice-president of the government party, Golkar. Family ties made it possible for her to become a front-runner, as in some other Asian countries dominated by dynastic political elites. Yet until very recently it has been difficult for women to play political roles, largely as a result of military domination of politics. Even in the last years of the New Order, if one belonged to the opposition, being a woman was little protection against repression, as the other prominent daughter of a president, Megawati Sukarnoputri, found when she tried to challenge the regime. She was summarily evicted from her position as leader of the small opposition party, Partai Demokrasi Indonesia (Indonesian Democracy Party – PDI).

As far as the majority of the population is concerned, during the New Order political participation was limited to voting at the elections held every five years from 1971 onwards. This was considered a duty rather than a right of Indonesian citizens, since the result was a foregone con- clusion: Golkar always won by a comfortable margin due to government manipulation of the opposition and the solid support of the state appara- tus in getting out the vote. Those who were elected to parliament played an insignificant political role, since parliament was largely a rubber- stamp for government legislation: Golkar members predominated and even 'opposition' members rarely criticised the government. Every five years the People's Consultative Assembly (consisting of the parliament supplemented by government appointees) obediently voted in Suharto as President, unopposed. Opposition political parties were not permitted to operate at village level except during short election campaigns, effec- tively removing the majority of the population from party political life. In the eyes of the New Order Government, the responsibility of ordinary citizens was to devote themselves to the effort of national development.

Under Suharto, women were channelled into various organisations intended to help them carry out tasks suited to their feminine nature, or *kodrat*. One of them was Dharma Wanita, comprising the wives of all civil servants, a large contingent in a country where the state plays such a prominent role. The tasks enumerated for these women give some idea of the New Order's priorities for women as citizens: they were to be companions to their husbands, educators of children, supplementary income-earners, housekeepers, and members of Indonesian society – in that order (Ilhami 1995: 74–5).

Under international pressure during the United Nations Decade for Women, the New Order regime did set up a Ministry for Women's Role and for the first time in 1978 began to appoint a few women to the Cabinet, but these positions provided little scope for effective political action. Moreover, the refusal of the government to allow new parties to be established meant there was no opportunity for new ideas to be channelled upwards through the political system. Even the new-style women's organisations that began to appear in the last decade of the regime suffered occasional harassment at the hands of the authorities, particularly if they tried to extend their activities beyond the level of the urban elite.

Certain responsibilities were carved out for women as citizens, but apart from the meaningless act of 'voting' in elections, political participation in state-level decision-making was made very difficult for them. For women, this created particular problems. Because women are more inexperienced in politics than men, practice in meetings and political discussion is especially important. Poorer women in particular lack the time, inclination and confidence to participate in public meetings, meaning that in organised politics, unless there are groups like Gerwani that make a special effort to elicit their views, poor women lack a voice. Although there is a popular perception that there is equality of the sexes among poor Indonesians, research shows that lower levels of education among rural women, their longer working hours and their lower wages are all testimony to the real subordination of women that helps to explain their lack of political efficacy (White and Hastuti 1980).

This point reinforces the importance of women's membership of local collectivities in explaining their citizenship behaviour. Practical difficulties and popular mythology at the level of villages and kinship networks create obstacles to women's political participation which will take a long time to overcome. In Indonesia, Islam constitutes a particular case of collective restriction on women's political participation, as was shown with unexpected force at the end of the twentieth century, notably in the debate about whether Megawati Sukarnoputri, as a woman, could become president of a Muslim nation.

Islam and women's political participation

During Indonesian women's struggle for suffrage, Islam played a relatively subdued role in the debate. There were very few cases of open confrontation between protagonists of women's political rights and Islamic leaders. Indeed, in 1999–2000, when the possibility that Megawati might become President of Indonesia was the focus of debate, the resurgence of Islamic assertiveness about women in politics surprised most people.

How do we explain the relatively low profile of Islam on the matter of the political participation of women? Firstly we should recognise that in Indonesia, Islam has very rarely interfered with the public role of women. Since pre-Islamic times, women have been free to work in the fields and in the markets, to participate in festivals alongside men and even, in exceptional cases, to take on roles as political leaders. With the rise of modern political movements in Indonesia since the early twentieth century, there was no objection to women becoming members, although they very rarely played a prominent role. Indeed, most political parties wanted to recruit women to swell their ranks and to raise children as loyal Indonesians.

Overtly Islamic parties and organisations did, however, have some difficulty in overcoming religious and sometimes customary objections to women playing a public political role. They preferred women to join separate wings or auxiliary bodies, and during the colonial period some Islamic organisations erected curtains at public meetings to separate men from women in the audience. Sometimes they objected to women speaking before male audiences (Blackburn 2002).

As the support of Islamic organisations for the nationalist movement grew, and their practices of gender discrimination were challenged by secular nationalists, they quietly modified their behaviour. It was exceptional to hear Islamic leaders object to women taking on public roles; more commonly they just remained silent on the matter of women's political rights. Women members of Islamic organisations took no part in the struggle for women to gain the vote during the colonial period – but neither did they oppose it. Within Gapi, in 1939 Islamic parties joined with secular ones in supporting the idea of universal suffrage, thus committing themselves to women's right to vote without spelling it out in ways that might prove embarrassing. This gave tacit permission for at least one leader of the women's wing of an Islamic party (S. Yati of Pergerakan Isteri PSII) to pronounce that 'In civic matters, surely we women have a right to a say like other citizens in the running of the country, but up to now we have had no satisfaction in this respect, rather only disappointment' (Madjelis Departement 1940: 82). After 1945, tacit acceptance of universal suffrage continued, for equally pragmatic reasons, such as the desire to win international support. Although some Islamic groups placed themselves outside the consensus by campaigning for an Islamic state where the rights of women might have been reduced (although that was never spelled out), they were marginalised and swept away by the post-war democratic tide.

In subsequent years nothing further was heard from the Islamic movement in Indonesia about women's political rights, until the next wave of democratisation in the 1990s. By then the issue was not whether women should be allowed to vote or to be represented in parliament, rights which were not contested, but whether they should be allowed to take the position of president.

Suharto's regime finally fell in 1998, brought down by the Asian financial crisis that undermined the economic development so important to its legitimacy. In 1999 fully fledged democracy returned to Indonesia with its first free elections for decades. Women like men revelled in their new political rights. There was a big voter turn-out and many new parties participated. Women were not well-placed, however, to take full advantage of opportunities. Despite massively increased literacy rates as a result of the New Order and foreign aid to help inform women about the true meaning of elections, women did not have enough time and resources to prepare for the election. As in 1955, there were relatively few women candidates and the percentage of women in the new parliament, at 8 per cent, represented a dramatic decline compared with the composition of the previous body (Blackburn 1999b). This follows the pattern of the aftermath of democratisation in other authoritarian regimes: when the parliament gains in prestige and power, men are increasingly unwilling to pre-select women, especially for safe seats.

However, the big issue of women's political rights that took everyone by surprise was the question of whether the country should have a female president. Megawati Sukarnoputri led the Partai Demokrasi Indonesia – Perjuangan (Indonesian Democracy Party of Struggle – PDI-P) which gained the largest number of votes in the 1999 election. Representing the legacy of her late father, Sukarno, she was immensely popular in areas where support for secular nationalism was strong, such as among less devout Muslims and in non-Islamic areas like Hindu Bali. Any government emerging from the 1999 elections was going to have to rely on a coalition within the parliament, and intense negotiations took place to establish the new government and determine the president, who was to be elected by the People's Consultative Assembly.[8] Since under the prevailing 1945 Constitution the president has wide powers, this was a critical matter. The largest parties based on Islam formed a united front to oppose the selection of Megawati as president in favour of someone more identified with the Islamic cause. Some Islamic leaders maintained that their rejection of Megawati was based on Islamic teachings that a woman should not lead men. For months there was controversy, with verses of the Koran and *Hadis* (sayings of the Prophet) being bandied about by both sides, and many pointed out that the Constitution precluded such discrimination against women.[9] Finally when the vote was held in the

---

[8] In 1998 the composition of both the People's Consultative Assembly and the Parliament were reformed to bring them more into line with democratic principles. By 1999 the majority of the former consisted of elected members.

[9] For examples of the publications marking the debate, see Jaiz (1998) and Hidayah (1998).

People's Consultative Assembly in October 1999, the strongly Islamic leader Abdurrachman Wahid was elected president with Megawati as his vice-president. That the opposition to Megawati by many politicians was a purely tactical one, was shown two years later when the parliament had lost patience with Wahid's erratic leadership. In 2001 Islamic leaders declared they had dropped their objections to a female leader; Wahid was ousted from office by the People's Consultative Assembly, which then voted Megawati into power, giving Indonesia its first female president.

Such was the irony of the situation that, as women's organisations glumly pointed out, Megawati was actually less interested in women's issues than Wahid. The latter had, for instance, appointed the first truly feminist (and Islamic) minister for women's affairs – who insisted that her department be renamed Ministry for Women's Empowerment (Parawansa 2002). However, the appointment of a woman president is clearly of immense symbolic significance for women's political rights.

Regardless of the reasons for the Islamic case against Megawati, it did represent a challenge to women's political leadership and as such was strongly opposed by many women's organisations. The battle now seems to have been won. There is no noticeable opposition on religious grounds to women taking any public political roles. Women have taken seats in parliament and in the highest positions in the land. The question of numbers is a different matter: as we have seen, women are still in a small minority. This in itself may be in part influenced by Islamic ideology, which in practice discourages women from entering publicly prominent positions. It is significant, however, that Indonesian Muslims avoid taking overtly antagonistic stances on such matters: there is no legitimacy within Indonesian Islam for opposing women's equal political rights as citizens. The 'Megawati debate' seems to have been a flash in the pan, motivated more by political expediency than religious principle.

As was frequently pointed out during that controversy, other Islamic countries (Turkey, Bangladesh and Pakistan) had already elected woman leaders. And despite their symbolic importance, their accession to power did not in the short term signify any change in the position of women, which was admittedly far lower in those countries than in Indonesia. As will be noted in the Conclusion, since the end of the twentieth century a successful campaign was waged by many women's organisations for quotas for women among party candidates. So the fight for women's political rights continues. The right to vote is only one of the changes necessary to empower women.

There are contradictory elements within Islam. Influences from the Middle East, fuelled by anti-Western elements and the accompanying fear of globalisation, push towards the domestication of women, while more moderate trends, including the growing Muslim feminist movement, favour a more public role (Blackburn 2004). Because Islam is expected to play a stronger political part in the post-Suharto era, this is a debate to watch carefully.

As has been shown, Indonesian women have experienced political participation in quite varied ways. Although there now appears to be a great desire among many women to choose their own channels of political participation, free from state intervention, it is not clear that the level of their political activity will necessarily rise. Only a minority of Indonesian women have ever been 'active citizens' in democratic parlance, because they have not had the opportunity to become involved in public politics, and because they have been socialised to think that politics is for men.

In many ways political participation is critical to resolving the problems associated with the gendered nature of citizenship. Only as women enter the sphere of public politics and voice their concerns can it be fully understood how the rights of citizens, formulated on the basis of the male citizen, frequently do not apply to women because the obstacles to implementing such rights are too great, and/or because they lack relevance. As a plural society, Indonesia needs to accommodate gender difference within its notion of citizenship, and only women can ensure that this accommodation is worked through in an equitable manner (Dzuhayatin 2001). Whether or not the reforms to the Indonesian state will permit this remains to be seen.

Conclusion

With greater opportunities for political organisation and expression, many more women are now exerting their rights as citizens to make claims upon the state. In so far as these claims involve more state expenditure, they are likely to fail for the time being at least, but claims which cost little may have a chance of success. It is likely, however, that governments for some time will comprise coalitions, in which case any demands by women which threaten party alliances may well fail as they did in the 1950s. Now that there are more well-educated women available, they are more likely to form and lead parties, as Megawati has done. Yet this may do little to affect gender policies, to judge from experiences elsewhere: the political system will continue to be male-dominated.

The history of Latin American countries emerging from authoritarian rule teaches us that as societies move into more democratic scenarios, the diversity among women as citizens may get lost from view. It is the elite and middle-class women who are more politically astute and vocal, and frequently they claim to represent all women (Schild 1997). It seems almost inevitable that in Indonesia, with a move towards a more liberal model of the state, the articulate and knowledgeable urban middle-class women of Java will come to represent Indonesian women citizens in the national parliament, continuing to exclude rural and poorer women, as well as women from more remote regions. Class may well play an even more prominent role in defining effective citizenship among women. The current move to political decentralisation does, however, offer women in the regions more chance to play a role in representative bodies.

The strong history of nationalism in Indonesia has made citizenship into an influential symbol which could be exploited by women if they managed to remould it into something closer to their wishes. The communitarianism implicit in Indonesian citizenship has attracted many women in the past, causing them to expend their best efforts in voluntary work for others. The current turbulent situation in Indonesia will undoubtedly call on this altruism yet again. The very fact that innumerable women will again prove themselves to be exemplary, altruistic citizens puts them firmly in the communitarian camp: they find it hard to use the language of rights.

As an example of a highly plural society, Indonesia highlights the importance for women of their layered membership of groups. Where the state is poor, as it has been for most of Indonesia's history, women are likely to be seen and to see themselves more as members of those subordinate groups, based on ethnicity, kinship networks and religion, than as members of the polity. Those groups differ so greatly in their expectations of women that it is not possible to read from this situation whether women are more or less limited in their rights and political participation as members of those groups than as Indonesian citizens. This has important implications for discussions of the impact of 'modernisation' or 'globalisation' on women as citizens. There are contradictory forces at work here: women may well be 'freed' from the bonds of their immediate communities only to have to struggle with new burdens preventing them from effectively exercising their rights as citizens. Western experience would seem to support this view.

Finally, the Indonesian experience illustrates the significance of different types of authoritarian states for women's role as citizens, offering a rich range from Western colonialism through military occupation to 'revolutionary' and 'developmental' versions of nationalist repressive regimes.

They have called upon ideologies of citizenship that reverberate with organicist and communitarian thinking in Western thought, and there has been little scope for liberal notions or ideas about 'active citizenship'. At present, as a form of democracy takes hold again in Indonesia, we may see how it manages to accommodate the nation's many forms of difference, including that of gender, within its discourse on citizenship.

5   Polygamy

Many Indonesian women have passionately opposed polygamy. Of all the issues canvassed in this book, it is the one that has aroused the greatest depth of feeling among the largest number of Indonesian women. In 1900 Kartini wrote in Java that 'Almost every woman I know here, curses [the] right that men have' to take up to four wives (Kartini 1995: 45–6). In 1913 in Minangkabau another woman wrote in equally sombre terms: 'Polygamy is the poison of the world for us women. There is nothing so painful, so troublesome' (*Soenting Melajoe*, 1913: 1). This characterisation of polygamy as poison was common among Indonesian women.[1] In the early 1960s an anthropologist talking to Sasak village women in Lombok found that they were unusually emotional about polygamy. 'One young woman who had been married for two years related the recurrent nightmares she had about her husband taking another wife, or having another wife and not telling her about it.' In a society where violence was strongly deprecated, 'The wife of a village official talked of fighting with her husband's second wife, stating that such conflicts between co-wives were frequent . . . Another woman said that she dreamed of scratching her co-wife's eyes out.' Women reported that others had committed suicide or become insane as a result of polygamy (Krulfeld 1986: 204).

Opposition to polygamy has driven Indonesian women to public action on many occasions. Examples of public expressions include speeches in the first Indonesian Women's Congress in 1928; street demonstrations in 1952 against a regulation giving pensions to all widows of polygamous civil servants; protests in 1955 against President Sukarno's polygamous marriage; campaigns for a marriage law from the 1940s to the 1970s; and

---

[1] Significantly, the use of the term poison contradicted the root of the Indonesian word for polygamy, *permaduan*, which is *madu* meaning honey. Jennaway (2000:147) notes that in Bali the analogy of extra wives with honey is often made, consistent with many references in Balinese literature and popular discourse likening girls to honey and men to bees that drink their nectar. The association of polygyny with sweetness, she comments, 'would seem to represent the male perspective; for many co-wives the term *madu* parodies the bitterness it almost inevitably entails.'

demonstrations against polygamists in 2003 (*Jakarta Post* 30 July 2003). Even Muslim women's organisations, while unwilling to speak out against the institution of polygamy, wished to see what they considered 'abuses' of polygamy eradicated to protect women.

Despite the very low incidence of polygamy in Indonesia, it has been a central issue in relations between Indonesian women and the state in the twentieth century. Indonesian women's organisations have long wanted the state to legislate on this matter, yet it was most reluctant to do so until the passage of the 1974 Marriage Law. After that the fire went out of the issue as far as women's organisations were concerned, although in very recent years there has been a revival of interest. This chapter will first address the question of why polygamy has been so central in Indonesian debates about marriage. Unlike most other issues discussed in this book, polygamy engaged women's organisations in public debate with one another and with men, and in particular Islamic women's organisations felt involved, in the kind of public manner they generally avoided. What exactly has been at stake here in the eyes of Indonesian women? A substantial part of the chapter analyses the arguments put forward by women themselves.

Secondly, given that polygamy was the issue on which women's organisations pressed governments most strongly for the longest period of time, what have Indonesian women wanted the state to do about it? What have been the interests of the state at different times in responding or not responding to women's pressure on this issue?

Finally, why did the polygamy debate decline in the last part of the twentieth century, only to revive more recently? What if anything has the state contributed to this fluctuating concern about polygamy?

The question of polygamy, like that of pornography or prostitution in Western societies, with which indeed it often overlaps, has generated heated debate as it tears at the heart of people's private feelings about sexual morality. So far at least, in Indonesia prostitution and pornography, while popular targets of some Islamic groups, have not given rise to such strong and ambivalent public feelings about sexuality as has polygamy: the polygamy debate exposes normally hidden views on this subject and tests what the state's role should be in relation to it. And like prostitution, polygamy touches on a range of other issues relating to gender differences, most particularly that of power within marriage. What does equality mean within marriage: does it create marital stability or happiness, and does the state have any interest or influence in these matters?

As a controversial issue, polygamy in Indonesia has had considerable coverage. Legal analysts have examined the problems it poses for the unification of law and legal administration. Politically it is usually treated purely as a source of tension between the state and Islamic groups. Such a view completely overlooks the significance of polygamy in women's lives. For them it has been a symbol of men's power within marriage, and more generally of the willingness of a male-dominated state to uphold that power. The significance of the debate for gender relations and the state's role in shaping those relations has been ignored except within histories of the Indonesian women's movement (Stuers 1960; Soebadio 1981; Suwondo 1981). The latter have tended to see the issue from the perspective of women's organisations, without attempting to gauge what the state can effectively do on the matter and what its interests might be. This chapter aims to examine where women's interests in polygamy have converged with or diverged from those of the state, why and with what results.

Polygamy in Indonesia: incidence and legal status

Strictly speaking, the subject of this chapter is polygyny (marriages involving more than one wife simultaneously), but common usage refers to polygamy, a broader term meaning the practice of having more than one spouse. In Indonesia only polygyny has been legal. Although it is commonly associated with Islam, and much of the debate about it in Indonesia has certainly revolved around Islam, polygamy has a much older history in the archipelago and was permitted according to a number of different customary legal systems (*adat*), including in Hindu Bali and among Chinese Indonesians. The custom of Javanese aristocrats having unlimited numbers of *selir* or secondary wives was also not based on Islam but predated it.

Marriage law in Indonesia has been a highly complex matter due to the legal pluralism that has prevailed in family matters. The Dutch permitted differing and even conflicting *adat* and religious laws to govern marriage, while adding the additional layer of the choice of marrying under a civil marriage code. In general, however, people were governed by what their religion ruled on marriage, modified by local *adat*. The independent state of Indonesia had to wrestle with this pluralistic legal heritage, over which it had little effective control until the latter part of the last century.

It is unfortunate that most opponents of polygamy have singled out Islam for attack, since polygamy has been practised under *adat* as well as Muslim law, and in some respects Islam has provided women with more freedom in marriage than have other religions or traditions in the archipelago. (It was, for instance, impossible for Catholics to divorce, and Balinese women who married men of lower caste were severely punished.) Considering that Islam is the dominant religion in Indonesia, however, this focus is understandable. Certainly from the state point of view, the political force to be reckoned with on the issue of polygamy is organised Islam. Until 1974 Islamic law on marriage was virtually independent of state control although governments had attempted to regulate its administration by religious authorities. Under Islamic law, men were permitted to have up to four wives at the one time. No conditions applied, and similarly men could divorce their wives at will, whereas women had to apply to religious officials for a divorce which was permitted only under limited conditions and at some expense. Also, as we have seen in Chapter 3, under Islamic law there was no minimum age of marriage, nor was the bride required to give consent. On the other hand, husbands had responsibility for supporting their families, although their obligation to support former wives and children after divorce was extremely limited. For most of the twentieth century, these marriage laws depended on enforcement by male religious officials. Lack of codification and central control over the administration of religious courts meant that uncertainty was added to manifest inequity in the eyes of many women.

As far as the role of the state is concerned, defenders of polygamy have wanted the state to stay out of the matter, leaving it in the realm of religious and *adat* officials. It was the opponents of polygamy who lobbied for the state to intervene. The reluctance of the state to do so is understandable in the light of strong political resistance and the great complexity of the legal situation in Indonesia, especially the vexed question of whether marriage law should be dealt with by means of a uniform law or through a perpetuation of the existing plural system.

The incidence of polygamy in Indonesia has apparently always been low but varies considerably between regions. According to the 1920 census, only 1.5 per cent of husbands in Java were polygamous. The 1930 census indicated an overall incidence of 2.6 per cent throughout Indonesia, with the rate for Java being about half that in the Outer Islands. The regions with the highest incidence were non-Islamic areas (Sumba with 13.5 per cent and Flores with 12 per cent), whilst among Islamic areas the rates were highest in West Sumatra (9 per cent) and Lampung (5.9 per cent) (Jones 1994: 269). A 1973 survey revealed a rather lower incidence of polygamous marriages but with the same regional variation. Significantly, it showed a lower proportion of younger women in polygamous marriages and lower rates in urban areas as compared with the countryside, indicating the trend of social change (Jones 1994: 272–3). Unfortunately no more recent surveys have been conducted on the incidence of polygamy. (There are also disappointingly few studies of the experience of polygamy by women in Indonesia.[2])

---

[2] Some of these few studies include Krulfeld (1986), Jennaway (2000) and Grace (1996).

During most of the twentieth century, polygamy was practised within a context of easy (male) access to and very high rates of divorce and remarriage, so that divorce was an alternative to polygamy. In the 1960s there were almost half as many divorces as marriages across Indonesia, with even higher rates in some regions like West Java. In the last few decades, the divorce rate has declined, in contrast with the trend in Western countries. As the demographer Gavin Jones has pointed out, this appears to be a consequence both of socioeconomic developments that favour marriage stability (such as increased education, marriage at later ages and by personal choice rather than parental arrangement) and also of attitudinal change: ironically Muslims in Southeast Asia have come to regard divorce as 'not modern' and less acceptable than in the past (Jones 1994: 184–90).

The fact that until recently polygamy has existed within the context of a high divorce rate, has added to the general fears among women about marital instability. It is unknown how many divorces were caused by women refusing to tolerate sharing their husband with other wives, but it must have been a contributing factor (Jones 1994: 210, 277).

Debates about polygamy and the state's role

Polygamy is notable as an issue where it was almost exclusively women calling on the state to take action. At the same time, women have also been divided on the matter, thus weakening their own stand. Muslim women who defended Koranic views of women as 'separate but equal', often defended polygamy or at least opposed any state interference with Islam.

Indonesian women's concerns about polygamy are a complex mixture, touching on economic, sexual, emotional, moral, social, legal and religious aspects of marriage. Many of the protagonists were personally affected by the issue. Kartini not only typified those who feared being married off by their parents into a polygamous union – a fate she ultimately experienced – but was also the child of a polygamous marriage. Her anger may have also reflected the suffering of her mother, a *selir* or secondary wife of a high-ranking Javanese *priyayi*. The core of women's concerns was the threat of polygamy to a wife's love and self-esteem when the husband took what was almost invariably a younger woman as a new wife; repugnance at having to share a husband's sexual life with other women; and the threat to the economic basis of the marriage when resources had to be spread amongst more wives and children. Finally, there was outrage at the inequality of polygamy: why should a man be privileged to have more than one legal sexual partner while women were prevented (by lack of ready access to divorce or through lack of alternative support) from escaping a fate that many abhorred – that is becoming a co-wife?

While the most outspoken critics of polygamy were often driven by personal experience of the practice, the leaders of women's Islamic organisations were often silenced by their proximity to polygamists. The male leaders of Islamic organisations, particularly the religious leaders known as *kiais*, frequently had more than one wife, and female leaders were commonly their wives, sisters or daughters. In this environment, to attack polygamy was to impugn relatives and revered elders.

In what follows I have identified different aspects of this heady brew in order to ascertain what women thought the state might do about the issue. The debates have been divided into arguments focussing on economic, social and moral aspects of polygamy, since each of these approaches had different implications for state action. It should be noted, however, that many women, preoccupied by the personal emotions stirred by polygamy, did not always consider political consequences.

Economic damage to the polygamous family

Debates about the economic aspect of polygamy centred around the husband's role in supporting his family. According to the Islamic conception of gender roles in marriage, the husband was first and foremost responsible for the economic support of his wife and children. And if a wife fled the house when her husband took a second wife, according to Islamic law she lost the right to his economic support. How then was a polygamous husband going to support more wives and their children in a satisfactory manner?

In 1939 the lawyer Maria Ullfah Santoso cited the example of a metalworker with a wife and three children and an income that was not enough to support all of them unless they lived simply. One day when she was six months pregnant he told her to go back to her parents, and she subsequently learnt he had taken another wife. Her husband left her without any support but would not divorce her, and the Islamic official responsible for marriage matters would help her only if she paid him money she could not afford. Maria Ullfah commented that most men who took a new wife would not support their children from the old wife (BBPIP 1939: 58).

For many, the argument that the husband was obliged to support his family involved an inherent paradox. The reality of Indonesian life was that most women were not solely dependent on their husbands. They were accustomed to supporting themselves and their children, either through agricultural pursuits or through earning an income by trading, handicrafts or waged work. And in a climate of high divorce rates, women kept up their ties with their natal families, on whom they could call for support if their marriage failed. The economic aspect of the debate should be seen in the context of general poverty in Indonesia: for most wives, a husband's support was important regardless of their other sources of income. On the other hand, economic arguments also reflected a class bias within the anti-polygamy lobby: many of these protagonists were middle- or upper-class women who were not accustomed to supporting themselves and/or fearful of losing the wealthy living conditions to which their husbands' income had accustomed them. This lobby tended to blame second or subsequent wives as attracted by pecuniary interests. They felt it inequitable that wives who supported their husbands in an unpaid capacity should, in later life, be obliged to share the family income with younger women who had contributed nothing.

Most members of the women's movement advocated that women should be able to earn their own living, to protect them from marital insecurity caused either by polygamy or by the high divorce rate. Kartini was one of the foremost of the early advocates of women's need to be self-supporting. She was followed by others like the redoubtable Suyatin Kartowiyono, a leader of the women's movement from the 1920s to the 1950s. In her memoirs Suyatin recalled a conversation with other women activists at the 1935 women's congress where there had been heated debate between Suwarni Pringgodigdo and Islamic groups over polygamy.

While five of us were having lunch at the conference, I said to . . . Suwarni Pringgodigdo, 'You are very worked up about polygamy. What would you do if your husband took another wife?'

Suwarni replied passionately, 'I would take a revolver and kill him. And then kill myself.'

Another participant responded, 'Yes, what can you do? You're forced just to accept it.'

I was the only one of the five who made her own living. My reaction was just to smile, 'But I could go on living. Because I can find my own money . . . So for that reason you should all earn a living for yourselves so you have economic power.' (Kartowijono 1983: 219)

Economic alternatives to marriage would also reduce the temptation for single, divorced or widowed women to become co-wives. In Bali, for instance, where the patrilineal system meant that women's access to natal family property and support was more limited than in some other parts of Indonesia, economic imperatives forced many women into less than desirable marriages (Jennaway 2000). Better incomes would mean that these women could marry (or not) according to their own choice and reduce the economic pressure on women and children in polygamous marriages.

On the other hand, strict Islamic defenders of polygamy were trapped in their need to demand that husbands support their wives and children and that women's role was in the home, not out in the workforce. Going against the tide of Indonesian life meant that they were placing extra demands on men, and in the process making polygamy harder for them to realise. For some Muslim women, it is possible that this outcome suited their basic antagonism to the institution of polygamy.

In claiming that the state should take an interest in polygamy, some economic analysts appealed to the drain on the nation's resources and earning potential of neglected mothers and children abandoned by polygamous husbands. But what should the state do about it? Everyone knew that it was impossible to shift the burden of supporting these women and children onto the state, because governments in Indonesia have never espoused a welfare ideology or had the resources to finance extensive welfare measures. Support of family members has been left almost exclusively in the hands of families or charitable institutions, except in the case of civil servants who are entitled to modest pensions. In this situation, the only direct action that could be expected of the state was that it do what it could to enforce the duty of husbands to support their families.

Indirectly the state could do much more, by creating or permitting an environment in which women could earn their own living. This involved resourcing education and training for women and economic growth that made better paid work available for them. In this way solutions to polygamy dovetailed with other demands the women's movement made for education of girls, as discussed in Chapter 2. Those most passionately opposed to polygamy, however, were unlikely to expend their energy demanding that the state take this indirect (if effective) route, and at the same time the state had many other reasons for its interest in education and the economy. These issues rarely featured in the public controversy about polygamy, relevant though they might be to its resolution.

Social damage caused by polygamy

Most debates about polygamy were concerned with the wider social context of marriage, in particular with the age of women at marriage, their ability to resist the pressures of kinfolk, their knowledge of their rights, their access to divorce and their status in society outside marriage. In the Indonesian context, many women argued, the social outcomes of polygamy were pernicious. For such critics of polygamy, the solutions were to be found mainly in education and in legal reform to give women greater equality in marriage. Behind all this lay the vexed question of how change in social attitudes was to be achieved and what role the state should play in leading that change.

For those who advocated reform, it was most important to establish the social consequences of polygamy. It was common to point to the deleterious effects on society of divided families where children of different wives and their mothers competed and fought over their share of their father's resources during his life and after his death.

Muslim women who felt obliged to defend polygamy nevertheless often joined forces with social critics because of common concerns about marital and family stability. Such women (e.g. Jumawar 1952) argued polygamy could be condoned only under very restricted conditions, and that it was important that women be educated as to the limitations on the practice of polygamy as decreed in the Koran. In order to protect women, they should also be taught to be self-supporting. These shared interests made it possible for women even from strict Muslim organisations to work together on practical projects with more secularly minded women, as will be discussed below.

Muslim women leaders have often been concerned that women did not know their rights according to Islam, which could in their view also offer protection against abuses of polygamy. In the Islamic journal *El Fadjar* in 1927, for instance, Supinah Isti Kasiati wrote:

Islam offers polygamy only as a variety of marriage permitted (but not obliged) . . . I am therefore convinced that I am not opposing the spirit of Islam when I express the opinion that one should by all means combat polygamy as it is practised in our country today . . . There is no longer a question of extenuating circumstances . . . Polygamy has become nothing other than disguised prostitution. The best way to contend polygamy lies in a more thorough study of Islam itself. (cited in Stuers 1960: 105)

Particularly in the light of current reinterpretations of Islam more sympathetic to equality for women, many Muslim leaders have emphasised these new teachings and practices. Concurrently, Islamic women's organisations have supported teaching women how to get their rights in Islamic courts of law, as well as educating male judges in this respect.[3]

---

[3] See Sejarah Muslimat (1979) for evidence of this concern on the part of the women's wing of the Muslim organisation Nahdlatul Ulama.

While some, like Kartini, advocated education as the antidote to polygamy, others placed their hope in legal reform to outlaw forced marriages, set a minimum age for marriage and give women better access to divorce to allow them to escape from polygamous unions. The aim was to give women greater legal equality, to make marriage more of a partnership of equals. From an early date, women's organisations began pursuing legal options. Yet the legal path entailed huge problems caused by the pluralism of legal systems relating to marriage and the political resistance of male-dominated Islamic organisations to any perceived weakening of the autonomy of Islamic law. Negotiating these obstacles proved a complex matter beyond the understanding or expertise of most women. The strength of feeling generated by polygamy meant that many women demanded its abolition without considering how the state might embark on this perilous path. Very few wrestled with the hard facts and those who attempted to negotiate feasible legal solutions found it an arduous and lengthy task. In this respect Maria Ullfah Santoso (later Subadio) and Nani Suwondo displayed outstanding dedication. From the late 1930s to the 1970s, they made serious efforts to draw up proposed legislation restricting polygamy.

Throughout the century, in fact, education and legal reform have been regarded by most interested parties as the best ways of dealing with the problems associated with polygamy because they best address its social causes and consequences. Since the state is heavily involved in education and legislation, it clearly has a role to play here.

The immorality of polygamy

Finally there were women whose strongest feelings were aroused by what they saw as the moral outrage of polygamy, by the assumption that men were considered to have stronger sexual urges and should therefore be allowed more than one wife. The basis for the moral debate shifted over the century. In the first half of the century such protagonists demanded an end to the double standard, posing the goal as chastity for both men and women within monogamy. In more recent decades, the 'moral purity' argument has tended to give way to discourse based on human rights as the moral foundation for legal equality between the sexes.

During much of the last century, many women viewed the fight against polygamy as a battle against the demon of male lust. For instance, in 1929 an outspoken Minangkabau critic, Rohana, wrote in a local paper in response to a Minangkabau leader who supported polygamy as a means of 'combating illicit sex' that he 'seems to see women as created by Allah to satisfy the desires of men'.

We should let him know that the inner feelings of men and women do not differ, there is only a difference in the shape of their bodies. If you know that a woman is a human, you will certainly know how she feels if her husband takes another wife . . . If a wife goes looking for another husband, what would her husband do? . . . It is an incomparable shame, isn't it? That's how we women feel too.

It is a falsehood to say that polygamy restricts illicit sex. Illicit sex arises from desire that cannot be governed by an individual. But a human who is not a man but a woman must govern her desires.

In conclusion she appealed to Islam: 'Religion teaches that lust is one of the most extraordinarily intense things on earth. And a person who does not restrain it will be consigned by Allah to hell' (*Harian Radio* March 1929, cited in Toemenggoeng 1958: 20–1). Thus opponents of polygamy were often those conducting the struggle against illicit sex on all fronts, the aim being to restrain lust.

One of the best-known and most passionate exponents of this moralistic view was the well-known pre-war feminist Suwarni Pringgodigdo, the president of the nationalist and feminist organisation Istri Sedar (Aware Women). A most articulate and strong-minded young woman, she opposed polygamy in the context of her desire for secure, stable marriages based on sexual fidelity. She held fast to an ideal of lifetime monogamy for men and women, rejecting anything that made it easier for a couple to abandon their commitment to each other. Her image of 'strong marriage' depended on a notion of sexual 'purity' reminiscent of some European suffragists.

Rebutting the view that the main reason for polygamy was the polygamous nature of men and their desire for change, she asked sarcastically, 'We know that there are men who are kleptomaniacs, or who have a cruel nature, are sadistic: should we allow them to steal or kill?' Moreover, she queried, 'Why should one think that a man driven by lust will be cured by being given an opportunity to be polygamous: he would also like to take the wife of someone else, or have sex with a prostitute.' In her view, marriage was 'something pure, not just for "satisfying one's desires"' (Pringgodigdo 1937: 30–1).

Suwarni's hard line on marriage was reflected in her attitude toward divorce, which she was reluctant to consider as an escape from polygamy. When it came to the point it appeared that she was not very concerned to remove the barriers to divorce that faced women because she feared anything, including divorce, that threatened marital stability. 'It's not the right of *talak* [divorce] that we want but strong marriage which can raise and strengthen the status of humanity in Indonesia' (Pringgodigdo 1937: 36). It is to be hoped that her feelings on the matter had changed by the time she herself was divorced in the 1950s.

In the Islamic camp, too, there was some sympathy from Muslim women for this kind of moral critique of polygamy, at least of what they saw as its abuse in practice. In the parliamentary debate on marriage law proposals in 1959, for instance, Mrs Mahmudah-Mawardi of Nahdlatul Ulama, while upholding the right of Muslim men to have up to four wives, said feelingly: 'Many men are all too ready to make a hobby of polygamy, so it results in very tragic outcomes in the life of a family . . . The right of polygamy as given by Islam has become a disguise to satisfy lust without full responsibility for its consequences' (cited in Surya-Hadi 1959: 11)

But the moral attack on polygamy divided women. Some Islamic women reacted with their own moral retort, most commonly based on an appeal to authority. Since Islam and custom permitted polygamy, it must be accepted by women, however painful it might sometimes be. They must learn to fight jealousy, to purge their hearts of hatred, in the interests of the greater good, either of religion or society at large. Women's sense of self-sacrifice was appealed to, playing on the stereotype of women's altruistic and restrained nature. For example in the Minangkabau women's paper, *Sunting Melayu*, in 1912 one woman correspondent called on co-wives to exorcise hatred which would be 'punished in the life hereafter': 'The teaching of our religion has much knowledge for purifying the heart, only thus can we be free of enmity between co-wives' (Rafiah 1912). The fiery Muslim nationalist from West Sumatra, Rasuna Said, also attempted to turn the moral tables on those who rejected polygamy. She argued that women should be self-sacrificing enough to allow needy women to become co-wives, and to allow husbands to 'fulfil their desire' legally (cited in Pringgodigdo 1937: 25).

Thus female defenders of polygamy also could appeal to the 'finer side' of women's feelings for unity amongst them. Some were also inclined to join the male-led defence of Islam against depraved Western customs, arguing that polygamy provided an outlet for men's stronger sexual urges that was preferable to prostitution and illicit affairs which they considered to be rife in the West. It offered legal protection and status for women in a way that prostitutes and mistresses lacked.

In the Indonesian situation, men claimed religious leadership, but in the matter of marriage many women were quick to point to men's moral flaws and claim their own greater spiritual strength. This constituted part of a contested ideology within Indonesia about the 'nature' of men and women, with both sexes claiming greater control over their passions (Brenner 1995). In 1954 a female critic of polygamy wrote that referring to men's irresistible sexual urges was 'not a strong argument if man is considered to be a higher being able to control his desires because he has a sense of responsibility . . . People who cannot exercise self-control are considered weak and of low character' (Soedomo 1954: 13).

As with all attempts to generalise about the 'nature' of men or women, it was difficult for protagonists to be consistent. Defenders of polygamy were sometimes put in the difficult position of assuming women's greater sexual restraint while arguing that they were too weak in character to be trusted with the power to declare divorce.[4] It was unarguable too, that if polygamy involved moral ambiguity, it lay not just among men but amongst the women who became second, third and fourth wives. Opponents of polygamy were obliged to appeal to their 'sisters' to refrain from such polygamous marriages. The post-war years in particular were characterised by high marital instability with increased rates of divorce and polygamy. In an attempt to bridge the gap between wives and women who contributed to the break-up of marriages, one woman, Siti Danilah, like Rasuna Said before her, appealed in 1950 to a spirit of self-sacrifice but for a very different end, to avoid 'causing another woman to break her tie with her husband' (Danilah 1950). That all women did not conform to idealistic standards of 'purity' was only too clear. The attempt to unite women on the issue was a forlorn one, as their perceptions of their own interests differed. In this respect it very much resembled the related issue of prostitution, about which similar arguments have waged to and fro over the years.

Was there a role for the state in upholding morality in relation to polygamy? Some women leaders – and a few men[5] – argued that the state must ban polygamy for nationalist reasons. At the 1928 women's congress a strong opponent of polygamy, Siti Sundari, made a connection between moral outrage and nationalism. 'If the Indonesian nation wants to become a nation that has a place of dignity in the world', she argued, it must be built on households based on mutual love. Polygamy was indefensible; 'The stronger our households the stronger the Indonesian nation; the happier and more secure the marriages of Indonesians, the happier and safer the Indonesian nation' (Congres Perempoean, 1929: 55). It was common for proponents of this point of view to refer to action against polygamy in other Muslim countries, most notably Turkey which banned polygamy in the 1920s. The implication was that Indonesia was backward. In 1937 Suwarni Pringgodigdo also appealed to nationalist sentiment,

---

[4] Thus at the 1928 women's congress, Siti Munjiyah, a member of the executive of the Islamic women's organisation Aisyiyah said that it was proper that women did not have the power to repudiate their husbands (*talak*), because women were too impulsive, while men were 'patient and firm' (Congres Perempoean 1929: 43).

[5] The nationalist argument against polygamy as lowering the status of the nation was argued by Bahder Djohan at the 1926 Indonesian Youth Congress (Djohan and Adam 1977).

arguing that only people who were not modern and not idealistic would allow men to follow their base appetites by supporting polygamy (Pringgodigdo 1937: 31–2).

For those, like Suwarni Pringgodigdo, who claimed that men could not be relied on in this matter, there was of course some irony in expecting a patriarchal state to move against polygamy. If there was any opportunity to undermine polygamy, however, opponents of the institution were generally prepared to take it, however contradictory it might seem. Problems arose, however, when the moralists were not prepared to compromise, insisting on an outright ban on polygamy. Prohibition was never an option from the state's point of view, as we shall see: politically and legally the matter was far too complex to permit this solution. Divisions among women offered the state an excuse not to take action for moral reasons.

By the latter half of the twentieth century, the zeal of the moralising opponents of polygamy had faded. Campaigns for sexual purity declined in popularity among the ranks of the secular women's movement, as they did around the world. That torch was taken up more enthusiastically by the Islamic revival movement, which was precluded from using it to attack polygamy. A different and more legalistic approach to moral argumentation was that based on conceptions of human rights, advocating equal rights for men and women in marriage as elsewhere. A strong proponent of this viewpoint, before and after independence, was the lawyer Maria Ullfah Santoso (later Subadio). Just before the war, she made an appeal to Indonesian men: 'How can Indonesian women fulfil our hopes to nurture a new, strong nation if Indonesian men don't want to relinquish their position as kings in marriage? Relinquish this power. Women have feelings, women have thoughts, like men. We, Indonesian women, want to have human rights' (BBPIP 1939: 67).

The argument about rights, begun before the war, gained in strength after independence and proved to be the most popular source of appeal for those opposing polygamy. In supporting the Sumari marriage bill of 1959, for instance, Communist Party (PKI) members of parliament emphasised the need for 'a democratic marriage law that guarantees equal rights in the family' (Surya-Hadi 1959: 31, 56). External forces were invoked to bolster this pressure on the state, as it was pointed out that Indonesia ratified United Nations conventions respecting human rights. Propounded generally by those with a Western-style education and knowledge of legal procedure, the human rights approach could cut some ice with governments that were susceptible to international pressure. Its advocates were more ready to accept incremental change than were the opponents of polygamy who had in the past argued from a basis of sexual morality.

Action and inaction on polygamy by the state

Throughout most of the twentieth century Indonesian women's organisations appealed to the state to intervene in the issue of polygamy, either
directly or indirectly. Requests to introduce a marriage law that outlawed
polygamy were at one extreme and were regarded very warily by whichever
government was in power, because of anticipated implacable opposition
from Islamic organisations. Other ways of approaching the problem met
with more cooperation. The history of these efforts reveals the way that
the state in Indonesia has perceived its own interests in the matter.

The colonial state, 1900–1942

Education and improved communications, fostered by the colonial Ethical Policy adopted in 1901, radicalised a small number of women like
Kartini to challenge traditions that oppressed women. Officially the
Dutch supported social change of this kind that was in line with Christian
and liberal thinking, but they were unwilling to confront male leadership
within the Indonesian community that felt threatened by such change.
To attack polygamy was to attack organised Islam, and the colonial state
had little interest in arousing such enmity. Under the circumstances it
was surprising that the state took any direct action at all.

The colonial state took note of the Indonesian women's movement's
requests for action on polygamy. An early formal request came from the
1928 women's congress as a proposal to promote the notion of *taklik*. In
the face of resistance by Muslim groups to direct opposition to polygamy,
the conference resorted to advocating that women make use of the option
of marriage contracts, called *taklik*, that permitted women to specify at
the time of marriage the conditions under which a divorce would be
automatic; these conditions could include that the husband wished to
take a second wife. The congress requested the government to 'oblige
the Religious Court to give a letter explaining *taklik* to both parties at the
time of marriage' (Congres Perempoean 1929: 21). Clearly the Christian
colonial government was sympathetic: it complied by tightening control
over Islamic officials responsible for registering marriages and divorces
in Java and Madura, and instructing them to explain *taklik* (Stuers 1960:
101–2). Little was at stake in taking this small step.

It took more than the Indonesian women's movement to propel the
state to the stage of contemplating a reform of the marriage law. Marriages between European women and Muslim Indonesian men, although
relatively few in number, brought a dilemma for the government. Most
mixed marriages involving Europeans were with Indonesian women,

which in Dutch eyes was safely covered by the law of 1896 stating that the law of the husband prevailed over that of the wife's racial or religious group. With increasing numbers of Indonesians seeking an education in the Netherlands, however, some unions of Indonesian men and Dutch women occurred. The Dutch parliament, which after 1920 contained female members, began to agitate about the problem of European women who, by marrying Muslims, faced the possibility of polygamous marriage. This was considered intolerable, polygamy having all the orientalist connotations for Europeans of Turkish harems: no white woman should be subjected to such barbarity. The Minister for Colonies pressed a reluctant Governor-General to do something about it (Department of Colonies 1932). The colonial state was reluctant because the marriage law system in the Indies was already very complex and any changes that pinpointed polygamy were likely to arouse the wrath of Muslim organisations (Department of Justice 1932).

Hounded by the home government, the colonial government pondered different legislative alternatives and finally came up with a proposal that made it possible for couples to register monogamous marriages if they so wished. Unlike the compulsorily monogamous marriages for Christian couples, this was intended to be a kind of civil marriage law available to people proposing mixed marriages or for those of any faith who wished to bind themselves legally to a monogamous union, with divorce permitted under certain conditions. It was seen as a response to pressure from Indonesian women seeking more equal marriages as well as a solution to the mixed-marriage problem (Department of Justice 1936). As Locher-Scholten has commented (2000: 209–10), the colonial state was willing to intervene in marriage matters in a very limited way to propitiate the narrow stratum of Dutch women and Westernised urban Indonesian women who shared its notions of civilised, stable family life.

The 1937 Marriage Ordinance proposal was floated publicly to test the waters before being introduced into the colonial People's Council. As a first step, the Officer for Native Affairs, Pijper, called a meeting with prominent Indonesian women leaders in June 1937. He found that almost all of them were sympathetic to the proposal, although some cautiously reserved their judgment until they had had more time to consider it (Netherlands Indies Government 1937). Suwarni Pringgodigdo was an immediate supporter and commenced a campaign on behalf of the ordinance. However, under pressure from the male-dominated nationalist and religious organisations most other women activists fell silent. The government then faced a barrage of opposition from men (and some Muslim women, including Rasuna Said) who interpreted the proposal as an attack on Islam and an unwarranted intrusion into private affairs by Christian colonialists intent on dividing the ranks of the nationalists (Pijper 1937). The government decided that discretion was the better part of valour and withdrew the proposal. It never resolved the legal problem of European women marrying Muslim men.

Suwarni Pringgodigdo was scathing about the withdrawal of the 1937 Marriage Ordinance, seeing it as evidence of state racism and patriarchy. 'The colonial Government doesn't care much for us women either. It is afraid to attack polygamy because it fears a revolt by Indonesian men. It is only when Dutch women are humiliated by our men that there arises this "plan for registered marriages" and *at the same time* we also *are given the scope* to be protected.' Responding to the argument that Indonesian women should be careful in making up their minds about the Ordinance, because 'it might upset people, especially the nationalists and the Muslims', she issued this appeal:

Sisters, we can only achieve humanism and freedom by being brave . . . ! This is not a matter of *Nationalists* against *Muslims*, the new Ordinance is just a matter of *men* and *women*!

31 million women ask for their rights and 30 million men want to protect their right to divorce and to polygamy, so the fate of the Indonesian people is in disorder! In the nationalist camp there are people who want to protect these rights and in Muslim circles also there are people of broader views who want to raise the status of the people by giving humanitarian treatment to women.

In her view it was Indonesian women who had to decide the issue (Pringgodigdo 1937: 20–2). Despite her protest, however, the Marriage Ordinance, the closest that Indonesian women got to undermining the legal foundations of polygamy during the colonial period, was dead in the water. The state could see little to be gained by antagonising the already restive nationalist and Islamic movements.

The failure of the 1937 Marriage Ordinance, however, spurred on the women's movement to establish a committee to investigate ways of formulating a law that would win support from Islamic organisations as well as secular ones. Islamic and secular women leaders cooperated for decades in search of an acceptable legal formula (Soebadio 1981: 11–12). They agreed on the need to restrict rather than prohibit polygamy, but until 1973 it was not possible to win agreement from the other interested parties – male-dominated parties and the state – on a uniform marriage law.

The democratic republic, 1950s

In theory, governments in the period of parliamentary democracy in Indonesia were well disposed to women's equality. Much legislation of these years enshrined this principle, and Indonesia ratified the International Convention on the Political Rights of Women in 1958. But the country was very poor, lacking resources to implement many of the governments' aims, and the political obstacles were formidable.

From the end of 1945 when the first Cabinet of the newly independent Indonesian Republic was formed until President Sukarno imposed Guided Democracy in 1959, Indonesian governments were characterised by instability as Cabinets formed and reformed among the numerous political parties that vied for power. The general elections held in 1955 did not resolve this situation, since they showed that four main parties had strong roots in Indonesian society and no combination of them formed a reliable coalition. Two of the largest parties were Islamic. Plagued with coalition problems and grappling with the devastation of years of Japanese Occupation and the subsequent struggle for independence against the Dutch, none of the successive governments was seriously prepared to contemplate putting before the parliament a marriage law of the kind the women's organisations wanted. In 1950 all the women members of parliament joined to urge the government to draw up a marriage proposal suited to the new era (Suwondo 1981: 79). Every congress of the federation of Indonesian women's organisations in the 1950s passed resolutions urging the government to pass marriage laws to protect women (Panitia Peringatan 1958). Governments prevaricated by referring the matter to committees which struggled with the perennial question of whether to retain legal pluralism or propose a uniform marriage law. Strongly Islamic groups were opposed to the latter (Soebadio 1981: 15–16).

During these years the state's most positive contribution to resolving problems associated with polygamy was to support literacy campaigns and the spread of education, although the weak economy did not allow great expenditure on either. Some ministers were also prepared to issue regulations affecting the implementation of marriage law in favour of women, a move that was not as public and confrontational as legislation. In an important step, in 1946 the Ministry of Religion was created and made responsible for appointing as civil servants those responsible for the registration of marriages and divorces. As urged by the women's organisations, this ensured that religious marriage officials were brought more closely under the state supervision of the Department of Religion and were paid regular wages so that they were not dependent on fees from clients and thus likely to ignore wives who could not afford to pay them. They were also instructed as civil servants to follow certain directions such as to explain to would-be polygamous husbands their responsibilities according to Islam (Suwondo 1981: 78–9). The women's federation urged the government to permit women to become judges in religious courts, to overcome the male bias they had long observed amongst Islamic officials. In conjunction with the women's federation, the Ministry for Religion began in 1956 to conduct courses training women as judges (Panitia Penasehat 1957: 2). This step constituted a significant break-through: it was the first time women held the position of Islamic judge anywhere in the world. From 1954, also, the Ministry of Religion estab-lished marriage guidance councils to advise couples concerning matters like polygamy that caused conflict within marriage, indicating official con-cern about high divorce rates that may have been in part connected with polygamy. Islamic women's organisations, which felt constrained about speaking about polygamy in public, were happy to participate in these kinds of practical, low-key measures (Sejarah Muslimat 1979).

On the other hand, another administrative measure taken during these years enraged much of the women's movement. In 1952 the government issued a regulation providing government pensions to the multiple wid-ows of polygamous civil servants, thus implying state endorsement of polygamy. Under colonial rule only one wife had been entitled to a civil servant's pension. In 1952 and 1953 the move brought protesting dele-gations from women's organisations to the government and even a street demonstration (Suwondo 1981: 81–4). This regulation applying to civil servants was balanced by much stricter control of polygamy in the armed forces, where members were required to obtain the permission of their commanding officer before taking a second wife (Rasid 1982: 116–17). Commanded by secular nationalists, the military rarely gave permission, and this practice presaged the wider control of state employees that fol-lowed under the New Order.

Exasperated by government failure to enact marriage reform, in 1958 a Nationalist Party (PNI) member of parliament, Sumari, proposed her own private bill for a uniform marriage law. It had the support of a number of leading non-religious women's organisations. The Sumari bill attempted to combine elements of uniformity (covering all citizens) with the right of all citizens to marry according to their own religion. It stipu-lated that the basis of marriage was monogamy, provided divorce on the same terms for both men and women and fixed minimum marriage ages. Polygamy was not permitted under the Sumari proposal, in the name of 'the peace and happiness of the family' and of equality of men and women. When it was discussed by the parliament in early 1959, members of Islamic parties predictably lined up to denounce the bill as contrary to Islamic law. It did however have the effect of impelling the government in 1959 to present its own bill for Islamic marriages to the parliament, thus avoiding the problems posed by uniform legislation but at the same time alienating those (notably the secular women's organisations) who would only accept a uniform law. The government bill proved more acceptable to most Muslims. It permitted polygamy so long as a man could give a witnessed written promise that his existing wife/wives had given permission, that he would treat all his wives fairly and that he could guarantee their needs. The parliament, the public and the women's movement were all divided in their attitudes to both the Sumari bill and that for Islamic marriages when they were debated simultaneously in 1959. However, before any vote could be taken on either bill, there was a Cabinet reshuffle and then President Sukarno dissolved the parliament as part of his introduction of Guided Democracy (Suwondo 1981).

While democratic governments in the 1950s had been reluctant to antagonise the Muslim parties by pushing the issue of a marriage law, and too weak to enforce many measures in favour of the equality of women in marriage, the new dictatorial government of Sukarno clearly had no interest at all in introducing any bill that would weaken men's right to polygamy. After all, Sukarno himself had entered a polygamous marriage in 1954, infuriating the secular women's organisations which protested against his new wife, and he proceeded to take further wives in the course of his dictatorship.

The New Order state, 1965–1998

The prospects for marriage law reform improved significantly with the introduction of Suharto's New Order Government, which effectively took power in late 1965. The new regime was motivated by several imperatives that worked in favour of women who opposed polygamy. First, it wished to domesticate and de-politicise Islam. Secondly, it aimed to develop Indonesia economically and socially, which included harnessing women's organisations behind its development agenda, especially family planning. Marriage law reform fitted into a project of establishing smaller and more stable families. And legal unification suited the government's desire for strong, centralised control over the archipelago. Thirdly, unlike the Sukarno regime the New Order was more sensitive to international opinion: it rejoined the United Nations and participated in the conferences and conventions associated with the International Decade for Women 1975–85. Especially after the prices of its oil exports rose dramatically in the 1970s, the New Order was able to implement many of its objectives far better than previous governments: this was a strong state.

From 1966 the Ministries of Justice and Religion began examining how to introduce a marriage law that would apply nationwide and be based on the state ideology of Pancasila. In 1967 the Minister of Religion proposed an Islamic marriage law to the parliament, followed in 1968 by a law establishing basic principles of marriage introduced by the Minister of Justice. Meeting opposition from various religious groups, these bills were withdrawn (*Tempo* 8 September 1973: 7).

Around the time of the 1971 elections that delivered a resounding victory to the government party, the government appointed as Ministers of Religion men whose prime loyalties did not, as in the past, lie with Nahdlatul Ulama (Cammack 1997: 150). Its plan for a marriage law, issued in 1973, defied Islamic law on many points and had the support of the women's federation, Kowani (Soebadio 1981: 17–19). A uniform law laying the basis for marriage for all Indonesians, it included tight restrictions on both divorce and polygamy. The desire to weaken political Islam may have been an important motivation, but one should also not ignore the role of women in this matter. As explained in Chapter 1, the New Order Government developed a specific ideology of the family and the role of women within the family and in development, the strength of the family unit being seen as indispensable to political stability and socioeconomic growth. This line suited perfectly the wives' organisations that had come to dominate the official women's movement. In particular Dharma Wanita, the organisation of civil servants' wives, had campaigned strongly against polygamy (Suryakusuma 1996). In fact, as Nursyahbani Kacasungkana (Katjasungkana 1992) has pointed out, the year of the promulgation of the new Marriage Law, 1974, was the same year in which women's organisations were 'restructured' to draw them further under government control, and in which the official family-planning programme really took off, assisted by foreign aid. The Marriage Law served to buy off women's organisations as they were incorporated into the government's development plans. It was suspected, too, that the President's wife, Tien Suharto, played an important role behind the scenes in instigating the bill (Katz and Katz 1975: 660).

Requiring as it did civil registration for marriage and overview by civil courts, the 1973 bill was a tremendous blow to the Islamic court system, whose main jurisdiction had been family law matters. Not surprisingly there was outrage in Islamic quarters, far stronger than the government seemed to have anticipated. Although seven hundred representatives of women's organisations attended in support of the bill, at one stage parliament had to be suspended when the floor was occupied by young Muslim protesters (*Tempo* 8 September 1973: 6–8).

Despite having the numbers in the parliament, the government was unwilling to jeopardise national harmony by riding roughshod over the intense opposition of the Islamic movement. It deputed military officers to negotiate concessions that allowed family law matters to remain with the religious courts while putting restrictions on access by men to polygamy and giving women more access to divorce. However, much of the original proposal remained in the final law promulgated in 1974. The result is an uneasy compromise. It claims to be a uniform marriage law, setting out the guidelines within which marriage must be conducted by all citizens, while stipulating that marriages are legal if performed according to religious requirements, and some articles allow exceptions if one's religion provides otherwise. Monogamy was declared the norm in marriage (Article 3), with very strictly defined conditions allowing those men whose religion permitted polygamy to take more than one wife only with the permission of prior wife/wives and if the husband could show that he was able to support more than one wife and their children, and if he undertook to treat all wives and children fairly. He required the approval of the local religious court, which could be given only if the existing wife could not fulfil her responsibilities as a wife or was incurably ill or infertile (Articles 4 and 5). There are also requirements for minimum age at marriage (nineteen for men and sixteen for women), for all divorces to have the approval of the court, and penalties for infringing the law. In effect, under the 1974 law, people are subject to marriage law according to their religion as in the past but now also within the overarching requirements of the new law.

Veterans of the women's movement who had long campaigned for a marriage law declared themselves largely satisfied with the 1974 law (Soebadio 1981; Suwondo 1981). As will be shown below, more recent observers have been less willing to remain silent in light of the strongly gendered notion of the role of men and women embodied in the 1974 Marriage Law, which stipulated that the husband was the public head of the family and the breadwinner while the wife was in charge of the household in the private sphere. Equality of the sexes, acknowledged in the Constitution and in international covenants ratified by the government, was clearly modified in domestic rhetoric and practice. However, since the 1974 law was passed there have been no further efforts at legislative reform in this area, despite various problems with the law such as the apparent impossibility of marriage between people of different religions (Soebadio 1981: 23–9; Butt 1999). As far as polygamy, divorce and age of marriage are concerned, however, no major complaints were expressed.

It was not just the passage of the 1974 Marriage Law that mattered, however, but its implementation. From early in the twentieth century it had been recognised that much of the problem lay with the religious courts that administered Islamic marriage law. The New Order Government moved to exert more control over the Muslim court system by taking

over the training of judges and appointing women judges and undermined the religious conservatives' domination of the Ministry of Religion
by appointing modernists to the highest ranks (Cammack 1997; Butt
1999). A further step in state control over the religious judiciary was
taken with the codification of Islamic law in 1991. The general trend has
been to modernise the Islamic judicial system with results more sympathetic to women. One legal analyst had concluded that whereas the
state underestimated the danger of confronting Islam in 1973, it has now
learnt that it can get its way on marriage matters more indirectly via
greater influence over the Islamic courts (Cammack 1997: 168).

Although the New Order Government was not able to achieve all it
intended through the 1974 Marriage Law, it used its control over state
employees to enforce far stricter adherence to monogamy. Following in
the footsteps of earlier practice within the armed forces, as mentioned
above, regulations in 1983 required civil service employees to seek permission from their superiors if they wanted a divorce or a polygamous
marriage. A later amendment went further, prohibiting female state
employees from contracting polygamous marriages. This was unprecedented intervention into the private lives of state servants, who were
clearly expected to provide a model for the rest of society. In this we
can see the influence of the 'wives' organisations' patronised by the New
Order: the state appropriated the voluntary work of wives of state employees, and in return they won regulations enforcing monogamy, something
for which these organisations had been pressing for years. Whether or
not this was a Faustian bargain can be debated: it was noted that the
practice of keeping mistresses spread among the wealthier civil servants,
and women may have been trapped in unhappy marriages just as much as
men (Suryakusuma 1996). Nevertheless, the state had clearly signalled
for the first time since independence that it disapproved of polygamy,
strengthening the decline in social tolerance of the practice.

Just as important as any direct moves by the state to combat polygamy
were its efforts to raise the standard of living of Indonesians. Education, improved communications and the proliferation of non-government
organisations made information available to girls and women about their
legal rights and gave them access to new ideas about their role in the world
that often helped them challenge custom, at the same time as they also
modified the views of their kin and peer groups. A very early effect was
to increase the age of marriage of girls. Education and training, accompanied by better employment opportunities as economic development
occurred, made women more able to earn their own living and thus
less dependent on their families, whose influence on them was consequently diminished. A marked decline in poverty reduced the likelihood

that parents would marry their daughters off young, that widows, single women and divorcees would find themselves forced into marriage by need and that wives would feel obliged to stay in marriages where their husband took a second or subsequent wife.

The current context of polygamy

In the eyes of some women, polygamy remains a threat to married women. Feelings still run strong, as illustrated by an interview with a prominent woman academic, Miriam Budiarjo, who stated that the fact that a man can take another wife 'determines the position and outlook' of a wife. 'Every other woman may be a threat to your marriage. I think that is the weak point of our situation. Why are not more women vocal or more progressive in having a career? It's the fear of the second wife. It's very real.' Despite the law, she claimed, men frequently did not take care of the children of their first marriage. In her view, 'the fear of a second wife really makes the position of Indonesian women weaker than in Western countries or even in the Philippines. It accounts for the reputation of Indonesian women as very jealous. It makes a woman very careful in her choice of career and execution of career because you don't want your children to be fatherless' (Budiardjo 1997). A well-known feminist legal-rights activist, Nursyahbani Kacasungkana, singles out polygamy as an example of the way in which the 1974 Marriage Law embodies inequality between men and women. Men are permitted to do things that are forbidden to women. Moreover, she claims, what happens in practice is rather different from what the law indicates. Because of various pressures, a wife's permission for her husband to marry again is not too difficult to obtain. It also often happens, she says, that polygamy occurs secretly, conducted according to religious regulations, although not legally. Furthermore, she argues, religious courts continue to discriminate against women, based on an unrealistic view of them as wives and housewives who must depend on their husbands as heads of families and breadwinners (Katjasungkana 1993 and 1997; *Jakarta Post* 27 August 2003b).

The state is vulnerable to international accusations about women's human rights within marriage. Required to report regularly to UN bodies on equal rights, the Indonesian Government officially admits that the continued legality of polygamy is evidence of the continuing inequality of women before the law (Indonesia Country Report 1996). But the domestic opposition to pursuing the matter clearly precludes further action for the foreseeable future.

Throughout the twentieth century, governments in Indonesia have hoped that social change would resolve the problem of polygamy, that it would just become unfashionable like child marriage. To a large extent this has occurred. For example, polygamy used to be widely practised among the Javanese and Balinese aristocracy, and young women were attracted to the position of *selir* or junior wife because of the prestige and wealth that attached to the aristocracy in pre-war times. Since independence, however, the power, status and resources of the aristocracy have dwindled and with them the willingness of young women to enter polygamous marriages.

The Islamic resurgence in recent years has complicated the picture as far as support for polygamy is concerned. On the one hand are the very prominent Islamic reformers, who now take the line that polygamy was something suited to the Prophet's time but no longer necessary today: monogamy is desirable and polygamy is justifiable only under extraordinary circumstances and only with the consent of all concerned.[6] There is a strong and growing movement within Islam pushing for a reinterpretation of the scriptures to allow for greater gender equality, and even within traditionally conservative Islamic institutions like *pesantren* (Islamic boarding schools) women and men are attempting to reform the gender discourse. On the other hand, the concern of people like Nursyahbani is justified given the deeply conservative line on gender taken by many Islamic leaders and publications, which continue to argue that wives must obey their husbands, that women's career is as a wife and that women are more emotional and unreliable than men.[7] Translations of Arabic works on Islam and women abound, some of them defending polygamy (e.g. Aj-Jahrani 1997). For Indonesian Islam, polygamy represents one of the last bastions of inequality in marriage. It has rejected forced marriages, it condones women earning their own living, but devout Muslims cannot denounce polygamy without being accused of disavowing their religion (Kuypers 1993). In fact, for some Islamic conservatives, polygamy is something to be proud of, the badge of a devout Muslim Efforts are currently being made by feminists within the Islamic movement to counter such notions, as witness a flurry of publications from the liberal camp (e.g. Mulia 1999).

Some women are concerned that polygamy is practised secretly (with religious but not legal sanction) and may even be on the rise. The prominent feminist academic Saparinah Sadli, never one to exaggerate situations, has been quoted as saying 'Polygamy has become fashionable now in elite circles' (cited in Feillard 1996: 19). For those undertaking illegal

---

[6] See Andree Feillard who interviewed Muslim women leaders and found that 'Even in circles considered conservative, polygamy is viewed as improper' (1996: 19).

[7] See, for example, Thayib (1994) and Djawas (1996).

multiple marriages, the fines against infringement of the 1974 Marriage Law are so low as to make them scarcely a deterrent (Butt 1999: 132).

With democratisation, the heavy hand of official control of marriage has lifted. In her efforts to compromise with Islamic groups to engineer more political stability, President Megawati (herself the daughter of a polygamous president) has turned a blind eye to concerns about polygamy. The fact that her vice-president, Hamzah Haz (leader of an Islamic party), has three wives attests to the state's current lack of interest in the issue. Many women's organisations fear this tolerance is allowing polygamy to gain ground, and the fact that some men openly flaunt their polygamous status, and claim it to be evidence of Islamic identity, has alarmed many women (*Jakarta Post* 30 July 2003). Data on the current incidence of polygamy is lacking, but as this chapter has shown, for many women the actual incidence of polygamy is irrelevant: its sheer existence and social sanction is enough to make them feel insecure about marriage.

Conclusion

By the late twentieth century, the Indonesian state had done much to restrict polygamy, without making it illegal. The 1974 Marriage Law imposed tight conditions and state control over religious courts, and civil servants further impeded the practice.

What study of this issue reveals, among other things, is the fact that polygamy cannot be viewed in isolation if one wants to understand its impact on women and families. In circumstances where women have considerable autonomy, the legal existence of polygamy is less threatening to women. Those conditions include where it is not only little practised but devalued socially; where women are free to escape from unwanted polygamous marriage and sufficiently independent economically not to feel forced into a polygamous marriage; where marriage occurs at an age when both partners can make informed decisions free from family coercion; where women are sufficiently educated to be well-informed about their rights in marriage and to have access to relatively well-paid employment; where support and lack of stigma exist for divorced women and their children; and where the law ensures that the agreement of the first wife is a precondition for polygamy and that a woman who does not wish to share her husband can easily obtain a divorce. The state has a role to play in bringing about these conditions. It can promote education for girls; encourage economic development of a kind that enables women to have reasonably rewarding work, pass and enforce laws ensuring that women do not marry too young and that polygamy is consensual, that women have easy access to divorce, and that women are informed about their marriage rights.

But there are limits to what the state can do. It can only lead in so far as powerful forces in society will allow it to. Indonesian men have shown almost no interest in combating polygamy, and women have been divided in their attitudes to laws that might be seen to confront religious sensitivities. In these circumstances the Indonesian state for decades moved slowly on polygamy. With the recent Islamic revival and the importance of Islamic groups in the current democratic polity, the state is again reticent to intervene.

In any case, the state acts in the public sphere, influencing but distant from the world of private emotions. It can do little to assuage the hurt that women feel when their husbands take other sexual partners. Here non-state actors, and in particular other women, are important in creating a supportive environment. The world of statistics and legislation tells us little about whether Indonesian women are happier in their marriages.[8] But there is cause for optimism if we reflect that there now seems to be greater legal equality and protection for women in marriage than before, that their social and economic position also seems to offer them more possibility of autonomy if they choose to take it, and that the echoes of Kartini's anguished polemic against polygamy seem to have died down.

---

[8] For discussion about the interpretation of statistics showing declining divorce rates in Indonesia, see Jones (1994: 265, 310) and Guest (1991).

6   Motherhood

For both Indonesian women and the state, motherhood has been a concept of crucial importance. Governments have wanted responsible modern mothers, who can raise healthy children of good moral character. In
the late twentieth century, the main concern of the state in relation to
women was that they should have fewer children. Most of the research
commissioned by the New Order Government on the subject of women
related to fertility and how to limit it, and the largest single area of state
expenditure on women has been devoted to birth control. Unlike other
issues studied in this book, this one was largely initiated and pursued by
the state.

For organised Indonesian women, on the other hand, it is striking how
seldom they advanced any needs or rights that they had as mothers. More
frequently, they fell in with the dominant state ideology concerning the
responsibilities of mothers. Motherhood in the service of the nation-state
was the prevailing theme of their activities and rhetoric. Only occasionally
in modern Indonesian history have women taken a prominent political
stand to demand that the needs of mothers be met.

Most notably, the issue of the health needs of mothers received little
attention from either women's organisations or the state. It was not until
the late twentieth century, as a result of external pressure, that the state
began to address the high level of maternal mortality in Indonesia, and
some women's groups took up the international call for reproductive
health rights. Those rights are still narrowly conceived: for instance the
issue of abortion is still largely ignored.

This chapter seeks to understand the causes and consequences of the
convergence of approaches to motherhood by the state and the Indonesian women's movement and the way in which women's rights as mothers
were neglected until international forces permitted them to be addressed
in public.

The legacy: Indonesian meanings of motherhood

Anthropologists and historians have documented the great importance of motherhood in Indonesian societies and the richness of traditions associated with the concept. In the modern period it has been possible for women to draw on many strands of these traditions.

Women take pride in their public role as mothers. In Indonesia an adult woman is commonly referred to as *Ibu* (mother), on the assumption that she is one. Because motherhood is considered by most Indonesians as clearly the desirable state for women, ineluctably bound up with their *kodrat* (nature), even single or childless women are thus honorary mothers, although they are constantly called to account for themselves. It is considered perfectly acceptable to question a single woman as to why she is not married, or a married woman without children as to why she is delaying motherhood.

The notion of *kodrat* helps explain dominant Indonesian views on sexuality. The fact that it is a woman's destiny to be a mother would seem to rule out any possibility that women can acceptably be lesbians. Officially people are expected by religion, state and society to conform to the gender expectations of *kodrat* with its heavy emphasis on marriage and parenthood.

In practice, some ethnic groups in Indonesia have fluid attitudes towards sexuality, avoiding a strict categorisation into male/female, heterosexual/ homosexual. Male transvestism in religion, the arts and prostitution is well known in Java and South Sulawesi, for instance. Identifying as a bisexual or homosexual, with its implications of fixed sexual identity, is unusual. The important thing is that the social sanctity of marriage and motherhood is preserved, regardless of private behaviour. Until recently, the existence of lesbianism was denied by Indonesians, and it was regarded in official and Islamic circles under the New Order as a perversion (Gayatri 1996; Wieringa 1999). Owing to the efforts of homosexuals who no longer wish to remain 'in the closet', male and female homosexual groups began to emerge in a very small way in a few Javanese cities in the 1980s (Jeumpa and Ulil 2001). As in the West, it has been men who tend to 'come out' as homosexuals rather than women; lesbianism has had far less recognition in Indonesia and there is no legitimation of it within local traditions (Blackwood 1999; Murray 1999). The women's movement has been most reluctant to acknowledge lesbianism as a legitimate choice for women, or to include sexual preference in any of its programmes. Bringing such matters into the open only increases the likelihood of a confrontation with religious taboos (Murray 1999;

Amnesty International, 2001: 47–8). The accepted norm, the destiny of all Indonesians, is to form a family of heterosexual parents and children.

The centrality of parenthood in daily life is illustrated by the fact that in some areas of Indonesia it is common for both parents to be referred to as mothers or fathers of particular children rather than by their personal names. Amongst some ethnic groups like the patrilineal Balinese or the matrilineal Minangkabauers, it is imperative for purposes of perpetuating the lineage that wives give birth to a boy or girl respectively. As the previous chapter on polygamy has pointed out, being childless is also grounds for a husband to divorce his wife or take a second wife. In poor communities to be a mother without a husband makes more sense than to be a wife without children: being widowed or divorced with children is common, and having children is even more important than having a husband, since children are insurance for the future and soon contribute to household income.

It is not just social endorsement that makes motherhood so central: the maternal instinct is considered to be universal among women, and children are widely enjoyed and celebrated. Consider Kartini: although opposed to being married, she still wanted children, and when her birth is celebrated on Kartini Day it is always as *Ibu* Kartini, although she was only very briefly a mother, having died shortly after childbirth.

The established religions of Indonesia also offer strong support for women as mothers. Islam, Christianity, Hinduism and Buddhism all express reverence for the status of motherhood and identify it as women's main role. Indonesian mythology abounds with stories about the origin of different ethnic groups from earth mother figures: thus Minangkabau has Bundo Kanduang and Minahasa has Lumimu'ut.

Mythology also offers less dutiful and peaceful aspects of motherhood than have been drawn upon in public debate. For instance, Javanese pre-Islamic tradition included the Hindu goddess Durga, a demon-slayer whose mission is 'to combat cosmic disorder'. Although Hinduism died out in Java, it is still dominant in Bali, which is famous for its own version of Durga, the bloodthirsty and child-eating witch Rangda (Dowling 1994). Even after the coming of Islam, Javanese tradition retained Nyai Lara Kidul, who is associated both with fertility and with 'disease, death, the underworld, and demonic creatures' (Jordaan 1984: 107). Although the idea of the destructive mother-goddess, 'ready to destroy the demon of evil', played a prominent role in the radical tradition of Indian nationalism (Forbes 1996: 136–42), it was not taken up in Indonesia's nationalist movement. Instead, public debate about motherhood in Indonesia has been dominated by the elite whose images of mothers have been benign and self-sacrificing. This chapter will suggest that the identification of the

Indonesian women's movement with such images has been the source of some power but has also restricted its ability to assert the rights of mothers.

Motherhood in Indonesia has always carried its own meanings, often distinct from those in Western societies. Amongst ordinary Indonesians, an *ibu* has many roles (Locher-Scholten and Niehof 1987; Sullivan 1994). They go beyond domestic care of husband, children and the household and include activities outside the home to support the family. In other words, motherhood was associated with the 'private' world of the home as distinct from the 'public' world dominated by men. Mothers had a right to be active in the public world – so long as it was justified in the name of the family. Hence, from early times, it has been common to see Indonesian women working in the fields and markets. Nor was this view of motherhood restricted to working-class people, since Javanese *priyayi* women had a tradition of trade and other activities in support of the material needs of the family (Djadjadiningrat-Nieuwenhuis 1987). In fact, because a woman might well operate a business, her family was extended to include her employees. Just as a man was a *bapak* or father to his subordinates, so a woman could be an *ibu* with responsibilities to the 'family' at work. Indonesians are adept at manufacturing quasi-family relations in any situation. This legitimised the extensive activities of women, so long as they were framed in terms of responsibilities to dependants. Such ideas were also acceptable to modernist Islam. Founders of Muhammadiyah and Aisyiyah, after all, came from the area of Yogyakarta renowned for its devout Muslim manufacturers of *batik* (waxed and dyed cloth), where the industries were usually run by women (Marcoes-Natsir 2000).

Just as motherhood was not exclusively domestic, neither was it attached only to the biological mother. Indonesian children were accustomed to multiple mothering, to care by servants, co-wives, grandparents, aunts and older siblings, depending on parental wealth and status. No Western-style notions of child psychology (specifically maternal deprivation) hindered mothers in sharing child-rearing. There was even a casual approach to adoption, whereby parents gave their children into the more-or-less permanent care of a member of their wider family, either because that person lacked children, or because the parents were not in a position to raise their child. In turn, multiple mothering facilitated the multiple roles of mothers mentioned above.

The flexibility of Indonesian concepts of motherhood has allowed women to interpret it in their own ways, often to expand their own options. For instance, Indonesian women have long been interested in controlling fertility. Various traditional methods have been employed, some depending on practices for physical or spiritual wellbeing, such as abstention, or the prolonging of amenorrhea after childbirth by breast-feeding infants for long periods. Regardless of the strong prohibitions of all the main religions of the archipelago against abortion, traditional methods (like swallowing herbal concoctions, and vigorous massage) were employed to prevent the growth of the foetus (Hull 1999). Clearly the widespread acceptance of these practices meant that people acknowledged the need for women to restrict child-bearing, for the sake not just of the individual woman but also of the family. It was compatible with responsible motherhood.

From time to time in the twentieth century there has been tension in incorporating notions of modern motherhood into Indonesian understandings of *ibu*. Overall, however, it has been a remarkably resilient and flexible concept. In particular it is imbued with a strong sense of responsibility that both women and the state have used frequently in public discourse. The notion of mothers having rights, however, was more alien.

Motherhood and the colonial state

The colonial Dutch joined with Indonesians in having a high regard for motherhood, but they construed it in the contemporary middle-class European fashion, more narrowly and rigidly than was the tradition in Indonesia. Moreover, to a certain extent they saw it as a matter of interest to the modern state. Their own gender ideology exerted considerable influence over the emerging discourse about motherhood in the early twentieth century.

With the adoption of the Ethical Policy in 1901, the Dutch acknowledged some responsibility for the welfare of their colonial subjects. For many Indonesians colonial rule brought the benefits of peace, better transport, better clean water supplies and greater economic prosperity. Patchy though the data is, the evidence indicates a decline in mortality in the first half of the twentieth century, with temporal and regional fluctuations (Gooszen 2000).

Nevertheless, the authorities were concerned that the infant mortality rate was high. They tackled the problem in two ways, through direct health measures and through the education of mothers. Although these approaches had little impact at the time, they had a substantial long-term influence on state attitudes to motherhood, reflecting as they did a desire to recreate Indonesian mothers in a 'modern' light.

Health expenditure increased markedly but still provided little for the vast bulk of the population. By 1930 there were still only 404 doctors in government service and 324 private doctors on Java, mostly based in urban areas, in an overwhelmingly rural population of more than 40 million. Growth in medical personnel was even slower in the Outer Islands. The small health budget was skewed towards fighting epidemics, like cholera and the plague, towards preventing disease in urban areas where most Europeans lived, and towards key employment sectors like military and plantation workers (Gooszen 2000). In cases of ill health, there was often little of a curative nature that the state could do, given the medical knowledge of the time.

The colonial state began to document the extent of maternal morbidity and mortality, while acknowledging that in the absence of proper registration of deaths good data was lacking. In 1941 Verdoorn estimated that the maternal mortality rate for the whole of the Indies must have been at least 15 per cent (slightly less in towns), a high level which he attributed not just to lack of proper assistance for birthing women but also to unsatisfactory nutrition and chronic undermining illnesses like anaemia and malaria (Verdoorn 1941: 163–75).

Before the twentieth century there was no public discussion of maternal health. As individuals, Indonesian women cared for their own health as best they could, with the knowledge and means available to them. Herbal medicines were assiduously taken and the help of traditional healers sought. The village experts in childbirth have always been the traditional birth attendants (TBAs), known in Java as *dukun bayi*, who surround the crisis of childbirth with practices intended to ward off evil spirits and misfortune. Poor women have sought their own best interests and those of their families in circumstances that have often been very difficult and fraught with dangers.[1]

The colonial period marked the start of the clash between Western and traditional healthcare that had special significance for Indonesian women. Most Dutch observers despised the TBAs, whom they regarded as utterly ignorant of scientific medical knowledge, especially hygiene. In order to replace them, the government opened a few maternity hospitals and training institutions for Western-style doctors, nurses and midwives. Not only were the numbers of such trainees woefully inadequate, however, but the Dutch also found their midwives were not accepted by Indonesian women, who preferred the comfort, convenience and low cost of the care of TBAs during and after childbirth, even when midwives were available (Verdoorn 1941: 211).

TBAs were also criticised by the Dutch for their role in providing abortions, which in 1918 they made a criminal offence just as it was back in

---

[1] For sympathetic depictions of Indonesian women's experience of childbirth and associated health issues, see contributions in Rice and Manderson (1996).

the Netherlands. From their point of view, abortion was the worst form of birth control, which they viewed as erroneous, unsafe and irreligious.

Like most colonial powers, the Dutch had a poor opinion not only of TBAs but also of the standard of mothering by Indonesians, who needed to learn from the superior Dutch example.[2] Superstition and bad practices such as feeding babies solid food were held to cause high infant mortality (Habich-Veenhuijzen 1920). Fearful that the lax standards of Indonesian mothering might degrade Europeans and Eurasians, the Dutch wished to inculcate their current bourgeois ideas about the 'modern mother' who followed scientific notions on childbirth, health, hygiene and child care (Stoler 1996). The infant mortality rate had recently begun to decline in the Netherlands at the same time as notions of 'scientific' mothering gained in adherents.

Apart from the limited medium of education, however, lack of funding and a fear of the political consequences of interfering too far in social life prevented the colonial state from taking effective measures to implement their ideology of mothering among the mass of Indonesians. As usual, it was left mainly to 'social forces' to bring about change in attitudes and practices.

Those forces included the early Indonesian women's organisations, which were indeed profoundly influenced by Dutch notions of maternal care. Women most frequently justified their entry into public life, as well as their need for schooling, by referring to the need to promote new notions of responsible modern motherhood.

At first some educated Indonesian women failed to recognise the risks and contradictions involved in embracing 'modern motherhood' along Dutch lines. For poor Indonesians, even soap was a luxury in the early twentieth century. Borrowing the colonial perception of poor women as irresponsible mothers was invidious, considering the heavy burdens that rested on the shoulders of those mothers. Nevertheless, many of the early women's organisations were mainly concerned with teaching poor women how to take better care of their families, where better meant more 'scientific', hygienic and systematic. Demonstrations of how to bathe infants, advice about nutrition and competitions for the best baby were standard fare.

Some of the early women's organisations also adopted Dutch attitudes to maternal health: they established and maintained maternity hospitals and trained midwives. A well-known example was Budi Kemuliaan (Noble Character), formed in 1915 in Jakarta, which established a midwife training school (Ikatan Bidan Indonesia 1996: 15).

[2] Comparative insights on colonial criticisms of mothering practices among their colonial subjects can be found in Jolly (1998) and Manderson (1996).

Midwives began to make their mark on public debate about women's health, a prominent example being the midwife from Bandung named Jarisah who has already been mentioned as making a submission to the colonial enquiry into the declining welfare of the Javanese people in 1914. In an unusually frank way she spoke out about the problems of mothers she assisted in childbirth. 'There is a need for girls to know things, not to be innocent and ignorant in their relations with men', she said, 'to avoid the danger of unwanted pregnancies'. Moreover, she deplored the symptoms of venereal disease that she had seen 'even in married women, spread by their husbands' and passed on to their babies at birth, leading to the danger of blindness. She recommended that men should be examined before marriage to arouse their sense of responsibility for this evil. Concerned about the dangers of childbirth, she called for 'help in cases of difficult births in the *kampung*: it needs cooperation from *kampung* people and from the Government, for instance in transporting women to my home' (Netherlands Indies Government 1914: Bijdrage van Mevrouw Djarisah).

As we shall see, Jarisah might just as well have been speaking at the end of the century as near its outset. While the dangers facing pregnant and parturient women were great, they received little public attention and officials were slow to address them. In general, the dangers of pregnancy and childbirth for women were largely taken for granted as part of women's destiny, and aroused little discussion. Even when the well-loved Kartini died of a haemorrhage after the birth of her child in 1904, her death constituted an everyday tragedy. It might even have been better not to mention it, because in many parts of Indonesia it is believed that women who die in childbirth reappear as evil spirits, or *pontianak*, to take revenge on the living (Pontianak 1919). Amid the public sanctification of Kartini, exhibited every year on Kartini Day, it is almost refreshing to think of her as a *pontianak*. In the light of Indonesia's poor record on reducing maternal mortality, *pontianaks* might be seen as crying out for justice.

The nationalist movement and motherhood

From the 1920s onwards, Indonesian women's organisations increasingly identified with the nationalist movement. For Indonesian nationalists the nation was the mother: '*Ibu Indonesia*'. The motherland, *Ibu Pertiwi*, was often symbolised by nationalists as a nurturing mother and a suffering beauty who needed to be rescued from colonial oppression, as portrayed in the popular song 'Kulihat Ibu Pertiwi' (I See the Motherland) (Sunindyo 1998). For women in the nationalist movement, this symbolism offered certain advantages, elevating motherhood as it did to a position of national reverence. The discourse of the women's organisations mostly reinforced the nationalist image: mothers appeared as child-rearers, as selfless carers for others, as bearers of tradition, for whose honour their sons would sacrifice themselves.

At the first congress of nationalist-oriented women's organisations in 1928, there was agreement across the board, from religious and non-religious groups, that motherhood was their highest calling. Siti Sundari, whom we have seen in previous chapters clashing with Muslim groups, on this occasion found general support in speaking of the 'responsibilities and ideals of Indonesian women'. She claimed 'there is no other work in this world as weighty as' the role of the mother 'as educator of her children and the educator of our nation': this was 'the work which we consider the most noble' (Congres Perempoean 1929: 49–61). Her words were echoed by other speakers of different persuasions, who all stressed the obligations of mothers. It is not surprising, then, that when the women's movement, and subsequently the Indonesian Republic, chose to com-memorate 22 December, the opening date of the first Women's Congress in 1928, as a national day of celebration, it was called *Hari Ibu* or Mothers' Day, playing on the popular tendency to conflate 'woman' and 'mother'.[3] A later critic complained, 'Every other role has been subsumed to that one role' (Katoppo 1996).

The women of 1928 spoke of 'modern motherhood', enlightened by Western education. The publications of women's organisations reflected an ideal of Indonesian motherhood that was greatly influenced by Dutch thinking. It conceived of mothers within a nuclear family, with no men-tion of grandparents or other kin: mothering was exclusively the domain of the biological mother. Nor did unmarried mothers or single mothers (divorced or widowed) have any place in the idealised version of Indone-sian motherhood. Good mothers were married, apparently at home all the time and devoted to bringing up their children in the modern manner. In women's journals and magazines of the time, mothers in advertisements fed milk to their children, although in Indonesian society milk was an acquired taste and afforded by only a small minority of the population (Hatley and Blackburn 2000). In reality, most women were poor, most mothers worked outside the home and depended on established kinship networks to provide children with 'multiple mothering', and most chil-dren never saw the inside of a school.

---

[3] The Women's Congress held in July 1938 decided to commemorate 22 December as 'Hari Ibu' and the independent government declared it a national day in 1959. It was supposed both to mark the start of the awakening of Indonesian women (commemorating the 1928 conference) and to 'honour our mothers for their services in the family circle' (*Suara Indonesia* 22 December 1959).

Within the women's movement itself, some criticised the projected image of motherhood. A contributor to *Sedar*, the journal of the radical women's organisation Istri Sedar, noted that most Indonesian working-class women worked long hours.

You women who are always demanding that women should stay at home to look after the household and children: do you remember the women who work in your homes as servants, do your remember that those mothers must leave their homes and children and there is no nursemaid to look after their children, who are neglected and miserable? Do you feel the hardship of those who must work until half dead while their children suffer? (*Sedar* 1930: 5)

She was reminding women that the reality of motherhood differed from the version being constructed by middle-class women's organisations and media. Her criticism of the treatment of servants forms a link with the next chapter of this book, about women's work.

Indonesian women's organisations recognised the danger of painting themselves into a domestic corner. They wished to expand the image of motherhood taught to them in colonial schools to include duties to society at large rather than just to the family. Mothers must be free to be active in wider society and to carry their nurturing function even into the public political realm. In this way women's organisations dominated by elite women were developing an ideology that Madelon Djajadiningrat-Nieuwenhuis (1987) has called 'Ibuism': one that 'sanctions any action provided that it is taken as a mother who is looking after her family, a group, a class, a company or the state, without demanding power or prestige in return'. Djajadiningrat-Nieuwenhuis linked it to the traditions of the Javanese *priyayi*, amongst whom women were expected to contribute in an unobtrusive way to the material and moral support of their families to keep their menfolk free from mundane cares and able to exercise their higher spiritual calling. In her view, elite women educated in the colonial period found it easy to combine this tradition with the middle-class Dutch notions of motherhood imbibed with Western schooling. In keeping with the Javanese *priyayi* tradition, women could engage in activities, including income-earning ones, outside the home, so long as they did so in a way that did not detract from the husband's prestige as head of household. In both Javanese and Dutch teachings, women's motherly qualities tied them to the everyday, practical world and excluded them from 'real' power conceived of as belonging to higher spheres.

During the 1930s, the organised women's movement identified Indonesian motherhood with the demands of nationalism. *Isteri*, the journal of the women's federation, PPII, continued the refrain of the 1928 congress in extolling women's role as mothers of the nation and calling attention to the nationalist responsibilities of mothers. Contributors from both secular and religious organisations were at pains to point out that mothers' duties were not limited to their immediate family but extended to the wider family of Indonesia.

Most strikingly, no requests were put to the colonial state to attend to the needs of mothers, an issue that was treated very differently from schooling for girls or early marriage, discussed in earlier chapters. Nor, as the nationalist movement grew, did women use their role in that movement to put forward such demands as ones that an independent Indonesian state should heed. Collaborating in the creation of a mystique of self-sacrificing, responsible motherhood made it difficult for organised women to assert their own needs.

Motherhood in the early Republic

Indonesian women were considered by the nationalist movement to have proved their commitment to the nation during the trials of the Japanese Occupation and the subsequent period known as the Revolution (1945–9). Women had an important role in caring for soldiers and others during this period of upheaval, and in circumstances of deprivation and hardship the needs of mothers were acutely visible. In particular there were large numbers of refugees, mostly mothers and children.

More than ever, after the Declaration of Independence in 1945, organised women were expected to continue to honour a notion of motherhood that included caring for the wider society. As vice-president Mohamad Hatta put it in 1958:

The task for the present is raising new people with good character and a sense of responsibility. Next to school teachers it is the mother in the home who must lay the basis for the character formation of children. For this reason, the education and training of children, especially girls who will mostly become mothers in future, must be the subject of great efforts by the women's movement, as well as the health and education of society.

The issue now is not to make demands but to participate in carrying out measures, in taking initiatives.

The social problems in the development of state and society are remarkably intense, more intense probably than political issues. The women's movement must concentrate its efforts on that, adding its initiatives to those of the government. (Buku Peringatan 1958: 110)

Hatta's words, relegating the women's movement to a 'non-political', 'social' role supportive of the state, foreshadowed the later style of the New Order. It was women's maternal, nurturing efforts that the state wanted to coordinate. Madelon Djajadiningrat-Nieuwenhuis later commented, 'the new Indonesian society called upon the "kaum Ibu" [women/mothers] to put their shoulders to the task of building a new national state; and more than the men, they were expected to do this disinterestedly. The honour they could gain was that of being a good Ibu. Power and prestige remained the privilege of men' (Djadjadiningrat-Nieuwenhuis 1987: 43).

The decade or so following the Declaration of Independence was a period of heroic social work performed by many women in a voluntary capacity. Starting with women's work in first-aid and feeding the soldiers and public servants of the fledgling Republican government during the Revolution of 1945–9 and stretching into the reconstruction years of the early 1950s, women were the mothers of the infant Republic. Again, motherhood was interpreted broadly and used as a justification for women's wider role.

Most of the endeavours of women's organisations in the early years of the Republic were devoted to working hand in hand with state institutions on behalf of families, to provide much-needed welfare. Their efforts bore fruit in a continuous decline in childhood mortality during the 1950s (Iskandar 1997). Little was done by the state, however, to meet women's health needs, apart from the launch in 1951 of the Mother and Child Health programme, setting up clinics in towns and villages run by midwives. They were supposed to conduct examinations before and after childbirth and give vaccinations and immunisations and advice on health and nutrition. These were the first of many such programmes that until recently have faltered due to lack of funding, shortage of midwives and lack of participation by village mothers. At the same time, in 1951 the midwives' association (Ikatan Bidan Indonesia – IBI) was formed and became an important lobby group for mother and child healthcare (Ikatan Bidan Indonesia 1996).

In the 1950s women's organisations were learning to participate in democratic politics, and beginning to address the needs of mothers. The second post-independence congress of the women's movement in 1952, representing sixty-three organisations from many regions, called for child care for working women, a radical demand. The third congress in 1955 approved a Charter of Women's Rights that included a section on the welfare of mothers and children. They demanded 'the establishment of hospitals and consultation bureaux in sufficient numbers throughout the country, and child care provision in industrial and plantation centres'. And in 1953, on the twenty-fifth anniversary of the Indonesian women's movement, the president of the IBI wrote that her organisation was concerned that 1.2 per cent of women still died in childbirth, and that maternity hospitals were still inadequate and midwives few in number (Buku Peringatan 1958: 46, 52, 135–6). Some women were pointing to the failure of state action in addressing the health needs of Indonesian mothers. Perwari, one of the largest women's organisations of the time, and in particular its very active president, Suyatin Kartowiyono, frequently attempted to draw public attention to the high maternal mortality rate and the need for better health services for women (Martyn 2001: 123–4).

Most women's organisations of the time, religious and secular, were heavily involved in providing health services, such as setting up health information bureaux and Mother and Child Health clinics, and training midwives. It was the practical experience thus gained that allowed them to speak authoritatively in lobbying the state on behalf of the health of mothers and children (Martyn 2001: 124–6).

During the period of liberal democracy, some people took advantage of the freedom of association to work towards greater availability of contraception. In 1957 the Indonesian Planned Parenthood Association (Perkumpulan Keluarga Berencana Indonesia) was formed to provide advisory services in Jakarta on birth control. It was a modest beginning to what proved to be a massive venture, as will be discussed below. At the time it was a controversial move: some Muslim leaders publicly opposed birth control and Islamic women's organisations refused to discuss the issue. While the Ministry of Health was supportive, the rest of the government was not (Martyn 2001: 126–9).

President Sukarno himself was strongly opposed to limiting the rapid growth in Indonesia's population. Obsessed with threats from neo-colonialism, he felt that a large population made for a strong country. Sukarno had nothing to offer mothers except more opportunities for self-sacrifice on behalf of the nation as the economy stumbled further into disarray under his rule.

The perils of militant motherhood: Gerwani

Under Sukarno's Guided Democracy and the New Order, there were more official restrictions and more efforts by the state to harness women's organisations to its programmes. The transition was reflected in the work of Gerwani, one of the dominant women's organisations of the 1950s and early 1960s. In the 1950s it strove to project an image of motherhood that would conform to the needs of working and peasant mothers, the vast majority of the population. More than other women's organisations, it stressed that although women were necessarily mothers, they were also working women and should participate fully in politics. Gerwani encouraged the setting up of creches to care for infants so that mothers could be freed up for other tasks: by 1964 it was reported that nearly 1,500 crèches had been established. Such services were popular and constituted part of Gerwani's appeal to village and urban working women.

Saskia Wieringa (2002), who has made a close study of Gerwani literature and interviewed many former members of the organisation, notes that in the 1950s the organisation focussed on women's home responsibilities and their political ramifications such as concern over rising prices. Gerwani leaders strove to reconcile notions of the *kodrat* of mothers with a wider agenda, in much the same way as other nationalist-oriented secular women's organisations. Thus Umi Sarjono, in opening the Third Plenary of Gerwani in 1956, pronounced: 'We must not give up our womanly attitude . . . This womanly attitude is the love for husband and children, the organization of the household, being dressed properly and in a simple manner, and join in the struggle of women to defend the rights of women and children and for peace' (quoted in Wieringa 2002: 272).

As Gerwani became more closely aligned with the PKI from the late 1950s and the PKI itself prioritised support for President Sukarno and his international ventures (leading the Afro-Asian bloc, winning back West Irian, opposing the formation of Malaysia), Gerwani relegated the needs of mothers to a secondary place and tended rather to emphasise their identification with the on-going revolution. Mothers should educate their children in revolutionary beliefs and participate in drills and other preparations for armed struggle against neo-imperialism. Wieringa calls this the period of Gerwani's 'motherly militancy'. By cleaving ever more closely to the PKI, Gerwani had become coopted into the Sukarnoist political agenda.

Pursuing this militant path cost Gerwani dear. It was perceived by the enemies of the PKI (principally the army and Islamic organisations) as part and parcel of the communist movement which must be crushed at all costs. When the army took power at the end of 1965, Gerwani suffered along with the PKI and its other 'front' organisations: thousands of its members were killed and arrested, thrown into jail for many years without trial. The New Order regime identified Gerwani followers as deviants from the feminine order, in a way that is neatly portrayed on the Pancasila monument erected to commemorate the killing of ten generals in October 1965, an event in which it claimed Gerwani members were implicated. The frieze on the monument shows women 'before' and 'after' the New Order regime. 'Before' is clearly meant to depict the stereotype of Gerwani women: they are indeed militant, shouting, gesticulating and generally in revolt. 'Afterwards' shows women in what the army presumably considered their rightful, orderly role, standing quietly in the background and nursing babies. In the New Order view of things, motherhood was incompatible with the Gerwani spirit, whereas in fact the organisation had identified as strongly as any with the needs of mothers.

The New Order's agenda for mothers

The New Order valued mothers as sources of stability in society, working for harmony in the smallest and most basic unit of the social order: the family. Not surprisingly for a regime led by military men, it made a very clear distinction between the roles of men and women, the latter being expected to keep the home fires burning. The main women's organisations created and promoted by the New Order regime – Dharma Wanita and the PKK – were devoted to wifely and motherly duties. Regarded as dangerously aberrant, Gerwani was purged from the women's movement.

Conducting research in rural Java in the early 1970s, Valerie Hull found middle-class people endorsing notions of the domesticated housewife, and criticising working women for neglecting their children (Hull 1996). For some mothers, the New Order gender ideology was attractive and even practicable. Through the PKK and official arms of the state some effort was made to extend these ideas to the wider population. Observers noted, for example, that PKK volunteers at health posts criticised poor women for neglecting their children by working outside the home (Robinson 1994: 79).

The New Order regime was clear about its first priority for mothers: limiting their fertility. After years in which President Sukarno had spurned birth control as unnecessary, President Suharto recognised that Indonesia's fertility rate, at 5.6 births per woman, was too high. His government became converted to spreading the message of contraception for three main reasons. Firstly, limiting the birth rate formed part of the government's far-reaching commitment to development, which was the basis for the New Order's legitimacy. Suharto was aware that a rapidly growing population made it so much more difficult to raise people's standard of living and put immense strain on government resources. Secondly, measures in the late 1960s by the Governor of Jakarta, Ali Sadikin, showed that Muslims could be persuaded to support state-sponsored family planning (Hull 1994: 129). Thirdly, family planning was urged upon the Indonesian Government by its main aid donors, Western countries like the USA. The Family Planning Programme adopted by Suharto in 1970 was largely dependent on foreign aid.[4] The West wanted to limit world

---

[4] The main donors to the Indonesian family-planning programme have been the World Bank, USAID and the United Nations Population Fund.

population growth, especially in large countries like Indonesia which was at the time the fifth largest country in the world (now the fourth largest). Thus family planning was part of the Western agenda which impinged upon Indonesia at a time when it was sensitive to the wishes of aid donors.

The state tackled family planning with enormous enthusiasm and resourcefulness. Suharto established a National Family Planning Coordination Board answerable directly to himself and accessing large amounts of foreign aid. Opposition from religious groups was overcome by omitting from the officially sponsored methods those most condemned by Islam and Christianity, that is abortion and sterilisation, and targeting propaganda only at married couples. Religious leaders were then successfully wooed to support the programme. 'Two children is enough' was its slogan. The civil service and social groups were mobilised to spread the family-planning word and means right down to the village level, making approved kinds of modern contraceptives freely available. To win further popular support, in the 1990s the government linked birth control to a range of other measures under its new slogan, Family Welfare. For instance it provided 'acceptors' of contraception with income-generating activities and small loans. This wider approach won it greater cooperation from Muslim organisations. In fact the government borrowed many of the ideas for the Family Welfare policy from Aisyiyah, the women's wing of Muhammadiyah, which had been working since 1985 with the Department of Religion and with UNICEF on a programme to improve the health of mothers and children. In exchange, Aisyiyah agreed to work with the Family Planning Coordination Board to promote contraception, although it did not agree with the Board that the ideal family should be limited to two children (Bright 1999).

By the end of the New Order the prevalence of contraceptive use among women of child-bearing age had risen to almost 60 per cent from less than 10 per cent at the start of the regime, and fertility had more than halved to 1.35 per cent per annum (*Jakarta Post* 8 January 2001). The international community hailed the programme as a great success and conferred two United Nations Population Awards on Suharto. There has been considerable debate as to how far the state was in fact responsible for the decline in fertility, because a range of factors are involved, and the fall in birth-rates began before the family-planning programme started. In evaluating the outcomes, research nevertheless indicates that the work of 'motivators' at the grass-roots and the availability of contraceptives throughout the country have at the very least been major stimuli (Hull 1987; Robinson 1989; Koning 1996; Hull, Widyatun, Raharto et al. 1999).

By the time Suharto's awards were conferred, criticism of the family-planning programme had begun to surface. The choice of contraceptives made available to women was limited to those the state considered most cost-effective, such as IUDs, injectables and, later, hormonal implants. Many observers considered these were imposed without sufficient consideration, or warning to women, of their side effects. There was evidence of undue pressure on women to adopt contraception, especially in the early days of the programme, when the military staged an intimidatory presence in villages, and later the requirement that civil servants achieve target numbers of 'acceptors' in their jurisdiction was also considered by many to amount to a form of coercion (Warwick 1986; Hull 1991; Smyth 1991; Hafidz, Taslim, Aripurnami et al. 1992; Adrina, Purwandari, Triwijati et al. 1998). In East Timor, the application of the family-planning programme was especially controversial: coercion and violence were associated with the programme, and informed user consent was often lacking, so that many saw it as part of Indonesian oppression inflicted on the territory since the invasion of 1975 (Sissons 1997).

The Family Planning Programme was the prime example of state domination of the women's movement by the New Order regime and of the way it mobilised women behind its development effort. With its broad access to women, the state sponsored PKK was well placed to recruit them as 'acceptors' of family planning, and that became one of its main tasks.

Despite the heavy dependence on women as 'acceptors' of contraception and as 'motivators' at the lowest levels, the decisions about the family-planning programme were made by men, in particular the powerful Haryono Suyono who led the Family Planning Coordination Board for decades. The bureaucracy of the programme was male-dominated throughout the New Order period.

By the 1990s persuading women to have fewer children needed less effort because of many economic and social changes (Hull 1987). Women were marrying later, they had more education and were consequently better placed to negotiate child-bearing decisions with their partners and kin. More parents wanted to keep their children at school for longer periods, making child-rearing more expensive. Thus the campaigns in which women's organisations had been engaged for many years, against early marriage and for the education of girls, were contributing to the fertility decline. In addition, the economic and political context had changed. With the decline in government revenue from oil in the 1980s and the international move towards economic rationalism, state and international support for the provision of free contraceptives and birth control advice declined. It was replaced by the notion that the increasing number of people who could afford to do so should seek private medical care for contraception, and the state should serve only the neediest.

International pressure puts reproductive
health on the agenda

Despite its emphasis on motherhood, the New Order Government was slow to attend to the health of mothers and their children. Like previous governments, it continued to rely on voluntary efforts by women to look after their own needs. One of the duties of women drafted into the PKK was to assist in monitoring the health of infants and pregnant women in conjunction with the staff of health posts.

On the other hand, it cannot be denied that women and infants bene-fited from the general contribution that the government made to improve Indonesians' health, both directly and indirectly. The New Order used part of the greatly increased revenue of the 1970s oil boom to create a much more extensive system of health centres, and, more importantly, its promotion of economic development helped greatly reduce poverty, raise nutrition levels and increase life expectancy for both men and women (Rahardjo 1997). In the 1980s it initiated the provision of Village Inte-grated Service Posts specialising in nutrition, immunisation, control of diarrhoeal diseases, mother and child care, and family planning. Infant mortality rates declined steeply under the New Order (from about 150 to 51 in the period 1960–93), and life expectancy rose from almost 46 in 1967 (47 for women and 42 for men) to almost 63 in 1993 (almost 65 for women and 61 for men) (Iskandar 1997). Indirectly, too, the drive to pro-mote birth control and make contraception readily available to all women undoubtedly helped reduce maternal mortality and morbidity. What was lacking was any special recognition of the health problems of women on the part of the state and the will to address them. Health in general has received low priority in state expenditure in Indonesia (Iskandar 1997).

In the last decade of the New Order, however, a number of interna-tional conferences legitimised and popularised the notion of reproductive health, incorporating the needs of women into a programme broader than that of fertility control. Most notable were the Safe Motherhood Con-ference, held in Nairobi in 1987, and the International Conference on Population and Development in Cairo in 1994. At the Cairo conference the notion of reproductive rights was officially adopted and an ambitious list of targets drawn up involving reduction in maternal mortality rates (MMR) and provision of reproductive health services. The term 'repro-ductive health' refers to health issues affecting the reproductive system, such as childbirth, abortion, infertility and sexually transmitted diseases.

The Safe Motherhood Conference in Nairobi in 1987 sounded the alarm about high levels of maternal mortality in developing countries like Indonesia, where reporting of childbirth-related deaths has always been very poor (Zahr and Royston 1991). International agencies began publishing their own estimates of MMR in different countries and making an issue of the persistent high levels of maternal deaths in poor countries, one of the most striking gaps between rich and poor nations.[5] It soon emerged that Indonesia performed particularly poorly compared with its regional neighbours: its MMR was estimated in 1986 to be about 4.5 deaths per 1,000 live births, very high for Southeast Asia (Government of Indonesia-UNICEF 1989: 46). Maternal mortality, then, became a matter of national shame that called for government attention, and international organisations presented proposals to solve the problem.

Explanations for Indonesia's high MMR varied. State health officials saw it in the wider health perspective, claiming that the main reasons included people's lack of knowledge and 'various damaging superstitions' as well as low nutrition levels and anaemia. Childbirth specialists tended to focus on immediate causes like haemorrhaging, infection, toxicity in pregnancy and abortion, within the medical context of high blood pressure, tuberculosis, diabetes, hepatitis, anaemia and malaria. Different diagnoses gave rise to different recommendations for action, some mainly by the state and others by the community. In any case, all were in agreement that women needed more support and trained assistance before, during and after childbirth.

In the case of state concern about maternal mortality, the Ministries of Health and Women's Role took the lead in responding to international pressure (Shiffman 1999: 135–7). Although the Family Planning Board cooperated, it clearly felt threatened by the competition (Hull and Hull 1995). The notion that birth control was just one aspect of a wider spectrum of reproductive health found only a reluctant response in the Board, established as it was with a different agenda. Supported by international aid, the government adopted the Safe Motherhood programme proposed by the World Health Organisation. The number of trained midwives was rapidly expanded, and by the late 1990s the government could claim that there was one in almost every village (Shiffman 1999: 140). Figures of women giving birth without trained medical care have dropped significantly in Indonesia in recent years, although most women still turn to the assistance of a TBA in childbirth. Indicating the trend, midwives are more common in urban areas (Indonesia 1997, 1999; *Kompas* 3 September 2000). Nevertheless, the class gap between trained health personnel and many of the mothers they are supposed to serve still creates distrust and disillusionment on both sides (Grace 1996;

[5] One in four women in developing countries suffers from acute or chronic conditions related to pregnancy, and a woman in such countries has a 1 in 48 chance of dying from pregnancy-related causes, compared with 1 in 1,800 in a rich country like Australia (World Bank 1999: 1).

Hunter 1996b), and village midwives, although now the most numerous single category of health personnel, have received poor quality training (Hull et al. 1999: 18).

A further measure, initiated in 1996 by the Ministry for Women's Role, attempted to generate broad community support for pregnant women to prevent deaths in childbirth: this was the 'Sayang Ibu' (Mother Friendly) programme which mobilised communities to identify pregnant women in risk categories and to ensure that they got medical care if they encountered difficulties in childbirth. The Ministry for Women's Role had taken on board the argument advanced at international conferences that the level of maternal mortality was related to women's status in society (Shiffman 1999: 144). In the Indonesian case this was thought to include customs such as the expectation that women would eat after they had served their families, which in poor households meant insufficient nutrition for expectant mothers. Dr Abdullah Cholil, a high-ranking official of the Ministry, took a prominent role in delivering the message, contrary to the gender ideology of the New Order state, that 'women are still subordinate in the family', causing the health problems of parturient women to be ignored (*Kompas* 17 December 1996; *Kompas* 19 February 1997). The Ministry recruited women's organisations to garner community support for pregnant women. For example, the Muslim women's wing of NU, Muslimat NU, persuaded religious leaders to speak in sermons in support of the Mother Friendly Programme (*Kompas* 10 March 1997). In 1997 the Ministry for Women's Role was authorised to act as coordinator of safe motherhood initiatives and was partially funded by UNICEF to take on further duties (Shiffman 1999: 147).

Again, it seems doubtful whether the Indonesian Government would have adopted the discourse of reproductive health without the international pressure and foreign aid that accompanied it. Indications of the lack of political will of the government were its continuing low expenditure on health generally and the high levels of corruption in the system, both of which contributed to underutilisation of public health services (Iskandar 1997: 221–3). Moreover, the authoritarian style of government militated against a truly 'bottom-up' approach to public health care, despite the rhetoric (Hull 1988; Achmad 1999). The continuing dominant legacy of Western-style healthcare, focussing on the medical care of the patient by the scientifically trained expert, is also at odds with the primary healthcare approach that is basic to the philosophy of reproductive healthcare: this approach sees health in a wider perspective and is preventive rather than curative. Despite the apparent endorsement by the Ministry of Health of primary healthcare principles, the training of health and administrative personnel, and the hierarchy of the health system have hampered the implementation of these ideas (Hunter 1996a). Finally, the state discourse on reproductive health continued to be dominated by the perspective of the family-planning programme.

Within Indonesia, few women were able to join the debate on reproductive health issues. An exception has been the midwives, who have formed a pressure group in favour of Western concepts of reproductive health, often in conjunction with gynaecologists and obstetricians. Fortified by the 1987 Nairobi Safe Motherhood Conference that drew attention to the maternal mortality issue, the 1988 congress of the IBI sent several recommendations to the Ministry of Health as to how to improve the health of mothers, all featuring the role of midwives very prominently (Ikatan Bidan Indonesia 1996: 23–4). To a large extent, however, midwives are part of the phalanx of 'experts' who speak with authority on health matters but in ways that are incomprehensible to or just unheard by most Indonesians. Differing from their clients not only in class but also in ethnicity in more remote areas, midwives may not even speak the same language as poor clients who have little if any schooling in Bahasa Indonesia, the national language. The TBAs to whom most rural women turn for support have no authority politically and are excluded from the health debate.

The dominance of reproductive health discourse by a small elite is striking. An experienced doctor, Januar Achmad, has argued (1999: 170) that 'no strong mass organisation has concerned itself with vast population issues such as health'. This has not been the case in all areas of public policy: Achmad points out that the Islamic lobby has been influential in the Ministries of Religion and Education. From 1983 the Minister for Women's Role participated in the Cabinet, but she relied on the cooperation of other ministries for any implementation of policies. Moreover, she suffered from the absence of a strong, autonomous women's movement that might have supported its policies in the community. Commenting on the lack of attention to reproductive tract infections in Indonesia, Valerie Hull and colleagues noted in 1996:

There is an absence of grassroots NGOs concerned with women's health in Indonesia, so there is no countervailing model to balance the top-down, authoritarian approach of government campaigns. Most importantly, little information exists about women's own health experiences and priorities. Programs to assist in areas such as abortion, adolescent reproductive health and wider sexual health are hampered by politico-religious sensitivities. (Hull, Widyantoro and Fetters 1996: 228–9)

Many women's organisations continued the tradition established earlier in the century of supporting private health facilities for women. For instance, Muslimat NU and Aisyiyah ran birth clinics and mother and child

healthcare centres, trained midwives and provided family-planning education (Rahman 2000). However, they did not lobby the state on behalf
of women's health because they saw their role as a social rather than
political one.

Women's organisations rally to the slogan
of reproductive health

It was only towards the end of the New Order that younger Indonesian
women were bold enough to pose demands on the state in relation to
reproductive health. The more overtly feminist organisations founded
in this period were attracted to the notion of reproductive health rights
and used it as a platform to put women's health on the political agenda.
Thus, for example, leaders of Solidaritas Perempuan (Women's Solidarity, founded in 1990) challenged the 1992 Health Law, saying that it
was too family centred and neglected the health needs of marginalised
people like single old people, unmarried women, and prostitutes. Echoing the words of the midwife Jarisah in 1914, they argued that adolescents needed information about reproduction. They also rejected the very
limited access to abortion permitted in the 1992 Law (*Media Indonesia*
17 February 1992). In this campaign they were joined by some prominent
medical men, notably Kartono Mohamad, a redoubtable leader of the
Indonesian Planned Parenthood Association (Mohamad 1998). Muslim
feminists, too, were outspoken about reproductive health, even arguing
that abortion was legal according to Islamic law within the first hundred
days of pregnancy (Muchtar 1999: 108). Islamic law is in fact divided on
the question (Huzaimah 1996; Hooker 1999).

The level of activity of organisations in the area of women's reproductive health rose rapidly at the end of the twentieth century, assisted by
foreign aid. This was by no means a Java-based movement: such NGOs
spread throughout the archipelago.

The new discourse amongst women's organisations locates reproductive health in the context of human rights, the approach popularised at
international women's conferences from the late 1980s onwards and at
the Cairo Conference in 1994. A powerful voice for this politicisation of
reproductive health has been Nursyahbani Kacasungkana, director of the
women's legal-rights organisation Indonesian Women's Association for
Justice (LBH-APIK), and, from 1999, secretary-general of the Indonesian Women's Coalition for Justice and Democracy (Koalisi Perempuan
Indonesia untuk Keadilan dan Demokrasi). At a symposium in 1995 following up the Cairo Conference, she said: 'In legal and social reality,
the issue of reproductive rights is an issue of power relations. Society,

especially women, are powerless. So they remain silent. They have no economic, social, cultural or political power, in their relations with men, the family, the society or the state' (Katjasungkana 1996: 123).

The examples she gave to support this statement were controversial. One referred to the failure of a woman in a maternity clinic to prevent the circumcision of her daughter. Female circumcision, practised in Indonesia in a very minimalist fashion, had not been publicly discussed (Feillard and Marcoes 1998). Another concerned a factory worker whose employer refused to give her maternity leave. Unbeknown to the employee, the leader of the government-run trade union in her work unit had signed a Work Agreement that limited the rights of employees who had more than three children, as part of a deal between the Ministry of Labour and the National Family Planning Coordination Board. Nursyahbani concluded her presentation by saying:

In our country the function of the mother is highly revered. It has become a common saying that heaven lies at the feet of the mother, and other similar remarks. The main thing is, the maternal function is highly esteemed, but demanding one's rights is completely prohibited. For example, we greatly honour a mother because she perpetuates human civilisation. But try looking at factories in the villages: mothers are forced to work for hours standing upright continuously, and the state does nothing about it. (Katjasungkana 1996: 150)

Elements within the largest Islamic organisation, Nahdlatul Ulama, have played an important part in advocating reproductive health rights in recent years. With foreign-aid funding, particularly from the Ford Foundation, NU under the leadership of Abdurrachman Wahid encouraged the promotion of the discourse of reproductive health in its widest sense within the organisation, despite opposition from some quarters. Individuals like Lies Markus-Natsir and Masdar Mas'udi worked hard to convince NU supporters that Islamic teachings were compatible with notions of reproductive health rights (Sehat 1998).

Most recently, the influence of Western aid on Indonesia has been seen in relation to another matter which can be regarded as an aspect of reproductive health: HIV/AIDS. In this case the Indonesian Government does not consider the issue central to its development planning and has approached the campaign against HIV/AIDS with far more reluctance than it displayed towards family planning. From its point of view the gains to be made in this campaign are negligible compared with the vast problems involved in confronting sexual issues, particularly relating to young, unmarried people. Part of its pact with religious groups underlying the family-planning programme, after all, was that only married couples might be assumed to have sex. Sex education is not provided in

Indonesian schools. Here, as in its pioneering campaign on birth control, the Indonesian Planned Parenthood Association has taken the lead,
opening sex education clinics for teenagers in the main cities (Dwiyanto
and Darwin 1996: 110). At the end of the century, the Family Planning
Board, using foreign aid, began cautiously to introduce a programme in
reproductive health for adolescents (*Media Indonesia* 8 August 2000).

Certain aspects of reproductive health that the Indonesian Government considers unacceptable have been neglected, regardless of women's
needs. Abortion is a good example here. Through the Family Planning
Programme modern contraceptives are available only to married couples, and this at a time when age of marriage is rising markedly while
premarital sex is known to be increasingly common. A high level of illegal (and botched) abortions show many women are still falling pregnant
against their will and are prepared to take high risks to get rid of the foetus
(Djohan, Indrawasih, Adenam et al. 1993; Hull, Sarwono, Widyantoro
et al. 1993). This is a significant contributing factor to the high maternal mortality rate.[6] Although there are no accurate statistics on abortion,
which is very difficult to acquire legally in Indonesia, currently more than
2 million are estimated to occur each year (*Kompas* 3 March 2000).

The independent Republic of Indonesia had inherited from colonial
times a 1918 law that made abortion a crime against morality and against
life, but loopholes and lack of clarity enabled some women to obtain
abortions. During the New Order period, attempts were made by some
medical professional associations and women's groups to regularise the
situation, legalising abortion under certain conditions. However, the government was extremely wary of tackling an issue that arouses a high level
of religious opposition. Like childbirth, abortion is also a bone of contention between specialists and others: physician specialists like obstetricians and gynaecologists, who are few in number, male and urban-based,
regard themselves as the only ones entitled to terminate pregnancies,
excluding the traditional practitioners, doctors, midwives and nurses who
in fact perform most abortions.

It was not until the passage of the national Health Law of 1992 that
legal abortions were made possible in certain restricted cases, so long
as they were performed by medical specialists. Such was the controversy
that the law itself could not even refer directly to abortion: instead it
uses the euphemism 'a certain medical procedure'. In practice religious

---

[6] In 2000 the president of the Family Planning Association of Indonesia (PKBI), Professor
Dr Azrul Azwar, was reported as claiming that abortions caused 13–15 per cent of the
maternal mortality rate in Indonesia (*Kompas* 3 March 2000). Another member of the
PKBI claimed half of the MMR was caused by unsafe abortions (Mohamad 1998: 84).
Later that year Azwar said up to half illegal abortions were fatal (*Kompas* 26 August 2000).

objections have made it very difficult for the government to authorise abortion, and the situation remains worryingly unclear for all concerned (Djohan et al. 1993; *Jakarta Post* 3 April 2000). The fact that there is no international consensus in favour of abortion has meant a lack of external support for the Indonesian Government in liberalising the availability of safe termination of pregnancy. Most Indonesian women's groups, too, have avoided the whole issue as abhorrent or excessively divisive.[7]

Other aspects of reproductive health have barely surfaced as yet. One example is the treatment of infertility. To be infertile in Indonesia is something of a tragedy for a woman, since all wives are expected to bear children. We do not know the level of infertility since diagnosis is inadequate and treatment available only to the wealthy few. Another neglected issue is that of sexually transmitted diseases (STDs), the dangers of which were raised by Jarisah in 1914. STDs are believed to be common but frequently undiagnosed among women and are linked to the spread of HIV/AIDS in Indonesia. Diseases of the reproductive tract make life miserable and/or short for innumerable women. Again, poor diagnosis and shame means we do not know the severity of this problem (Hull et al. 1996). The Indonesian state is highly unlikely to take such an interest in these aspects of reproductive health, or receive such a level of foreign assistance to attend to them, as it has done with HIV/AIDS or birth control.

It is a vexed question as to how Indonesian women can voice their demands for better reproductive health. Most women find it hard to articulate their health needs publicly: it is difficult enough to make choices at the individual level with the limited knowledge available to them. Matters of reproductive health, connected as they are to issues of sexuality that many women are socialised to regard as shameful, have not been considered suitable for public discussion (Adrina, et al. 1998). However, the fact that so many younger Indonesian women's organisations, including Islamic ones, have enthusiastically taken up the advocacy of reproductive rights in recent years, accepting foreign aid funding to do so, indicates potential for raising political awareness about such issues.

The return of political mothers

At the end of the Suharto era, motherhood was reclaimed by many Indonesian women as a far more complex and exciting symbol than it

---

[7] It should be noted that in Indonesia, there is little apparent public objection to 'regulation of menstruation', meaning the traditional use of herbal concoctions and modern methods such as suction syringe for pregnancy termination early in the pregnancy (Suyono et al. 1981; Piet Stirling, Djohan et al. 1993; Hull et al. 1993). The problem in accepting abortion arises when the pregnancy is well established.

had been for years. Barbara Hatley has documented the rise of women's literary forms at the end of the century that play upon powerful and even fearful mythic images of women resisting patriarchal oppression: the Balinese witch Rangda, for instance, features as a deeply wronged woman (Hatley 2002).

The Asian financial crisis hit Indonesia in late 1997, to devastating effect. As the value of the *rupiah* plummeted, prices rose dramatically. Suharto's government failed to control the economy, and students and then other urban dwellers took to the streets in protest. In this situation, some Indonesian women began to call on a politicised version of motherhood that had not been seen since the days of high inflation and political turmoil in the 1950s and 1960s. It resembled the 'mother-activism' more commonly associated with Latin America, where women have felt driven by their maternal responsibilities to protest against intolerable state oppression. As in Latin America, these women traded on the official idealisation of motherhood that 'creates a taboo around using physical force against women in general and mothers in particular' (Orleck 1996: 15). Faced with military repression of demonstrators, some Indonesian mothers turned out in Latin American style to protest the 'disappearance' and torture of their children.

The similarities with Latin America were quite conscious on the part of one new organisation, Suara Ibu Peduli (SIP – Voice of Concerned Mothers), formed by a group of women intellectuals in Jakarta in response to the economic crisis of 1997. It began by focussing on the rapidly rising prices of goods and services and organised funding to provide women with half-price milk powder, one of the items in short supply and skyrocketing in price.[8] In February 1998 the leading activists in SIP began gathering in a prominent spot in Jakarta to conduct a 'prayer for milk' protest, which gained great media coverage because it was carried out by middle-class educated women. The protesters repeatedly sang 'Ibu Pertiwi', the nationalist song about the suffering motherland, and held banners with slogans like 'Mothers Struggle for the Children of the Nation'. Three activists were arrested and charged with conducting a demonstration without a permit, for which they were subsequently given nominal fines (*Jurnal Perempuan* 1998, 2: 1–2).

The women behind SIP argued that women's political awareness could be heightened by starting with a focus on the failure of the state to meet their maternal need to provide for their families (*Jurnal Perempuan*

---

[8] This in itself marked it as a movement of middle-class women: only they can afford milk or think it essential for babies, children and pregnant mothers. Some concern has been expressed about the substitution of infant formula for breast-feeding in Indonesia (Lim and Kemp 1994).

1998b: 1–2). They moved on in May 1998 to protest the issue of 'disappeared children'. Most of SIP's work, however, was aimed at providing basic needs for Jakarta families suffering during the economic crisis.

During the demonstrations leading up to the fall of Suharto in May 1998, concerned mothers turned out in support of student protesters. In Jakarta, for instance, some women's organisations set up mobile kitchens to prepare meals for the demonstrators.

Among women's organisations, another significant new development in the post-Suharto period was the identification of mothers with peace movements as a response to the turbulence that has characterised Indonesian politics at the end of the century. This issue will be covered in more detail in Chapter 8, dealing with violence. Here it is enough to give one example, a protest against the brutal killings in East Timor that accompanied its final achievement of independence in 1999. A group called Mothers and Women of Indonesia (SERUNI – Kaum Ibu dan Seluruh Perempuan Indonesia) held demonstrations and on 10 September issued a statement to the Minister of Defence that included these words: 'In view of the continuing bloodshed in East Timor, we, Women of Indonesia state that we . . . feel saddened that the sons and daughters of this nation to whom we gave birth have become murderers of other human beings and have brought untold suffering to the families of victims of this violence' (SERUNI 1999). It took courage to take such a stand at a time when the Indonesian military was officially denying involvement in the killings in East Timor.

In 1999 the Wahid government took the momentous step of placing the Family Planning Programme within the Ministry for Women's Role, under the direction of Khofifah Indar Parawansa, who renamed her portfolio Women's Empowerment. This marked a huge change in the power dynamics of the administration of reproductive health. Subsequently Khofifah, as the new Chief of the Family Planning Coordination Board, made her mark by giving birth in office to her fourth child. Under her auspices, in 2000 the Family Planning Coordination Board put greater emphasis on the quality of family life as well as the need to gain greater participation by men in family planning. Clearly Khofifah did not believe the rhetoric of change had been realised by the Board (Parawansa 2002).

Unfortunately, Khofifah took office at a time when the government in Jakarta was in crisis, the economy struggling to recover from deep recession, and provincial administrations trying to come to terms with a new system of devolved autonomy. These were hard times for any initiatives requiring resources from government. Deprived of former levels of state support, contraceptive use dropped, apparently because fewer people could afford it (*Jakarta Post* 14 July 2003a). On the other hand, women were now freer to organise themselves and voice their concerns, which certainly included demands for better reproductive health.

As the century drew to a close, a new manifestation of political motherhood occurred. Megawati Sukarnoputri, a daughter of the late President Sukarno, had been the leader of one of the opposition parties in the dying years of the New Order and had experienced persecution at the hands of that regime, which feared the challenge she might pose. As a new democratic era dawned in Indonesia with the fall of Suharto in May 1998, Megawati campaigned in the 1999 elections as leader of her party, the PDI-P, which won more votes than any other party. Observers were struck by the way she played the mother role to her mostly very young followers. She had first developed the image of the long-suffering mother at the hands of New Order repression. Now she played the popular, well-loved mother at huge campaign rallies. Motherhood was clearly to her advantage in both defying the New Order state and creating a constituency. When, after the elections, she failed to be chosen as president by the People's Consultative Assembly, she calmed her disappointed supporters by referring to the fact that she was at least the vice-president: '"I now belong to the family of the nation," she told hundreds of supporters at her South Jakarta residence . . . "I'm still your mother and therefore urge you to remain loyal and follow my orders. Please go back home and return to your work," she said'(*Jakarta Post* 22 October 1999).

Serene, correct, soft and reticent, but remarkably resolute in the face of adversity, Megawati's style fitted a dominant Indonesian image of motherhood. By holding out for the position of president, which she finally won at the end of 2001, she demonstrated that the symbol of motherhood was no obstacle to access to power, but at the same time that power was unlikely to be used on behalf of mothers themselves. Women's organisations were under no illusion that Megawati held any brief for women's interests.

Conclusion

Throughout the twentieth century most Indonesian women's organisations have identified Indonesian women primarily as mothers and used an idealised image of motherhood to justify their role in the nation. Even when nationalist women insisted that women should offer maternal care not just to their children but also to the wider nation, they still ran the risk of essentialising women and thus limiting their scope. More particularly, many elite women attempted to present motherhood in Western, middle-class terms that implied a far greater level of domestication than had ever applied or could ever apply to the vast majority of Indonesian women. The maternal image rested on notions of nurture and self-sacrifice, on responsibility and not rights. By the time of the New Order, this had crystallised into ibuism, which was transformed by the regime into 'state ibuism' for its own purposes. Mothers were expected to do what was best for the nation, as interpreted by Suharto.

Under the New Order, the state took charge of the motherhood agenda, decreeing that the most important thing that women could do for national development was to have fewer children. The Family Planning Programme offered even poor women the means to limit their family size and recruited women into the programme in huge numbers. Fertility did indeed fall dramatically under the New Order. The consequences for mothers themselves of the family-planning programme were mixed: concerns about the side effects of contraception and heavy state pressure have to be balanced against the benefits of access to free or cheap modern methods of birth control.

Women's organisations were slow to make demands on the state concerning mothers' health needs. Such problems were not seen as something about which the state could or should do much. The impetus for change in attitudes towards the state's role in reproductive health came from outside. Shamed by international comparisons and backed by foreign funding, at the end of the twentieth century the Indonesian state took decisive moves to address maternal mortality. As a younger generation of well-educated and internationally connected women's organisations emerged in the late New Order period, women also began to take up the rhetoric of reproductive rights. This generation was unwilling to accept the state's definition of motherhood. At the end of the New Order, mothers began to present themselves in a militant way, legitimised by their concern for their children in a time of economic and political crisis. The democratic transition gave women the opportunity to present the concerns of mothers in a much more diverse way than in the past and to frame their demands in terms of rights.

The role played by outside forces on reproductive health gives a positive spin to Indonesia's experience of globalisation. The value of tapping into international networks will be further explored in Chapter 8 on violence against women.

7   Economic exploitation

Although Indonesian women are well known as economically independent and active within the workforce, their role as workers has rarely been
prominent in the eyes of either women's organisations or the state. Yet
evidence of the exploitation of women workers abounds throughout the
twentieth century. In this chapter, therefore, the interest lies in explaining why women have had such difficulty in drawing their work problems
to the attention of the state, and why the state has largely ignored the
issue. In public discourse, the sheer concept of economic exploitation of
women has been confronted at few times in Indonesian history, and only
in relation to a few groups of women. Why have those workers been in the
spotlight and not others, and who has proposed taking what actions to
improve their situation? Which elements within the state and the women's
movement have dealt with these issues and why?

The background to labour issues in Indonesia is, of course, the wider
context of the economy and the state's concern for economic growth.
In most of Indonesia (and more particularly Java), throughout the last
century too many poorly educated workers have sought too few unskilled
jobs. Such an environment favours the employer side in industrial relations and tends to silence all but the better-educated workers who are
less afraid of dismissal and replacement if they 'cause trouble'. Lagging
behind men in education levels, women have a worse negotiating position,
even without taking into account cultural pressures on them to be docile.
In such a situation it is difficult for the state to do a great deal, particularly
where it lacks resources to police labour protection laws. Governments
tend to take the view that the answer lies in long-term socioeconomic
change: when labour is better educated and the modern sector grows,
workers will be better off. Hence the preoccupation of most governments
in Indonesia with private investment and economic growth rather than
directly with the welfare of workers. Not surprisingly, the labour legislation that was most favourable to women workers dates from the period
immediately after independence when economic concerns ran second to
political and nationalist goals.

Debate on labour issues is remarkably gendered. Firstly, there is the problem of defining work. Unpaid work and thus much of the work done by women is usually disregarded. Studies have shown that Javanese women work longer hours than men if subsistence tasks like housework and gathering firewood are counted as work (Berninghausen and Kerstan 1992: 80). Secondly, discussion of the workforce has focussed on the formal sector, whereas most women still work in the informal sector, for example on family farms and in family enterprises; within the home, doing piece-work for factories; as domestic workers in other people's homes; as prostitutes; or as petty traders selling small quantities of goods. There has been a tendency to regard the informal sector as an area where exploitation is self-inflicted or the result of family relationships that are outside the purview of the state. Thirdly, women's work is considered supplementary to that of men. As the main wage-earners (and the main formal sector workers), men do the 'real' work which dominates the labour agenda, while women's income, however essential to the family, is of lesser importance and often unrecognised. Consequently it does not matter greatly that women receive lower pay than men for work of the same value or whether, for instance, women piece-workers are paid a pittance. For all these reasons, labour force surveys, based on male notions of work as full-time, regular and paid by an employer, miss much of women's work (Manning 1998: 235–6).

Under these circumstances the concept of exploitation is often difficult to grasp. Where does the injustice lie? If a worker has no clear employer (as in the case of women doing housework, or working at home for piece-rates, or as street-sellers), who is the exploiter? Some notion of exploitative working structures, based on the sexual division of labour, is required to deal with such cases. Such analysis has been largely lacking in Indonesia.

Gender stereotypes about work have been very pervasive in Indonesian society. They have affected not only state policies but also women's organisations. Even without such a cultural influence, however, the fact that most women's organisations have been made up of women who lack insight into the working lives of poor women has naturally been reflected in their priorities. State intervention to deter or suppress organisations working among poor working women has only exacerbated the neglect of economic exploitation by organised women. Combined with the weakness and repression of trade unions, this has meant that women workers have almost entirely lacked a voice. The exception, as we shall see, was during the 1950s and early 1960s.

As a result of these trends, there have been few occasions in the twentieth century when women's work has entered the political agenda. When it did, it was not purely because of concern with the economic plight of women workers; there has often been an overriding concern for the protection of these workers as women, and in particular as sexual beings. In other words, no one is surprised if women are overworked and underpaid (or even unpaid); concern arises when they are, in addition, exposed to moral jeopardy (as when they have to travel home at night) or actually raped or dishonoured in a public way that reflects upon their families and even on the nation. Justice is not the main motivation for public action here, but rather the need to protect women as mothers, wives and daughters – as weaker and sexual beings, fraught with moral significance. All of this reflects the difficulty that Indonesians have had in accepting the identity of women as workers, with rights as workers.

There have been forces operating in favour of women workers, however, and in this chapter a number of them will be identified. Some have been external, such as the International Labour Organisation (ILO) and pressure groups in Europe and the United States. Within the state itself, some elements have taken the side of women workers from time to time. And within the women's movement a few organisations have prioritised women workers. The forces arrayed against them, however, have been overwhelming, so that even when pressure resulted in changes to state policy favouring women workers, implementing such policies has been an uphill battle.

The colonial state and women workers

Colonial governments are notorious for neglecting the interests of workers, and the Dutch in the Indies were no different. Despite the introduction of the Ethical Policy in 1901, the colonial state was most reluctant to intervene in the economy on behalf of workers if to do so prejudiced investment and profit-making. The colonial power was closely aligned with the interests of foreign investors, a measure of successful colonialism being a flourishing export economy. Consequently workers lacked effective protective legislation, and the emerging union movement in the Indies suffered state repression (Ingleson 1986).

The Dutch were, however, sensitive to some criticisms about labour. Campaigns against the virtual enslavement of contract labour on Sumatran plantations finally led to some protective legislation relating to their employment in the early twentieth century (Furnivall 1939: 353–5). As far as women workers were concerned, it was pressure from the ILO and growing public concern within the Netherlands that led the government to a limited commitment to protect women and children in the workplace. As a member of the ILO, set up by the League of Nations after the First World War, in 1922 the Dutch committed themselves to legislation protective of workers not only in the Netherlands but also, to a lesser extent, in their colonies. The ILO had special stipulations concerning the protection of working women and children which the colonial government partially put into law in 1926, restricting women and children from working at night (between ten at night and five in the morning for women) in many industries. The law clearly favoured employers, because it spelt out exceptions that permitted the main employers of women as night labour (especially the sugar industry) to continue much as before (Locher-Scholten 2000).

In order to police its labour legislation, however weak it was, the colonial government created an inspectorate within the Labour Office. Although there were far too few inspectors and sanctions against offenders were too low to act as real deterrents, the Labour Office proceeded over the following years to produce a series of reports that provided some fuel for criticisms of industrial relations in the Indies, including the treatment of women workers. Their reports consistently showed that women were paid less than men for the same work. Lacking legal power to intervene on such matters as excessive hours of work, poor sanitation and low pay, the inspectorate could do little apart from expose poor conditions of work and prosecute employers who infringed the factory work safety laws and the night work law, both of which applied to only a limited number of workplaces (Tjoeng 1948).

Most workers were not affected by labour legislation. According to the 1930 census, 34 per cent of the Indonesian population of almost 61 million people were 'gainfully employed' (i.e. in paid employment), including about 21 per cent of women and 49 per cent of men. Most were employed in agriculture and were not subject to any labour protection or wage regulation (Elliot 1997: 130–3). Beyond the official workforce lay the bulk of women workers who received no recognition on the part of the state.

Labour concerns of women's organisations before independence

From within Indonesian society there was little pressure on the colonial government to take up issues concerning women workers. Although members and even leaders of women's organisations included employees (e.g. teachers and journalists), they rarely identified as such. Like Kartini, they defended women's right to work but took little public interest in the conditions experienced by women workers. Nor did they come from the most exploited groups in society, who in the colonial period included domestic servants, agricultural and plantation labourers, and piece-workers. They had no insight into those lives, except as employers. Many had domestic servants and some members of women's groups, particularly in Aisyiyah, the modernist Islamic organisation, were successful businesswomen and managed their own batik firms (Price 1983; Baried 1990; Marcoes-Natsir 2000). Since many of these women were in fact employers, they often viewed labour from that perspective, although women in traditional work situations were often not regarded as employees. Servants, for instance, were frequently bound by semi-feudal or patron-client relationships (Locher-Scholten 2000).

Moreover the organisations that one would expect to fight for workers – trade unions – were still in their infancy in the Indies. They had most success in organising skilled workers and those in the formal sector, which by definition excluded most workers and in particular most women workers. Even in the few sectors with large numbers of women, such as nursing and tea plantations, unions were led by men since women workers lacked organisational skills or were deterred by gender stereotyping. As colonial policy hardened in the late 1920s, any signs of militancy by workers were quickly suppressed by the authorities, and leaders were summarily dismissed (Ingleson 1986). Women's organisations had nothing to say about such matters.

In the 1930s women's groups began to show some interest in two cases related to labour exploitation: the 'Lasem affair' and trafficking in women. The former was in fact sparked by an initiative on the part of the state, or one element of it. In 1931 the second volume of the so-called Batik Report was released, a report by the Labour Office on conditions within the batik industry, a large employer of women (Angelino 1931). The report revealed widespread exploitation of women workers, who occupied the bottom layers of the industry's workforce, particularly the women outworkers who were paid a pittance by factory-owners to apply the wax to the cloth in their homes. As if that were nothing noteworthy, the only part of the report that led to public outcry was the section relating to the batik industry in Lasem, on the north coast of Central Java. As an egregious case, it received special attention from inspectors. The factory-owners made advance loans to outworkers and imposed heavy fines for mistakes, with the result that families quickly got into debt and were then forced to send their women to the factory to work off the debt – a virtual impossibility given the way the employers kept the accounts. These women were grossly overworked, starved and physically and sexually abused. If they tried to flee, their families and neighbouring families were held responsible, being forced to provide a replacement for the escapee, who was usually accused of theft and recaptured by the police. As the report said, these women were treated worse than common prisoners.

For at least two reasons, Indonesian nationalists and the Indonesian women's movement found it easier to tackle this case of exploitation than some others. Firstly, because the report was officially released by the colonial government authorities, it could hardly be dismissed or denied, nor could people be prevented from publicly discussing it. This came at a time when nationalist speakers were often silenced at meetings when raising 'sensitive' or 'subversive' matters, which in 1930s colonial parlance covered most issues relating to economic exploitation. Secondly, the employers in the Lasem case were Chinese, and therefore 'alien'. Plenty of exploiting batik industrialists were Indonesian, but nationalist and women's organisations (which included members who were batik entrepreneurs) avoided discussing such cases. It was popular with Indonesian nationalists to target Chinese business, which competed with their own and could stand as proxy for foreign capitalism.

Immediately after the publication of the Batik Report in 1931, nationalist media seized on the issue of Lasem and some Indonesian women's groups also began to discuss it. The question was, what should be done? Clearly the factory-owners should be brought to book, which was the responsibility of the colonial authorities. The Labour Office claimed that warnings to factory-owners, fines and jail terms had produced great improvements by 1931 (Angelino 1931: 319–20). But workers also needed to be informed of their rights. There were tasks here for Indonesian women's organisations if they claimed to be concerned about the fate of women workers.

At least two public meetings were held in Lasem. The women's federation, PPII, delegated the young Suyatin Kartowiyono to go to Lasem to address a protest meeting at a batik factory. She travelled there with R. A. Harjodiningrat, spokesperson for a newly established committee set up to defend women workers (*Isteri* 1931, 3(4): 97–9). The PPII organised a public meeting at Lasem at which Suyatin spoke, analysing the desperate situation of the women bonded labourers and calling for improvement. She was warned by police to be careful in her criticisms of the authorities (Kartowijono 1983: 43–4). In November 1931, a Committee for the Defence of Batik Workers (Komite Pembelaan Kaum Pengobeng) was established in Lasem, with the proclaimed goal of improving the women's situation 'through self-help'. It held a public meeting attended by about 1,200 people. Again, the findings of the Batik Report were described, but the difficulty that speakers (of whom four were women) had in freely discussing the situation was clear from the police harassment they experienced. The 'self-help' solutions proposed included literacy classes and the establishment by the committee of its own batik factory to offer alternative employment; money was collected for this purpose. Nothing further was reported about this venture. In the following year, the committee broadened its agenda to cover Indonesian women workers more generally, changing its name to Komite Pembela Kaum Buruh Perempuan Indonesia (Committee to Defend Indonesian Women Workers), based in Yogyakarta (*Isteri* 1932).

These accounts illustrate a rare occasion on which urban organised women took the trouble to visit a work-site. The difficulties involved in contacting and organising people outside the main towns overwhelmed most activists: the problems lay not just in the opposition of powerful local leaders but in the minds of urban educated people.[1]

It was easier to hold meetings in major towns. A protest meeting was held in Yogyakarta, organised by the executives of the PPII and the P4A (see below) and attended by about two thousand people. The tenor of the meeting was nationalist: not until the country was independent would discrimination such as that at Lasem be eliminated (*Isteri* 1931, 3(5): 108–9). In the short term it was unclear what could be done, particularly as the Depression was now upon the Indies, subduing labour still further.

A few activists attempted to expand the scope of women's organisations' interest in working women. Istri Sedar, closely aligned with the radical nationalist party PNI, pinpointed the lack of interest of most women's groups in ordinary working women. In a speech at the Istri Sedar congress in 1931, Mudinem, one of its leaders, expressed surprise that the plight of women workers was ignored by women's organisations. In her view, this was because middle-class women considered that work was not really legitimate for wives and mothers, who should devote themselves to household tasks, ignoring the fact that most women had to work for a living. She noted three groups of working women who deserved special attention. The first comprised women in the batik, weaving, sewing and home industries who did piece-work and had no fixed income or security. Lasem, she observed, was just one example of their oppression. But in her view attention should also be paid to women working as coolies or servants and those who sold goods in street-stalls or as itinerants. 'Most of us who have servants don't think of them as humans', she claimed. In Central Java, she said, they were not given wages, only two pieces of clothing a year. Street traders also had to work long hours and were usually heavily in debt (Moedinem 1931). Following Mudinem's speech, Istri Sedar adopted a resolution to promote the needs of women workers, and a committee to investigate women's work was established later that year

---

[1] Suwarsih Joyopuspito, the sister of Suwarni Pringgodigdo and a nationalist and feminist herself, has poignantly described the dilemma of activists in a famous autobiographical novel written in the 1930s (Djojopoespito 1940).

(Berita 1931). The second congress of Istri Sedar in 1932 heard a report from the committee, containing 'surprising and saddening' news of the plight of women workers in the grip of the Depression. They had investigated 383 cases of women working as day-labourers in factories and as domestic servants and traders. Although the congress resolved that Istri Sedar must strive to get 'better work regulations' for women workers, the stridently nationalist tenor of the congress made it clear that it expected nothing of a colonial state in this regard (*Sedar* 1932: 25).

Lasem was a classic case of gross exploitation of workers by employers. One aspect of the Lasem Affair that particularly shocked the women's movement was evidence of the sexual enslavement of some of the batik workers (Kartowijono 1983). Middle-class women found it easier to empathise with the plight of exploited women workers if they could see the situation in the light of sexual morality rather than of industrial relations, a matter that seemed to belong too much to the 'unfeminine' world of economics and politics.

Forced prostitution formed a link to the other case of women workers that aroused public concern during the colonial period: the issue of trafficking in women, which most viewed as a matter of moral turpitude as much as, or more than, of economic exploitation. These women were regarded as ruined morally, regardless of the health or financial consequences. What distressed women's organisations was the deception and/or abduction of 'innocent' girls and young women sold into sexual depravity, which was how they regarded the work of prostitutes. The nationalist press reported in outraged tones instances of trafficking in women within and outside the Indies. In 1931 the women's federation joined with nationalist men to establish the Organisation for the Eradication of Trade in Women and Children (Perkumpulan Pemberantasan Perdagangan Perempuan dan Anak-Anak – referred to as P4A), intended to assist women and children who were trafficked. Chaired for several years by Mrs Datu Tumenggung, who featured in earlier chapters as a champion of women's suffrage and opposition to child marriage, the concern of P4A was to rescue girls being enveigled or forced into prostitution and provide them with shelter and rehabilitation. Although accompanied by great moral fervour, it is unclear how successful their efforts were (Roeswo 1932; Toemenggoeng 1936). In the opinion of Mrs Datu Tumenggung, the answer lay in social change, in the upbringing of girls to provide them with a better education that would make them economically independent, and in the inculcation of sound religious principles (Toemenggoeng 1936). Others considered a basic problem was exploitation by moneylenders who took the daughters of poor peasants as payment for debts (Kartowijono 1977).

Like Lasem, this was a matter where the colonial authorities were also prepared to agree that something needed to be done. Middle-class Dutch morality was as strongly opposed to trafficking in women as that of middle-class Indonesians. Prostitution was illegal under colonial rule, although the state turned a blind eye to it in practice. Moreover, the colonial government had obligations through the League of Nations to combat trafficking (Boetzelaer 1933). In 1937 the League of Nations International Conference on the Traffic of Women and Children in the Far East was held in the Indies to discuss international trafficking, and the P4A along with other women's organisations was invited to participate (Pringgodigdo 1949: 198). Everyone was quick to condemn trafficking but so long as there was a demand for prostitutes and so long as poverty pushed women to meet that demand, it was unclear how it could be eliminated. The conference was followed by more propaganda against trafficking and promises of heightened vigilance by the authorities, but nothing effective was achieved.

Given the widespread poverty in the Indies, accompanied by the informal sector nature of most women's work, it was always going to be a difficult task to tackle economic exploitation of women. If the colonial period saw the first flickerings of interest in confronting it, they were extinguished during the Japanese Occupation. Although poverty and exploitation undoubtedly increased during the brief but disastrous war years, under harsh state repression it was almost impossible for anyone to resist. More positively, the war years increased the numbers of women in the formal workforce. Some women stepped into vacancies left by the Dutch or by men drafted to other duties, and others were mobilised on behalf of the war effort, or just worked to make ends meet. Any stigma that may have existed against women working was weakened during the war years and the subsequent Revolution (Suwondo 1981: 254–6). Finally, with the achievement of independence and the inauguration of liberal democracy in Indonesia, it became possible to explore the potential for political action on behalf of women workers.

Labour legislation in the early independence period

Soon after independence was declared in August 1945, the Republic took measures to protect workers. This was a unique period. Governments in these early years consisted of a group of nationalists committed to democratic reforms and state action to improve the lot of ordinary Indonesians. In part they were fulfilling their obligations to those who stood by them in the nationalist struggle, which continued until the transfer of sovereignty in 1949. In part they were proving to the democratic world, the triumphant Western allies who dominated the United Nations, that they were the legitimate and worthy rulers of a new democratic nation. Although they had little power over the economy, on the other hand there were no strong employer groups applying pressure to them, because the indigenous capitalist class was very weak: the modern sector and the sources of investment remained in the hands of 'aliens' – Europeans and the Chinese, who carried no political weight in the Republic. Governments saw themselves as taking the side of poor, exploited Indonesians against foreign capitalists.

In the early years of the Republic, moreover, there was for the only time in Indonesian history a woman Minister of Labour, the well-known journalist, nationalist and labour activist S. K. Trimurti. She had won her stripes in the nationalist struggle by being jailed by both the Dutch and the Japanese Governments. An executive member of Partai Buruh Indonesia (Indonesian Labour Party), established in 1946, Trimurti was chosen by Prime Minister Amir Syarifuddin, a socialist, as the Republic's first Minister of Labour in 1947. Governments at this time were short-lived, based on coalitions that fell when agreements were reached with the Dutch who were attempting to restore their colonial rule. Although the Syarifuddin government lasted only six months, at a time of turmoil when nothing could be done to improve the daily lot of workers, Trimurti initiated the legislation that was to become the first Labour Law in 1948, which was extended to cover the whole of Indonesia in 1951 (Soebagio 1982).

Despite deficiencies, the 1951 Labour Act served as a benchmark for the protection of women workers in Indonesia for many years. It included clauses prohibiting the employment of children below the age of fourteen, restricting women from being employed in mines and other places deemed dangerous for their health, safety or morality, and from working at night (with exceptions, including some relating to work considered appropriate for women, like nursing), and provided for mothers to be given time off for breastfeeding, three months' paid maternity leave and menstruation leave of two days a month. This last provision was something that very few countries have ever legislated. In the following years further democratic legislation was passed on labour matters, and in 1957 Indonesia confirmed its commitment to equality for women workers by ratifying the ILO Convention 100 on equal pay for equal work – one of the first nations to do so.

Criticisms of the 1951 Labour Act relate to its content and its implementation. Its 'protective' clauses were full of loopholes, and it applied only to formal sector, permanent employees. Employers could evade the leave provisions by demanding evidence of pregnancy or menstruation that was difficult or humiliating for the worker to provide (Surastro

1959: 28). Moreover, some clauses identifying women workers as requiring special treatment are questionable at best and at worst have played into the hands of those wishing to avoid employing women. While there can be no argument that maternity leave is necessary, other forms of protection are more debatable. For instance, the argument that women should not be employed in dangerous occupations merely raises the question of whether it would not be better to concentrate on eliminating unsafe working conditions. Similarly, the arguments against women working at night have often revolved around the need for women to be at home looking after the family in the evening, whereas men are not subject to such restrictions (Katjasungkana 1995). The case of menstruation leave is even more problematic. Indonesian women's organisations have argued that Indonesian women suffer badly from menstrual problems, especially related to the high rate of anaemia in the female population. The logical way to deal with this problem would surely be to tackle the malnutrition and other causes of anaemia, for example by ensuring that workers are provided with nutritious meals or earn enough to buy them. Deeper cultural attitudes to menstruation may be involved here. Islamic literature in Indonesia treats menstruation as a time of illness for women (and for men who are stupid enough to have sexual intercourse with menstruating women).[2] Singling out menstruating women as weak and unable to work properly represents them as undesirable workers. At the very least, the legislation confirmed basic stereotypes about the sexual division of labour (Elliot 1997).

Despite deficiencies, the years of liberal democracy produced laws that provided a useful bargaining tool for pressure groups for years to come. The main problem with the laws lay in implementation. Countervailing forces were brought to bear, and adequate implementing regulations were never enforced to accompany the laws; nor were the sanctions adequate to deter exploitative employers. Unions were reluctant to fight for the cause of equal pay for equal work. Probably the only place where it had considerable impact was in the public service. Large and rapidly growing though this sector was, it was scarcely the locus of the greatest exploitation of women workers, which was in unskilled and low-skilled occupations where women were consistently paid less than men and frequently worked in unsafe and unhealthy conditions (Elliot 1997). Even where equal pay nominally applied, what often happened was that men received extra allowances, on the grounds that they were the 'real breadwinners'.

---

[2] Indonesian bookshops are full of little books expounding Islamic rules on sex and body etiquette, often translated from the Arabic from Saudi Arabia or elsewhere, and always by men. Examples which discuss menstruation are Sahly (1994); Thalib (1995); Wasmukan, Waskito, Reksonotoprodjo et al. (1995); Al-Haq (1996); Al-Utsaimin (1996).

Moreover, since certain tasks (such as picking tea leaves) were deemed 'women's work', the notion of equal pay was not applied to them: they were done entirely by low-paid women (Surastro 1959: 27).

What the labour legislation of the 1950s did, above all, was to provide a rallying point for organisations that wished to see its principles applied to women workers. As Trimurti warned, the workers themselves had to struggle to win legislation and to ensure it was enforced: 'The bosses and the government are not going to give that protection if workers themselves do not really want it' (Tri 1950: 171). The independence era saw a mushrooming of unions and organisations aimed at representing and defending labour, the most notable of which, from the point of view of women, was Gerwani, the women's mass movement allied with the Communist Party of Indonesia (PKI).

Gerwani and women workers

Gerwani (Gerakan Wanita Indonesia – Indonesian Women's Movement) was founded in 1950 as Gerwis (Gerakan Wanita Indonesia Sedar – Movement of Conscious Indonesian Women) and changed its name in 1954 when it committed itself to becoming a mass movement. It has been the only women's organisation in Indonesia that could make a claim to represent poor women workers. Aligned with the PKI, ideologically Gerwani was impelled to seek a broad base among workers and peasants. Its membership grew from 100,000 in 1957 to 700,000 in 1960 and 1.5 million in 1963, with branches in every province and subbranches in 40 per cent of villages (Hindley 1964: 201–8). Such widespread membership was rivalled only by Islamic organisations, which, however, took no interest in the problems of women workers.

Gerwani was clearly pledged to improve the lot of female labour. The 1954 congress of the organisation adopted a platform that, in an ideological stance similar to that of the PKI, blamed the problems of Indonesian women on the continuing impact of colonialism and feudalism and expected the nationalist state to intervene on behalf of workers. Unlike other women's organisations, Gerwani had a clear notion of labour exploitation based on Marxism. It aimed to participate in women's struggles for daily needs and for their rights (Wieringa 2002: 153). In 1955 the Gerwani leader, Umi Sarjono, explained the rights of working women for which the organisation fought. It demanded social security and the implementation of the Labour Act; the same wages for the same work; crèches for children; the right of women to promotion and to training courses which would help them gain promotion; and the right to receive a family allowance and the same share of rations as male workers. Gerwani also recognised the needs of poor women working outside the formal workplace, stipulating that peasants and small traders needed sufficient wages and land to make a living; cheap and easy credit from the government; places to spend the night at the market; and light market taxes (Sardjono 1955: 18). Gerwani was very clear about the deficiencies in the implementation of Indonesian labour legislation intended to assist women. Women, they said, suffered wage discrimination, were the first victims of lay-offs and were often unable to gain leave for pregnancy and menstruation. The lack of crèches and clinics caused women to stop work after giving birth or because of illness, and this became a reason not to promote women or to dismiss them. Women peasants were not even covered by protective legislation. They suffered wage discrimination and had no social security at all (Gerakan Wanita Indonesia 1960).

Gerwani developed a clear strategy for improving the lot of working women. First, it decided to attract a mass membership amongst ordinary women, to give it a clear mandate to speak on their behalf. This involved offering assistance to poor women in practical ways, without which, Gerwani found, women had little interest in becoming politically involved, since their first priority was to fulfil basic material needs. Gerwani's practical work included setting up kindergartens, consumer co-operatives, mutual assistance and small-scale credit groups. The organisation worked hard to make women more politically aware and to train poor women as leaders. Literacy campaigns were a key part of this strategy, and courses for cadres were regularly held (Hindley 1964: 201–10).

Secondly, Gerwani recognised the value of alliances with other organisations, the relevant ones being trade unions, other women's organisations and the PKI. Not wishing to replicate the work of trade unions, but recognising that unions were too male-dominated, they worked to strengthen union awareness of women's issues and supported union actions and political advocacy that would benefit women and their families. Unions had direct access to workplaces and provided one way of raising women's consciousness of themselves as workers. Their size also gave them political clout in trying to influence governments. At the time, all unions were linked to political parties, and naturally Gerwani's alliances were with the large PKI-connected unions, the All-Indonesian Labour Unions Federation (Sentral Organisasi Buruh Seluruh Indonesia – SOBSI) and the Indonesian Farmers' Front (Barisan Tani Indonesia – BTI). Unions were active in the formal sector, where women made up a significant part of the workforce, always concentrated in the bottom layers.[3] Among

---

[3] In the late 1950s women made up about 30 per cent of manual wage-earners, of whom there were about 6 million in Indonesia. On plantations they constituted about 45 per cent of the workforce (as high as 70 per cent on coffee and tea estates); in the textile industry about 65 per cent, and in the cigarette industry 60 per cent (Surastro 1959: 26).

agricultural labourers, about half of whom were women, the BTI was active. By working with SOBSI and BTI, Gerwani helped ensure that women's needs gained a more prominent position in the communist-oriented union movement. Thus, for instance, SOBSI and BTI held special cadre courses for women, national seminars on women workers, and all-female meetings. More women rose to executive positions in unions in industries where the workforce was largely female, such as on estates and in the cigarette and textile industries (Hindley 1964: 208–10; Wieringa 2002: 197–205).

Gerwani's efforts to assist women in their workplaces were more successful than any Indonesian organisation before or since, not just in Java but elsewhere in the archipelago. It operated at a time when Indonesian employer groups were weak, and capital had little leverage with governments. Structurally, however, too much militated against improving the situation of workers at this time. The economy was in terminal decline, with inflation rising rapidly. All wage-earners were badly affected. The modern sector where workers were formally employed and could be most easily organised comprised only a minority of the real labour force, especially of women. Gerwani realised this and made efforts to assist other downtrodden workers like women harvesters and petty traders. Although like the PKI it contended that the core problem lay with imperialist control over the Indonesian economy, this argument wore thin in the 1960s when Sukarno's actions had more or less destroyed foreign investment in the country, and former Dutch firms became state enterprises.

Gerwani cooperated with other women's organisations in popular campaigns to demand decreases in the prices of essential commodities, and to lobby government on behalf of women. It played a prominent part in Kowani, stiffening its platform on behalf of working women. The federation's conferences throughout the 1950s passed resolutions concerning work. Thus, for instance, in 1955 the conference adopted a Charter of Women's Rights that contained a section on women as workers, claiming that women should be given the same rights as men to enter all fields of work and to be promoted, that they should have access to all vocational courses, that there should be equal pay for equal work, and that the rights guaranteed in the 1951 Labour Act should be implemented in practice. The 1957 conference decided to set up a Labour Section within the federation to study the problems of working women. While women's organisations continued to be dominated by middle-class women, however, the needs of the poorest workers were not likely to be centre stage. Of the member organisations in Kowani in 1958, the programmes of very few contained any reference at all to work (Panitia Peringatan 1958).

Saskia Wieringa (2002) has pointed out that Gerwani was able to cooperate with middle-class women's organisations in Kowani because in many ways it did not challenge their notions of gender identity. (The same observation may be made about its ability to work with unions and the PKI.) Like them, it strongly identified women as wives and mothers in addition to their role as workers and did not question the sexual division of labour within the household or the workplace.

Gerwani's alliance with the PKI proved difficult and ultimately fatal. As it became increasingly dominated by the party, it compromised its gender interests. Wieringa has described the process, which was reflected in the organisation's changing priorities. By the 1960s goals related to women, including working women, had taken a back seat to 'fighting imperialism'. Some long-established members who had helped set up Gerwis in 1950, like S. K. Trimurti, became disillusioned with Gerwani's loss of political independence. Finally, its identification as a 'front' organisation for the PKI condemned it to share the party's tragic fate in the massacres and incarcerations of 1965–6. In fact, Gerwani as a women's organisation was singled out for an orgy of misogynistic vilification. By attempting to stir poor women to a new consciousness of their rights as women and as workers, they had threatened many defenders of the status quo, both military, economic and religious (Wieringa 2002).

When the New Order regime came to power at the end of 1965, its destruction of Gerwani, along with other communist-dominated mass organisations like SOBSI and BTI, meant that the only organisation operating among poor women to advance their interests as workers was obliterated. Nothing replaced it, and the Indonesian women's movement has ever since failed to give a voice to such women. The expertise of Gerwani has been lost and will take a long time to rebuild.

Industrialisation and the rise of the new class of women factory workers

The New Order reversed the situation that working women had faced in the previous two decades. The government tackled the economy with determination, assisted by foreign aid and investment, and revenue generated by the oil boom. It had remarkable success in promoting economic stability and growth, but in the process it eliminated organisations that had any claim to represent workers. As a result, although employment expanded, particularly in the formal sector, and living standards rose for most people, even mentioning economic exploitation could be extremely dangerous: it laid one open to charges of being associated with communism at a time when such an accusation could lead to harassment, incarceration or worse. Consequently, the workers lacked a voice.

The state's policy was clear. It would achieve economic growth, and this would benefit everyone. Although modernisation might result in a decline in employment in some areas (such as harvesting and grain processing), in others (such as manufacturing) economic growth would lead to a compensatory expansion in jobs. Moreover, the military took a lively interest in labour relations, regarding it as a key security issue. They worked closely with business to suppress labour unrest. Some Ministers for Manpower were military men under the New Order, and one was a businessman. According to state ideology, a paternalistic state would bring harmony to relations between employers and employees. To allow free union activity would lead only to industrial unrest that would deter investment. Existing unions were disbanded in the aftermath of the communist purge, and the government decreed that only the SPSI (Serikat Pekerja Seluruh Indonesia – All-Indonesia Workers Union), a union firmly under state control, could represent workers. In fact the SPSI never operated in most workplaces, and where it did it was largely supine in the face of employer pressure.[4] Although the Ministry of Manpower undoubtedly contained staff who were genuinely concerned about worker protection, the fact that they had only a small number of inspectors showed the ambivalence within the ministry and, as in colonial times, the lack of political will.[5]

The Ministry for Women's Role, established in 1978, struggled even to create a profile for women as workers but won official acceptance for the notion that women had 'dual roles' (*peran ganda*), encompassing paid work as well as household responsibilities. Significantly, it seemed to be assumed that men did not have a domestic role. *Peran ganda* involved no challenge to the sexual division of labour which was well-entrenched in Indonesia, both at home and in the paid workforce (Katjasungkana 1995). Recognition of *peran ganda* did not involve any growth in awareness of the exploitation of women; rather, it was followed by a spate of speeches and media interviews celebrating the rise of professional women in Indonesia, who were all nevertheless careful to show that they did not neglect their home duties.

Economic exploitation did not enter the vocabulary of women's organisations in the first three decades of the New Order. The organisations affiliated with Kowani, which was 'restructured' following the elimination

[4] SPSI had a remarkably autonomous section, researching the conditions of women workers. Within the larger organisation, however, it had no clout (Eldridge, 1995: 163–5; Hadiz, 1997: 143–4).
[5] The director general of the Manpower Department acknowledged in 1995 that only 844 inspectors were in the field at any time, 'clearly insufficient to cover 157,103 firms and 7.76 million workers' (Binawas 1995: 47).

of Gerwani, had no links with poor working women. On work matters, their interests lay with professional and well-educated women workers. Only religious organisations, the wives' organisations and the state-run PKK could operate among women at the level of the village and the urban *kampung* where the poor lived. None of these evinced any interest in work conditions.

It was the new, feminist groups emerging from the 1980s outside state control that began to take up issues relating to poor working women. On two issues they succeeded in attracting considerable publicity: factory workers and migrant workers. Not that they generated this publicity entirely by themselves: factory women workers drew attention to themselves by going on strike with increasing frequency in the 1990s, and the plight of migrant workers became an international *cause célèbre*.

Women's participation in the workforce (which as we have seen was always an inadequate definition of women's real work) grew considerably during the New Order (Manning 1998). The percentage of women aged fifteen and above who were officially considered to be working rose from 37 per cent in 1971 to 47 per cent in 1995, apparently connected to a number of trends such as urbanisation, the rising age of marriage and the declining birth rate. When the oil boom ended in the early 1980s, the government looked to export-oriented manufacturing to fill the gap in export earnings. Its promotion of investment in this area was remarkably successful, and the preference for cheap and docile labour of young women led to the rapid growth of this section of the workforce. By 1990, for the first time in Indonesian history, more women were employed outside agriculture than in it, and the most rapid growth was in urban manufacturing, where women outnumbered men. (Trade and services each still employed more women than manufacturing, however.) Although women had worked in industry for decades, the new factories, being more capital-intensive and oriented to producing goods for export, were seen as more 'modern'. Most of this manufacturing was in Java, but growth occurred also in Bali and North Sumatra.

A number of studies have thrown light on the situation of these women workers, helping to explain the problems in organising them, apart from the obvious fact that state repression deterred them from making demands on employers (Mather 1983; Wolf 1992; White 1993; Grijns, Smyth, van Velzen et al. 1994; Singarimbun and Sairin 1995; Smyth and Grijns 1997; Kusyuniati 1998). Since the big surge in industrialisation occurred only from the 1980s, most of the women involved up to the end of the twentieth century were first generation factory workers. Girls from rural areas, they regarded factory work as superior to the alternatives: dirty and unpaid or very poorly remunerated work on farms or in petty trading, or the isolated drudgery of domestic service, which had previously been a major source of employment for unskilled, poorly educated women moving into town in search of work. These young women entered the formal workforce at a time when urban affluence was growing fast, and the lure of consumerism was met in a small way through the regular wage they received as factory employees. Finally, many factories were built on the urban fringes, meaning that girls could continue to live at home in their villages and commute to work. Such workers were still under the influence of their families and village life, which taught them to accept authority and to regard work as a temporary activity before the real responsibilities imposed by marriage. Married women usually sought more flexible work such as petty trade that allowed them to fulfil home duties.

Although what went on behind the high walls of factories was carefully screened from view by employers, working conditions soon received considerable publicity. It was well known that most factory workers received a wage that did not even meet subsistence needs, forcing them to do long hours of overtime. Although legislation was supposed to ensure not only maternity and menstruation leave, restrictions on child labour and night work, and some health and safety regulations as well as a series of allowances and overtime rates, in practice such regulations were most often ignored by employers.

Few tried to organise these women, who tended to take industrial action, when desperate, in a sporadic fashion. One of the new women's groups of the 1980s, Yayasan Annisa Swasti (Annisa Swasti Foundation – Yasanti), founded in 1982 in Yogyakarta, devoted itself to improving the lot of poor women workers in factories and shops in Central Java. It found that trying to raise awareness of their rights among these women was an uphill task. They responded better to efforts to improve their material situation, like credit and savings groups, and training courses to raise their skills levels. One of Yasanti's leaders, Sri Kusyuniati, finally decided it would take years before young women factory workers became sufficiently discontented and brave, and sufficiently identified as workers to undertake long-term organisation to improve their lot through industrial action and negotiating with employers. She recognised, however, that Yasanti's problems were connected with the location of the factory women among whom it worked, on the outskirts of towns in Central Java. Factory workers who lived in towns were more conscious and militant, and indeed in the 1990s strikes among these female workers grew rapidly despite repression. The main grievances concerned failure of factories to pay the official minimum wage and allowances (Singarimbun and Sairin 1995; Kusyuniati 1998).

Another women's organisation active among women workers was Yayasan Perempuan Mardhika (YPM – Foundation for Independent Women), operating in the factory areas around Jakarta. In order to reach women workers and raise their solidarity and awareness of their rights, it resorted to some new methods like theatre performances by workers. Significantly, both Yasanti and YPM faced enormous difficulties in maintaining direction. Starting out as groups of idealistic women university students, their leaders were dogged by disagreements which, in the case of YPM, led to the organisation dissolving itself in 1995. One of the founders felt that as middle-class activists they had 'gradually failed to listen to the voice of the workers' (Andriyani 1996).

Some non-government organisations attempted to act as unions in the 1990s, but met with quick repression by the New Order Government. One young woman activist, Dita Indah Sari, led the Pusat Perjuangan Buruh Indonesia (Centre for Indonesian Workers' Struggle) and was involved in a number of strikes in the mid-1990s. In 1996 she was arrested with three others under the anti-subversive law and condemned to twenty years in jail. Released by the Habibie government, she returned to union organising (McBeth 2001).

During the New Order there were many other examples of the perils of industrial action. For women, the most horrifying and well-publicised case was that of Marsinah. A young factory worker in East Java, Marsinah had been involved in a strike in 1993 to demand the official minimum wage and other rights to which workers were legally entitled. When the leaders of the strike were sacked, she went to the factory administration to protest and then disappeared. A few days later her mutilated body was found at some distance from the factory: she had been raped and tortured before being killed. Although the police attempted to cover the case up, pressure from a number of organisations including human rights groups and some women's groups put it under the spotlight, and Marsinah's martyrdom was commemorated by an extraordinarily wide range of people in Indonesia (Indonesian Legal Aid Foundation 1994; Weix 2002). When some individuals were finally brought to trial, it soon became clear that their confessions had been coerced, and they were released. No perpetrators were ever brought to justice, although there was strong evidence pointing to the military who had been involved in security at the factory. The failure of the judicial and law enforcement systems to solve the Marsinah case highlighted the state's denial of justice to workers and the power of the military in industrial affairs.

The case of Marsinah not only featured in campaigns within Indonesia by human rights, labour and women's organisations but was also taken up internationally. It became part of the evidence arrayed against the Indonesian government by American unions and human-rights groups pressuring the United States not to renew Indonesia's most-favoured-nation status. The many flagrant violations of labour rights in Indonesia came under close scrutiny, and for some months it appeared possible that the United States, under the more human-rights conscious President Clinton, elected at the end of 1992, would end Indonesia's status under the General System of Preferences. Such a move would have cost the country hundreds of millions of dollars in tariffs. Under pressure, the Indonesian Government introduced some minor reforms in industrial relations. For instance, the official minimum wage, nominally introduced in the 1970s, was increased, and an annual bonus for workers was made compulsory. The Minister for Labour at the time also made cosmetic reforms of SPSI to make it look more like a real union, but not being a military man he was unable to curb military involvement in suppressing industrial unrest. The right of workers to form unions was still effectively denied. Ultimately the US ceased to exert pressure for labour rights, and this source of external pressure faded away in 1995 (Bourchier 1994; Hadiz 1997; Smyth and Grijns, 1997).[6] In 1997 the government introduced a new labour law that did not, however, herald any new directions; nor was it ever enforced.

After the fall of the New Order, little attention was paid publicly to factory workers. The financial crisis hit some factories badly, with many workers being laid off. Naturally this dampened labour unrest, although with increased freedom strikes continued to occur (Hadiz 2002). The 1997 Labour Law was revoked, to be replaced in 2003 by a new bill that offered no improvement from the workers' point of view. An important change for women was that it eliminated menstruation leave (*Jakarta Post* 26 March 2003). Independent trade unions are re-emerging; it will be the business of women workers and women's organisations to ensure that they deal with gender-based issues.[7]

---

[6] At the level of particular firms, however, there was continued international campaigning, most notably on the question of Nike workers in Indonesia. Nike shoes were manufactured in a few factories in Java, where working conditions were held to be substandard (Hancock 1997 and 2000; INGI Labour Working Group 1991).

[7] A promising sign was a conference on working women organised jointly by fourteen unions and fifteen NGOs in October 2000, attended by 230 women workers. One of the coordinators was a former textile factory worker currently employed by the American Center for International Labor Solidarity. The US connection with Indonesian labour thus continues. The conference was partially funded by the US Embassy in Jakarta (*Media Indonesia* 23 October 2000). Subsequently a consortium of women's organisations and labour groups formed, called Kelompok Perempuan untuk Keadilan Buruh (Women's Group for Labour Justice).

Migrant workers

In Indonesia, of greater public concern than women factory workers has been the plight of women working overseas as domestic servants. Although the phenomenon of women migrant workers first gained wide attention at the end of the twentieth century, in fact it dates back to the colonial period when the problems first surfaced. Dutch families returning to the Netherlands on furlough were often accompanied by Indonesian nursemaids who cared for their children. Some of these women continued in employment in the Netherlands and faced considerable problems in a strange land where they frequently did not speak the language and lacked proper clothing for northern winters. Ultimately the Dutch Government felt obliged in 1919 to set up an institution especially to provide refuge, temporary housing and an employment exchange for Indonesian housemaids, cooks and sailors in Holland. Most of those seeking assistance were women. This was a foretaste of the problems that resurfaced in the 1980s (Poeze 1986).

One aspect of globalisation at the end of the twentieth century was rapid growth in the international movement of labour in search of better pay. Increasingly, Indonesian workers have sought better remunerated jobs overseas. In 1979 about 10,000 migrant workers, most of them male, were officially processed by the Department of Manpower. By 1992 the number had risen to almost 150,000, and in 2000 it shot up to more than 435,000. Since the 1980s, more than half of these workers have been women. In addition there are unknown but probably even larger numbers of illegal migrant workers, who are evading hefty official fees and lengthy and restrictive paperwork (Hugo 2002). Particularly during economic recessions, the Indonesian state has a great interest in encouraging labour migration, since it results in valuable remittances of foreign exchange. Between 1983 and 1989, remittances from migrant workers through official channels alone amounted to more than US $550 million, while in the first six months of 2001 they were estimated to be US $4 billion. Official figures constitute only a small proportion of the total amount (Hugo 1993 and 2002).

What was striking about the nature of worker migration in the last decades of the century was the rapid increase in the numbers of women seeking work overseas. Most of them found employment as domestic servants in wealthy regions, starting with the Middle-Eastern countries enriched by the oil boom in the 1970s and then expanding to include the newly industrialising states of Asia where menial labour became in short supply, notably Malaysia, Singapore, Taiwan and Hong Kong.

In the 1980s appalling stories began to filter back to Indonesia of mis-treatment of its women domestic workers in the Middle East. A mount-ing number of cases revealed not only inhumanly long hours of work but also employers failing to pay their housemaids, withholding their passports, refusing to let them contact people outside the home and ulti-mately rape and brutality. To add to the injustice, a number of women were brought before Islamic courts accused of adultery when seduced or raped by employers. Some were sentenced to death by stoning (Robinson 2000). The rapaciousness of recruiters and employers, the negligence of government authorities and the powerlessness of the workers led some Indonesians to compare the women migrant workers of the 1980s to Javanese contract coolie workers in Sumatra during the colonial period, whose slave-like fate had caused scandal in the late nineteenth century (Tobing, Hartiningsih, Dewabrata et al. 1990).

Well publicised in the Indonesian press, these cases could not be ignored, difficult though they were to handle for many Indonesians. The Indonesian state was anxious not to jeopardise the source of valuable remittances or its good relations with wealthy Middle-Eastern govern-ments. Islamic organisations in Indonesia were reluctant to admit wrong-doing by Muslims in the heartland of Islam, especially since many of them claimed that under Islam women were better protected than in the West. Indonesians who employed housemaids themselves also knew that many of the woes of women migrant workers were mirrored in Indone-sian homes. Neither the Indonesian state nor most women's organisations have shown any interest in the fate of local domestic servants, arguably one of the most exploited groups of women workers (Eldridge 1995: 164–7; Katjasungkana 1995; Thomson 1995).[8]

Nevertheless, feelings of national pride were outraged by the dishon-our experienced by Indonesian women overseas, and action was urged on many sides. The question was, what could be done? The Indone-sian Government had no control over treatment of its citizens in other countries, and in some countries, as in Indonesia itself, domestic service was regarded as outside the formal economic sector and therefore not regulated by industrial legislation. Many of the domestic servants who struck trouble were not registered with the Indonesian embassy, some-times because they were working illegally.

Under these circumstances, some Indonesians considered the only response was to prohibit women working as maids in the Middle East.

---

[8] In recent years a few women's organisations have begun to work with domestic servants to improve their conditions. They include the Yogyakarta-based Yayasan Cut Nyak Dien and LBH-APIK.

Many justifications were offered for this move, which has been proposed in different forms since the early 1990s. For some, this solution met not only their humanitarian concerns but also their repugnance at Indonesians working overseas in what were regarded as menial capacities. While it was acceptable for women to work as nurses, teachers or in other skilled jobs, the honour of the nation was sullied if its women were recruited to take lowly positions as servants. Moreover, according to Indonesian tradition, when domestic servants were admitted to the intimacy of the home they became part of the family (albeit at the lowest level of a family hierarchy). Although they might be grossly overworked and miserably paid, they were to be protected, given food and shelter and rewarded with gifts from time to time. Many of these pre-capitalist assumptions still clung to servants, the more particularly because most of them were women (Robinson 1991). If foreigners did not know how to treat servants properly, they clearly did not deserve to have them. The national honour too must be protected by not placing Indonesian womenfolk at risk.

Among the official women's organisations, this approach immediately struck a chord. Kowani announced that women workers should not be sent overseas for employment as domestic servants; rather 'in order not to lower the dignity and status of Indonesian women', they should be trained for jobs with higher skills (Mufti 1996). Some Islamic women's organisations also sought a solution through stopping the recruitment of housemaids to the offending countries. (It would be cynical but perhaps realistic to point to a conflict of interest here: some members of these organisations may have been influenced by the popular complaint that the growth in migration of domestic workers had affected the supply and cost of local servants.) The Minister for Women's Role was also known in 1997 to favour a halt to migration of maids to the Middle East (Robinson 2000).

A few of the new feminist organisations entered the fray on behalf of migrant female workers. Probably the best-known advocate is Solidaritas Perempuan (Solidarity of Women), founded in 1990 (Krisnawati 1995). Framing the issue as one of workers' rights, they were more ambivalent about attempts to halt migration. They recognised the dilemma facing unskilled workers for whom the home market was not growing fast enough to absorb them and who stood to gain much higher remuneration overseas. If too many obstacles were placed in their way, levels of illegal migration would just increase. Seeking practical ways of assisting migrant workers, they posed a range of demands. They included recognition by receiving countries of the rights of migrant workers and more support for workers from Indonesian embassies abroad, where officials often denigrated maidservants. Within Indonesia, Solidaritas Perempuan urged better control of recruiting agents who often deceived and grossly exploited women; training and information sessions for women before they left the country so that they were better prepared for what faced them; creation of crisis centres both at home and in foreign countries; and more broadly, development efforts to address the lack of remunerative employment that fed the migrant worker trade. Solidaritas Perempuan has succeeded in gaining widespread media coverage of the needs of migrant women workers, has documented many cases of rape, and has led these women in energetically lobbying government and the parliament (Krisnawati 1995; Robinson 2000; Hugo 2002). It helped form a coalition called Women's Movement for Justice for Migrant Labour.

The forces arrayed against any cessation in labour migration were varied. Employment agencies were, of course, aghast at the thought of failing to meet the overseas demand for Indonesian maids. Many within the government undoubtedly thought of the inevitable decline in remittances; the five-year plans had come to be predicated on assumptions about ever-growing amounts of foreign exchange earned by migrant labour. However, governments have suspended labour export for short periods in 2001 and 2003, on the grounds that they were helping to protect workers.

Governments have gradually responded to criticisms by implementing some reforms. The licences of some recruiting agents were revoked for not following regulations, and recruiters were required to train migrants before leaving Indonesia, so they were better prepared, and to maintain agents in Saudi Arabia who would help protect Indonesian workers (Robinson 2000; Hugo 2002). Problems persist in Saudi Arabia, however, with increasing numbers of Indonesian women sentenced to death and hundreds of rape cases reported every year.

In the 1990s attention turned to Asian countries where Indonesian maids were employed, as numbers to those destinations grew rapidly and cases of ill-treatment were replicated there. Mysterious deaths were a particular cause of concern. In the case of Malaysia the situation was compounded by the fact that most Indonesian workers were in the country illegally. Naturally it was even harder for Indonesian officials to provide assistance to such people in trouble. The expulsion by Malaysia of hundreds of thousands of illegal Indonesian migrant workers at the time of the financial crisis exacerbated the problem: in 2002 seventy-nine workers died when deported across the Malaysian border in Borneo (Jones 1996; Ford 2002).

Employment in Malaysia in particular draws women from all over the archipelago. This has helped to broaden the perspective on women's work, since understanding the reasons why these women seek work overseas has focussed more attention on the poverty in the sending areas and the impacts (both good and bad) on those communities of wives, mothers and daughters working overseas (Hugo 2002).

One of the aspects of migrant labour which reverberates most strongly with women's organisations is that which links it in their minds to sexual rather than sheer economic exploitation. There is no doubt that some young women accept jobs in the sex industry in lucrative markets like Malaysia, and others (including large numbers of children) are tricked into such work and treated virtually as slaves (Rochaida, Wicaksono and Tamtiari 2001; Hugo 2002). It has been difficult for women's organisations to distinguish between voluntary and involuntary work in the sex industry, and a tendency exists to see it all as part of trafficking in women. Since the work is generally illegal, it is extremely hard to police.

The number of Indonesian migrant workers continues to climb. While it offers great opportunities for these workers to earn far more than they could at home, it also poses one of the major dilemmas of globalisation when they strike trouble outside the jurisdiction of the state that owes them protection. The largest category of these workers, housemaids, combines old and new issues of economic exploitation in an intractable form over which the Indonesian state and women's organisations are still puzzling. The state can have little power over workers within the home, cut off from the outside world, and it is extremely difficult to organise them. How much more difficult is the task of dealing with such workers in a foreign country, isolated not only geographically but often also by poor command of the local language and lack of knowledge about the law and the social system. Remarkably, some Indonesian maidservants in Hong Kong succeeded in organising themselves into an Association of Indonesian Migrant Workers, which in 2001 staged a protest rally against exploitation by employers, recruitment agencies and the Indonesian Government – something which has never happened in Indonesia itself (*Jakarta Post* 21 July 2001).

In Indonesia, organisations have formed a Consortium to Defend Indonesian Migrant Workers (Konsorsium Pembela Buruh Migran Indonesia). In keeping with the international nature of the problem, they are working for the ratification of the United Nations Convention of 1990 on the Protection of the Rights of All Migrant Workers and Members of Their Families, which has not yet been ratified by Indonesia or the countries to which it sends migrant workers (Konsorsium 2002).

Conclusion: the controversies and the silences

Economic exploitation of women is something that has been taken for granted in a deeply ingrained way in Indonesian society. For many poor women it is the most basic form of oppression: they just cannot earn enough, no matter how hard they work, and their working lives are exhausting and debilitating, leaving little room for anything else, let alone political activity to redress their woes. Men also suffer, but women's situation is compounded by gender discrimination: much of their work is unrecognised and unpaid, and in the paid workforce they are concentrated in jobs deemed suitable for women, which are almost without exception worse paid and dead-end. The story is the same in most poor countries. What this chapter has shown is the political responses of women and the state to this situation.

The state in Indonesia in the twentieth century saw its main task in addressing the problem of women's exploitation as improving the economy, so that more and better-paid jobs were available to women. Related to this, the state envisaged improved education and training as a way to help Indonesians gain access to better positions. How high these priorities featured in a state's agenda varied with the nature of the state and the circumstances of the time. Most successful on the economic and educational fronts was the New Order regime, which helped to lift living standards, expand employment and boost the modern sector, while providing almost all Indonesians with basic schooling. In the wake of the Asian financial crisis and the chaos created by the fall of the New Order, the present Indonesian state is, like that of the 1950s, painfully attempting to get the economy back on track and restore employment levels.

From time to time the state has focussed on working women and passed legislation aimed at protecting them. Their responsibilities in the matter have been drawn to their attention at international levels, especially by the ILO. Indonesian legislation identifies women as a weak section of the workforce and is concerned about their role as mothers or housewives rather than seeking justice for them as workers. In fact, the notion that women workers have rights was discouraged by the state throughout most of the twentieth century. Efforts to single out women as in need of special protection have had the effect of disadvantaging them in the workforce, since they involve extra expense and effort on the part of employers. Experience has shown that employers often evade their responsibilities, even going so far as to sack women who are pregnant or demand their legal rights. It takes a very determined state to enforce such legislation, and the state in Indonesia, under every regime, has failed to show that determination.

As this chapter has shown, few Indonesian women's organisations have addressed questions of economic exploitation. At the very least, the task of women's organisations is to give a voice to all women, to represent their interests across the spectrum. Yet few Indonesian women's groups in the twentieth century have felt obliged to learn about the problems of poor working women and make them known to society and the state, let alone to help those women organise themselves. For middle-class and Islamic organisations, assumptions about men being the main income-earner pre-vailed, making the notion of exploitation rather irrelevant as far as women were concerned, unless it impinged on matters of sexual morality. The most successful organisation to address working women's concerns was Gerwani, and with its obliteration by the New Order state, poor work-ing women were silenced. Not until the last couple of decades have new women's groups emerged that tried to reach exploited working women. And only with the fall of the New Order could poor women really begin to organise in an independent way on the basis of their working interests – at a time of rising unemployment with the economic crisis. In the issues concerning working women that arose towards the end of the twentieth century, the links with sexual violence are striking. The Marsinah case, the afflictions of overseas women workers, all gained particular poignancy because of the sexual violence inflicted on factory workers and domestic servants. With established women's organisations, the chord struck was undoubtedly connected to their longstanding interest in sexual exploita-tion, and it was this aspect that scandalised the public. In the next chapter the question of violence against women is the focus, and we shall see how and why it gained in salience in the twentieth century.

8   Violence

Violence against women appeared as a prominent item on the agenda of the Indonesian women's movement only very late in the twentieth century. Earlier chapters have touched on aspects of sexual violence: domestic violence was related to marriage matters discussed in Chapters 2 and 5, and trafficking in women and sexual harassment (including the death of Marsinah) appeared in relation to work (Chapter 7). Yet these were regarded as important by very few organisations. The reasons are many, and most are not unique to Indonesia.

Firstly, there was no way of discussing violence against women in general terms until international institutions and conferences legitimised it. The watershed was the United Nations Declaration on the Elimination of Violence against Women of 1993. Article 1 of that declaration defined violence against women as 'any act of gender-based violence that results in, or is likely to result in, physical, sexual or psychological harm or suffering to women, including threats of such acts, coercion or arbitrary deprivation of liberty, whether occurring in public or in private life'. Article 2 distinguished three kinds of violence perpetrated more particularly against women: violence occurring within the family, including wife-battering, sexual abuse of female children and rape within marriage; violence occurring within the general community, including rape, sexual harassment (at work, in educational institutions, in the street), and trafficking in women and forced prostitution; and violence perpetrated or condoned by the state, such as torture and military rape. The Declaration called on members of the UN to work towards eliminating violence against women, for instance by collecting data on the subject, facilitating the work of women's movements and developing appropriate legislation and national plans of action to promote the protection of women.

Until recently, the only issues listed in the Declaration relating to gender violence that were on the Indonesian public agenda were rape and trafficking in women. Governments always had laws against both, as will be described below. Nevertheless, women's organisations were until recently very reluctant to discuss violence against women, especially such notions as rape in marriage, wife-beating, military rape and the gendered effects of war and communal violence on women. The UN Declaration of 1993 and the Beijing International Women's Conference of 1995 made it possible to discuss violence against women in Indonesia and provided foreign aid to organisations undertaking study and action on it.

Even when the subject of gender violence was broached in Indonesia, there was strong cultural resistance to accepting that it was relevant in that country. At first many Indonesians denied that, for instance, incest or sexual harassment of children happened in their society: such abuses were limited to the decadent West. In strongly Islamic circles there was an especially self-righteous culture of denial. People were slow to recognise that shame had kept these things hidden from public view. Violence against women has been connected to sexuality, which has been a taboo subject. Domestic violence was regarded as a private matter, not to be discussed with others. Rape casts a slur not only on the victim but also on her family. There is a common tendency for rape victims to internalise the problem, to regard it as somehow their own fault. Violated women are reduced to their most humiliated state: they do not wish their plight to be made public, hoping to preserve at least some scrap of dignity. Women have had no concept of rights against such violence. The problem is seen also in media discussions of violence against women. While the media are only too happy to publicise particular cases of violence against women, especially if they are regarded as titillating, there is great resistance to acknowledging structures of violence or a culture of violence, anything that appears to shift the blame from individuals to the wider society.

A strong reason for concealing violence against women is that victims fear the consequences of revealing cases of violence. Both self-interest and the protection of others affect their judgment. In the case of domestic violence, women are most reluctant to lay charges against their husbands on whom they and their children may be economically dependent. For the media, especially, it has always been difficult to accept the dilemmas facing women where no outcome is simple and someone apart from the culprit will always suffer as a result of disclosure.

Finally, victims have no confidence that anything is to be gained by going public. They lack faith in 'the system' to provide justice: police and the judiciary are not trusted, with considerable justification since they have treated women victims of violence with a callous lack of understanding and compounded their woes. Their problem is treated as personal, unable to be resolved at a public level. Their fate is often accepted as the natural course of events: soldiers are brutal; husbands will beat wives; men have sexual appetites that lead them to rape, and so on.

For all these reasons, the incidence of violence against Indonesian women is not really known. It is poorly reported. But clearly it has existed to varying degrees. This chapter investigates the emergence of interest among the Indonesian women's movement in violence against women and the response of the state to the issue. I do not argue that women are naturally opposed to violence or are only victims of it. Some Indonesian women have perpetrated or colluded in violence, including against other women. Such action may be officially endorsed, as with women in the fighting forces; it may be social, as when women urge men to rape or illtreat other women in communal strife; it may be domestic, as when women abuse their servants, or ignore men beating their neighbours' wives, or turn a blind eye to their husband's rape of children or maidservants. But it cannot be denied that women are more likely to be victims than perpetrators of violence, a fact connected to their position in the social and political structure, where they are more vulnerable than men and less able to voice their views.

A very limited agenda on violence against women

For most of the twentieth century the only matters on which women's organisations and the state showed any interest in relation to violence against women were rape and trafficking in women, and even on these matters the level of concern was low. Meanwhile the incidence of family, social and state violence against women was either unknown, unrecorded or unremarked.

The colonial legal code of 1918 created a precedent in the treatment of rape by classifying it as a 'crime against morality' rather than a crime against persons like assault. This has had important consequences for women's treatment as rape victims. Like pornography, adultery and abortion, which fell under the same heading in the criminal code, rape offended public morality. But if the woman raped was herself immoral because she was a prostitute or a 'loose woman', the public was not offended and thus the victim would have difficulty winning a legal case. Defence lawyers would therefore try to blacken the victim's character in order to save their clients. Conversely, the worst kind of rape was seen to be the rape of a virgin. Nursyahbani Kacasungkana, the human-rights lawyer, has pointed out that the whole morality of rape under existing law is predicated on the view that women are men's property, and that raping a woman is seen as a means of taking ownership of her, something only a husband can properly do. To restore moral order, the only logical solution in the case of rape of a virgin is to marry the victim to the rapist. After all, no one else would ever marry her, since she was 'someone else's' or 'damaged goods', and marriage was the fitting way for the rapist to make amends. Such ideas, according to Nursyahbani, ran deeper than just colonial law, since this logic has been widely accepted, including in contemporary Indonesia where authorities have occasionally insisted on the rapist marrying the victim (Katjasungkana 2001).

Since colonial and local views converged on the evil of rape, punishment was accepted. However, rape victims were extremely reluctant to report the crime, due to the shame involved, the frequent difficulty in proving its occurrence, the fear of retaliation and the unsympathetic response of male authorities. Apart from the few sensational rape cases that were covered by the press, little comment was made. No interest was displayed in the incidence of rape or its causes.

The logic of rape as a crime against morality also explains why the colonial legal code could not encompass the notion of marital rape. Since a wife was her husband's property, it was not possible for public morality to be offended by what a husband did to his wife in the way of sexual relations. Rape was simply not envisaged as a matter of unequal power relations between men and women, where women had no power to refuse sex and where sex could be used to impose dominance. As evidence, according to the colonial law which has continued until the present, although it was an offence for a man to have sexual relations with a woman below the age of fifteen years, the law does not apply if the woman is his wife (Katjasungkana 2001). The closest that the colonial authorities came to discussing marital rape was their concern about the fate of girls married off by their parents at an early age before they could be said to give informed consent to sexual intercourse (see Chapter 3). Interfering in such matters was, as we have seen, considered virtually impossible: only indirect approaches, such as promoting education for girls, could be attempted by the state. Finally, the law does not regard anything but penile insertion into the vagina as rape, excluding anal or oral rape or the use of objects in rape, which indicates a remarkably narrow view of this form of sexual assault, and one which, incidentally, excludes the possibility of rape of men (Harkrisnowo 2000).

For the women's movement, discussion of violence against women, impinging as it did on matters of sexuality, was virtually taboo. As was mentioned in the last chapter, they did, however, acknowledge the existence of sexual harassment in the workplace and trafficking in women, both of which they condemned strongly. Some organisations conducted activities on behalf of the victims of trafficking, but they had no way of publicly discussing how or why the practice occurred. Sexual violence was a private matter that should not be broached publicly.

Throughout the twentieth century there were numerous serious cases of state violence in which women were implicated, mostly as victims but occasionally as perpetrators. Not only were these never matters for public debate, but in some cases women's organisations condoned that violence by their endorsement of state policies.

The twentieth century opened with colonial violence and resistance in those parts of the archipelago that were still not incorporated into the Dutch East Indies. Little has been recorded about women's experience of or response to this conflict, apart from accounts of the exploits of some Acehnese women who led resistance against the Dutch in the decades-long war in northern Sumatra. Cut Nyak Dien and Cut Meutia are part of the nationalist pantheon: they fought together with their husbands and continued to lead troops into battle after they were widowed. Women's organisations never commented directly on how women were affected by state violence, although as they became more nationalist they might evoke such resistance fighters as heroines.

During the Second World War, there was a high level of violence in various parts of the archipelago, associated with the arrival and defeat of the Japanese, as well as the conduct of the Occupation, which was geared towards meeting the needs of Japan's war effort. The buried story of sexual violence during the war was the fate of the so-called 'comfort women' (*jugun ianfu*), Indonesian women forced into sexual slavery by the Japanese military. It is not known how many women were thus abused, because the issue did not come out into the open until quite recently. Like other countries from which these women were taken, Indonesia was silent on the matter until women took up the cause in the 1990s (Hartono and Juliantoro 1997).

At the time there was no notion that what the Japanese army had done was a crime. It was not recognised as such in international law, and the Japanese authorities always maintained that the women concerned were voluntarily working as prostitutes. In a recent book on the subject, Pramudya Ananta Tur considers the question of why the Indonesian Government did nothing about the issue, not even trying to assist the victims who were often abandoned a long way from their homes. He notes that immediately after the war, the Republic of Indonesia was struggling to gain international recognition and resist the return of the Dutch: it was not in a position to pursue any war crimes issues. After the transfer of sovereignty it had other priorities, and ultimately it must, says Tur, be regarded as negligent on the matter (Toer 2001).

But why did the women's movement not take up the issue or assist the victims? Some of the reasons have to do with the victims themselves: they were ashamed of what had happened to them and wanted to conceal it or to try to forget it and move on. From their point of view, nothing was to be gained by publicising their fate. Much later, some of these women were willing to talk and joined the international movement to put pressure on the Japanese Government to apologise and make reparations (*Surabaya Post* 21 November 2000; *Jakarta Post* 26 October 2001). From the perspective of women's groups at the time, the demand for attention from war victims was overwhelming: widows, orphans and displaced persons took all their time and efforts. They thought more about helping people to rebuild society and their lives, rather than about something as remote as international laws and rights, about which in any case they were largely ignorant.

The decades following the Japanese Occupation continued to be tumultuous and characterised by violence in several parts of the archipelago. Resisting the Dutch involved guerrilla warfare and a few massacres, including the killing and raping of women. Thousands of people were displaced, the majority being women and children.

The period of struggle for independence is rarely seen by Indonesians as a period of violence rather than one of heroism. As the historian William Frederick wrote recently, 'In the current blizzard of attention to violence in Indonesia, hardly a flurry has fallen on the Indonesian Revolution (1945–49), the modern nation's formative experience and by far its most extended period of violence' (Frederick 2002: 144). It will take some time for attention to turn to women's experience of violence during this period. So far, examples can only be gleaned from asides in historical accounts. The massacres of the Dutch soldier Westerling have been documented, although never from a gender perspective. Violence by Indonesians has had far less attention and has mainly focussed on their Chinese and European victims in an ungendered way. Frederick describes the actions of Zainul Sabaroeddin who, with a gang of youths, 'unleashed a whirlwind of brutal activity' in East Java in late 1945, killing Europeans and British-Indian soldiers and 'shooting, beheading, torturing, and burning alive dozens of men and women', including making a number of women into sex slaves (Frederick 2002: 151–2). Freed from the ultra-nationalist constraints that have dominated Indonesian historiography thus far, Indonesians themselves may well begin to unearth the less heroic aspects of their own past, including its effects on women (Nordholt 2002). Only a very few Indonesians have been able to contemplate this aspect of their history with the unflinching honesty of the great writer Pramudya Ananta Tur, whose short story 'The Vanquished' of 1951 might well serve as an inspiration for analysts of the effects of violence on women during this period. Pramudya portrays women as both perpetrators and victims of violence (Toer 1975).

The first impact of feminism on Indonesian historical studies was to inspire Indonesians to uncover and celebrate the role of women as part of the armed struggle for independence. The activities of the few women's paramilitary units (*laskar*) have been documented, and the work of women as intelligence gatherers, couriers, nurses and caterers for independence fighters is also recorded (Condronagoro 1979; Nurliana, Manus, Ohorella et al. 1986). These were voluntary and local actions, not coordinated or directed by a central body. The impact of all this violence on women receives less attention, although it is clear that many women's lives were devastated by the events of these years: apart from rape and injuries, they lost family, friends and property and were forced to flee and support themselves and their children single-handedly.

Even the transfer of sovereignty in 1949 did not see the end of armed violence in some areas. It was often hard to distinguish bandit attacks from guerrilla resistance to the Republic by extremist Islamic groups in West Java and elsewhere. Revolts flared again in the late 1950s as people in West Sumatra and Sulawesi resisted the policies of the Jakarta government, which they saw as deleterious to their regions. While the state was preoccupied with restoring order, women's organisations cared for refugees and tried to help people survive. The differential impact of the violence on women was not made a public issue (Martyn 2001; Nurliana et al. 1986).

Sukarno's Guided Democracy regime was unique in actually mobilising the women's movement behind military campaigns in Irian Jaya (now renamed Papua) and against the formation of Malaysia. For the first time the state organised women into volunteer military brigades and employed them in combat roles: for instance, one was parachuted into Irian Jaya as a paratrooper. The dominant ethos of the era was 'revolutionary', and the women's movement regularly referred to Sukarno by his official titles which included 'Great Leader of the Indonesian Revolution'. The women's movement was involved in the official state of alertness, ready for resistance to imperialist powers. Newspapers showed women drilling and doing target practice. Even the 'non-political' members of Islamic organisations, in their Islamic dress, joined in these activities (Ma'shum and Sawawi 1996). The military wives' organisations played a role in urging other women into a state of revolutionary preparedness (Suwondo 1981: 197–201).

Whereas most of the militarisation of Guided Democracy was just for outward show, the New Order regime was founded on a massacre, part of it explicitly aimed at women. The military in some places permitted, and in other places instigated and participated, in the murder of hundreds of thousands of suspected communists, including Gerwani members. In fact Gerwani was singled out for special hatred and accused in government propaganda of sexual depravity surrounding the murder of the six generals on the night of 1 October. A torrent of hatred was released that fed the killing, torture, rape and imprisonment of Gerwani women (Wieringa 2002). The restructured 'official' women's movement, headed by Kowani, echoed the government line. State repression was so strong that nothing was reported at the time about the treatment of Gerwani women: it came out only gradually and clandestinely in the late New Order period and received no official attention from women's organisations, who were afraid of being tarred with the same brush. Some organisations had encouraged the government in its suppression of Gerwani (Ma'shum and Sawawi 1996). But with the fall of the New Order, former Gerwani members began to appear publicly and demand recognition of their persecution. At the December 1998 women's congress, Sulami, a former Gerwani leader, spoke out in public for the first time in decades, denouncing the vilification of her colleagues. Some women's organisations responded sympathetically, but Kowani leaders at the conference regretted this turn of events.

Violence perpetrated by state elements against women continued throughout the New Order in different parts of the archipelago, but most notably where separatist movements occurred. Thus women in Aceh, East Timor and Papua were subject to on-going brutality. Rapes of women occurred regularly and women were abused to intimidate their menfolk. Because of censorship, this could not be reported in the media and most Indonesians elsewhere in the archipelago were ignorant of what was being done in their name, in defence of national unity. The fact that independent women's organisations did not exist in these areas until very late in the New Order period meant that these women had no voice.

Unlike during Guided Democracy, the New Order state did not seek to militarise women. The dominant force was a regular army that relied on an utterly masculine ethos. Fighting was for men; women should stay at home and support their husbands.[1] Encouraging women to become militant was part of the aberration of the 'Old Order' that had led to the breakdown of Indonesian society. The state would now return the nation to normality, including 'normal' gender roles.

A number of writers have pointed to the contradiction underlying the New Order as far as violence was concerned. It denied the existence of violence at the level of the family and stressed traditions of peace and cooperation at the social level. At the same time the state itself perpetrated violence on a wide scale, from the overt repression of any 'communist', separatist or 'extremist Islamic' elements to the clandestine terror

---

[1] Women have in fact been admitted to the Army into a special Army Women's Corps. Assigned to supporting roles such as aides and administrative personnel, they rarely participate in combat. Their training is similar to that of male recruits but they take additional classes, including in make-up and fashion (Sawitri 2001).

of the 'mysterious killings' kind in the 1980s, and the increasing use in the 1990s of bands of thugs associated with the military. The explanation of the state was that a high level of vigilance was required by the state apparatus (police, civil service, military, teachers, judiciary, intelligence) to prevent subversion of 'natural' Indonesian tendencies towards peace and harmony. Harmony was in fact fragile and depended on hierarchy and obedience. The mere discussion of differences within society (especially those of class, ethnicity, race and religion) was likely to give rise to dangerous tensions or conflict and must therefore be censored. Violence was the prerogative of the state and could be exercised in the interests of the nation. Because it was legitimate, it was not to be queried, and discussion of violence by non-state actors was to be avoided in the interests of preventing further conflict. Any notion of sexual violence had little hope of being aired in the face of this ideology. On the contrary, women as mothers were expected to spread harmony, not foment discord by claiming disruptive rights (Cooley 1992; Sciortino and Smyth 1997; Wessel and Wimhofer 2001).

The women's movement raises the issue of domestic violence

Often assisted by foreign aid, some of the newer women's organisations in the last years of the New Order began to emphasise the importance of violence against women as an issue requiring community and government action. Part of the international feminist programme, this topic received the attention of governments at the Beijing Conference on Women in 1995. The Indonesian Government, however, gave it little more than lip-service. The Ministry for Women's Role developed some policies on the matter but, lacking a line department of its own, had no power to enforce them. The existence in Indonesia of violence against women just did not fit the government's projected image of a harmonious society based on contented families.

In particular, domestic violence was felt to be too difficult to tackle, especially for a predominantly Islamic society in which the family life of Muslims is left largely to the realm of Muslim law. Strictly speaking, the criminal code contained sections about cruelty that could cover domestic violence, but in practice law-enforcers have not made use of the law to cover what they consider private affairs. On the other hand, the 1974 Marriage Law made it clear that women need not accept Islamic teachings that husbands could beat their wives: it was made grounds for divorce if a woman cared to take it to the Religious Court (Katjasungkana 2001).

The subject of sexual harassment was first raised at a seminar at the University of Indonesia in 1988, when it was beginning to be discussed at the global level. It was pointed out that although the criminal code appeared to cover cases of sexual harassment, it did not apply to workplace situations, apparently because the law did not acknowledge women's presence in the workforce (Katjasungkana 2001: 99–102).

In the early 1990s some of the new women's organisations began to address sexual violence in a direct way. As an indication of how attitudes were changing in Islamic circles, in 1993 the first Women's Crisis Centre was formed in Yogyakarta by Rifka Annisa, a group of young Islamic women. Women's organisations like Kalyanamitra in Jakarta monitored numbers of reported cases of sexual harassment and of domestic violence. Although patchy, the evidence was sufficient to show doubters that Indonesia was similar to other countries in that women across socioeconomic classes and in different regions suffered these abuses. Conferences were also held relating to gender violence, but it made little progress as an issue, either in public perceptions or with government (Sciortino and Smyth 1997). Rape, the most obvious form of gender violence, met with little sympathy: the tendency was to deny that it was a significant problem in Indonesia (due to its unique culture) or to argue that rapes occurred because of uncontrollable male sexual urges, especially when provoked by female licentiousness (such as the wearing of 'provocative' clothing). Reporting levels for rape were low, as women were inhibited by a culture of shame and by the unsympathetic treatment of rape by police and courts.

In the early 1990s some human rights-oriented women's organisations began to demand that marital rape be included in the criminal code. This was rejected by the Minister of Justice on the ground that the notion of marital rape was derived from Western individualistic notions of rights, whereas in Indonesia husband and wife 'have become one in the family'. Similarly the Minister for Women's Role considered marital rape 'against Pancasila and Indonesian culture'(Sciortino and Smyth 1997: 300).

The Indonesian women's movement was beginning to grasp the issue of violence against women in the 1990s and struggling to bring domestic violence onto the public agenda. What it did not anticipate was that the end of the century would witness social violence and state-instigated violence on a huge scale.

The violence of the transition to democracy: 1998

The end of the Suharto regime came quite quickly and unexpectedly in May 1998, for the most part in a peaceful manner but accompanied by some traumatic events, including riots and rapes. The cold-blooded shooting of Trisakti University students on 12 May was quickly followed by widespread looting in Jakarta and some other cities on 13–15 May. The main targets for looting were shops and other property of the Chinese Indonesian minority in identifiable 'Chinatown' areas. In these areas, especially in Jakarta, it was soon reported that rapes accompanied the rioting, and the last act was widespread burning of buildings in which hundreds of people died.

The extent of the violence shocked most Indonesians, more especially because the worst excesses occurred in the capital city, under the full scrutiny of domestic and foreign media. News of the rapes took a little while to emerge and longer to gain credibility and due attention.

Reports of the rapes were released in June by NGOs, a number of which cooperated in task forces specially formed to deal with the issue. Best known was the Team of Volunteers for Humanity (henceforth Volunteers' Team). Led by the Catholic priest Sandyawan Sumardi, the Volunteers' Team took an active role in monitoring the May riots and supporting its victims. They learnt of the existence of what they soon reported as mass rapes and sexual maltreatment coinciding with the riots and largely targeting women of Chinese descent. The Volunteers' Team set up a special women's section, coordinated by Ita F. Nadia of the feminist resource centre Kalyanamitra, to assist the rape victims with medical, psychological and legal support (*Republika* 24 August 1998).

The victims, their relatives and/or friends, doctors and other professionals approached members of the Volunteers' Team, and other trusted bodies like the National Commission on Human Rights, with reports of rapes, principally in Jakarta but also in Medan, Palembang, Surabaya and Solo. What was especially chilling about the phenomenon was the emerging picture of orchestrated gang rapes and sexual maltreatment conducted by groups of outsiders, men unknown in the locality. By 13 July the Volunteers' Team was claiming that 168 women (152 from Jakarta) had been raped in this way, supporting a picture of mass rape (*Kompas* 14 July 1998).

At first the reports were met with disbelief. The police, the military, and the Ministry for Women's Role made their own enquiries but met with a blank wall since no one would entrust them with relevant information. They then denied anything had happened. NGOs had to reiterate that victims did not wish to report cases to the police or public authorities because the women themselves were in trauma over what they considered a 'disgrace', that their families were afraid, and that the authorities had no credibility among rape victims or among the Chinese Indonesian community, since they had offered no security during the riots and were even suspected of complicity in the violence. Data collection was further complicated by the fact that many victims had fled overseas with their families as part of the exodus of Chinese Indonesians that marked the month of May.

On 9 July a strong statement on the matter was issued by the National Commission on Human Rights. It said that it could be clearly ascertained that there had been repeated cruel gang rapes of ethnic Chinese women and other Indonesian citizens in mid-May in Jakarta and other towns. It noted with concern the sceptical attitude of the government and condemned it as insensitive, requesting the government to acknowledge the violence, apologise for its failure to protect its citizens and punish those responsible. It was an example of racial rape that could be seen as a violation of human rights and a crime against humanity. At the same time even representatives of the Chinese community, normally reluctant to speak out on political issues, also asked the government to form an independent commission to investigate the riots (*Kompas* 10 July 1998).

Under pressure, the government admitted on 10 July that gang rapes had occurred and regretted and condemned them (*Jakarta Post* 11 July 1998). Belatedly, Kowani, the umbrella group of women's organisations that had the stamp of approval of the New Order, also came out with a condemnation of the rapes (*Jakarta Post* 13 July 1998). Rosita S. Nur, president of the Communication Body for Comprehensive National Unity, an organisation for interethnic unity, said that insufficient efforts had been made by the military to give any feeling of security to the ethnic Chinese community, more than 40,000 of whom had left Indonesia since May. Her organisation also lobbied parliament to investigate the riots and the rapes, calling attention to the importance of the ethnic aspect of the incidents (*Republika* 14 July 1998; *Republika* 21 July 1998).

On 15 July a delegation of prominent women activists from the coalition group called Community Opposed to Violence Against Women and a number of other women's organisations including Kowani and Dharma Wanita, visited President Habibie. Following lengthy discussions with them, Habibie issued a statement deploring the rapes and promising that the government would be more proactive in giving protection to women (*Kompas* 16 July 1998). In the following days, women's organisations kept up the pressure for action: for instance on 17 July about a hundred women dressed in white from the newly formed Coalition of Women for Justice and Democracy demonstrated outside the Department of Defence in Jakarta, demanding that the army explain and take responsibility for the rape victims. They carried banners and placards reading 'If you hurt one woman you hurt all women', 'We oppose racism', 'Indonesia, Republic of Fear, Republic of Terror, Republic of Rape' (*Suara Pembaruan* 20 July 1998).

Stories about the rapes proliferated and were spread around the world, often in sensationalised forms, via the mass media, including the Internet. Protests against the Indonesian Government for complicity or attempted cover-up began to emerge in places with strong ethnic Chinese lobby groups, such as Singapore, Taiwan, Malaysia, Hong Kong, Beijing, the Philippines and the USA. This negative publicity provoked reactions from Islamic organisations which had previously shown little interest in the rapes issue. Some Muslim groups in Indonesia felt that these stories were damaging not only to the Indonesian national image but also to Islam and tended to claim that the reports were fabrications by a global conspiracy against Islam. Various leaders of Islamic community organisations went so far as to form a League of Upholders of Truth and Justice expressly to counter the actions of NGO activists who they considered had damaged Indonesia in the eyes of the world, notably through spreading 'rumours' about the May rapes (*Gatra* 29 August 1998; Sumargono 1998). On 21 July the Coordinating Body of Indonesian Islamic Preachers met with the President to urge him to make a legal investigation of the rapes, drawing to his attention a *New York Times* report containing the sentence, 'Some of the rapers said, "You must be raped because you are Chinese and non-muslim"' (*Republika* 22 July 1998).

On 23 July the government finally announced the appointment of a representative and credible team of nineteen people to investigate the riots and associated events, including the rapes. This Fact Finding Team, consisting of representatives of government departments, the armed forces and NGOs, was given three months to report back.

During that time various prominent figures continued to express doubts that the rapes had actually occurred, since the victims still would not come forward to give public testimony. Further pressure was exerted on the Indonesian Government by foreign deputations, and the Volunteers' Team took the rapes case to a meeting of a sub-committee of the Human Rights Commission of the United Nations in Geneva in August (Polan 1998).

Although it found it difficult to reach consensus, the Fact Finding Team reported on 3 November 1998, stating that it had thoroughly investigated the evidence and found amongst other things, that at least fifty-two women, mostly of Chinese origin, were indeed raped in an apparently systematic fashion by gangs of men. This incident fitted into a pattern of events in mid-May when riots appeared to have been incited by groups with apparent military connections. It recommended that the role of Colonel Prabowo, Suharto's son-in-law and previous chief of the Kopassus (Special Forces), be further investigated. Prabowo had already been sacked for insubordination (*Tempo* 16 November 1998: 26–7).

The other big step forward in Indonesia's official recognition of the importance of violence against women was the government's decision, announced on 9 October, to institute a National Commission on Violence Against Women headed by the respected feminist academic Professor Saparinah Sadli, who was already a member of the National Commission on Human Rights. It contained eighteen members, many of them well-known feminist activists like Rita Serena Kolibonso from Mitra Perempuan, Myra Diarsi from Kalyanamitra, Nursyahbani Kacasungkana from LBH-APIK, and also representatives from Aceh, Irian Jaya, East Timor and the Chinese Indonesian community. According to the Commission, it consists of Indonesian women and men who are committed to eliminating all forms of violence against women in both domestic and public environments and who are resolved to voice the interests of women nationally. Intended to be an independent body that promotes understanding of violence against women in Indonesia, it assists efforts to prevent that violence and protect the human rights of women. It has a secretariat and three sections devoted to research, legal reform, and advocacy and public education.[2] Funding for its projects has to be found independently. For its first three years, its activities involved mapping the state of violence in Indonesia, services for survivors, responding to conflict, and institution building.

Thus by late 1998 Indonesia had publicly acknowledged that their country had in fact experienced gang rape on a mass scale, largely of women of Chinese descent. The result was widespread outrage: the notion of mass rape was unfamiliar in Indonesian national culture, prompting people to question its causes and significance, in particular its relationship to racism, sexism and militarism. James Siegel has argued, too, that the strength of feeling among middle-class Indonesians about the May violence was closely connected to their fear of 'the mob' (Siegel 2001).

The May rapes triggered a full-scale debate in Indonesia about all kinds of violence against women and about relations between the state and women. When some of the rape victims were subsequently reported to be pregnant, discussion arose about whether they were justified in seeking an abortion, another subject which had hitherto been taboo since it was unacceptable in religious circles and the law restricted access to abortion. The plight of the women who had been raped resulted in sympathetic media coverage of abortion and discussion of the unsatisfactory nature of the law.

---

[2] Description of the Commission, its purposes and origin come from the initial brochure produced by the commission (October 1998).

There were aspects of the responses to the rapes that demonstrated the need for considerable public education to change attitudes on the issue. Some newspapers, like the tabloid *Pos Kota*, carried sensationalist stories that catered to voyeurist tendencies in their readership, and pornographic photos of supposed rape victims were circulated on the Internet (Heryanto 1999). The continuing lack of understanding about the rapes was exemplified by a public speech on the matter by Dr Baharuddin Lopa, the chairman of the National Commission on Human Rights, normally a very enlightened group of people. Noting the great difficulty of bringing rape perpetrators to justice, he proposed that the alternative was for citizens to tighten security: 'Parents need to be reminded to forbid their daughters from wearing revealing clothing', he said (*Republika* 23 July 1998). The sale of 'chastity belts' in Indonesia after the May riots also served as an occasion for women leaders to criticise the objectification of women's sexuality. Feminists also had to spend some time countering the frequently quoted views of 'social experts' who found it difficult to accept accounts of the rapes because it was 'illogical' to believe that a man could get an erection in the confused atmosphere of looting and rioting. As their critics pointed out, such commentators were still clinging to the notion that rape was a matter of sexual desire (*Republika* 2 August 1998; Sadli 1998).

The extraordinary level of interest in the May rapes was seen in media coverage and a spate of publications about this incident and about the issue of rape more generally (e.g. Tim Relawan 1998; Kolibonso 1998). Coming at a time when the whole history of the New Order regime was being opened up for public scrutiny, the May rapes could be linked to more obvious forms of state violence against women. Evidence began to come forward of systematic rapes of women by the military in Aceh, East Timor and Papua, all places where there had been long-standing armed resistance to rule from Jakarta and where women were raped as a means of intimidating society.[3] Human rights organisations like LBH-APIK had been documenting these cases during the New Order and trying, with little success, to focus state and international attention on them.

Making this connection was important to women activists, because it put the May rapes in a context that broadened it beyond that of the ethnic Chinese, thus extending empathy for rape victims generally and shifting the view of the perpetrators so that they were seen not as Muslim

---

[3] These reports included one (in *Kompas* 25 August 1998), in which the report from the investigation by the National Commission on Human Rights in Aceh showed there had been 102 rape cases there.

Indonesians persecuting the Chinese non-Muslim minority but as part of a wider process of intimidation of dissidents or minority groups. Women's groups made a special effort to foster solidarity among women for all rape victims and organised demonstrations of mutual support such as joint prayer meetings attended by people of different ethnic and religious groups.

The extended debate in the media about proving that rape occurred also allowed activists to embark on public education about the nature of rape as a crime, that is how it differed from other crimes because of the way it was treated by society and the obstacles this placed in the way of victims providing public testimony. The whole treatment of rape in Indonesia was put in question and the existing law criticised, particularly the light punishments so often meted out for rape.

Although the May rapes issue focussed primarily on Jakarta, it had reverberations well beyond the capital, because in far-flung towns in the archipelago groups were working on sexual violence. In West Timor, for instance, the legal aid organisation Justitia had been struggling to raise awareness of what it claims is a very high level of rape and domestic violence there, and in East Timor organisations were beginning to fight legal battles on military rape in East Timor. The publicity gained by the May rapes was built on elsewhere for local campaigns.

Publicity and awareness was one thing; state action was another. The influence of the military in preventing investigation of its role in state violence was readily apparent in the years of transition following the fall of the New Order. Although it was discredited in the eyes of the public, the military's cooperation was essential for the weak governments of these years. One early example was the lack of follow-up on the report of the Fact Finding Team, particularly in relation to allegations of military involvement in fomenting the May riots and rapes. The report was accepted and then ignored by the authorities. Various protests since that time have been in vain. Worse than that, the government responded angrily to efforts by the United Nations to make its own investigation into the May rapes. Radhika Coomaraswamy, a Special Rapporteur to the United Nations Human Rights Commission, was dispatched to Indonesia in November 1998. She reported back to the Commission in March 1999, confirming that there had indeed been mass rapes of Chinese-Indonesian women, although she was unable to ascertain exact numbers. Moreover, the army had rarely intervened to protect them, and the victims had subsequently received death threats to prevent them from laying charges. She also referred to state violence against women in regions where separatist movements were active (*Jakarta Post* 27 March 1999). The response of the Indonesian Government to the UN report was remarkably negative and defensive (Bianpoen 1999). By that time the May rapes issue had been eclipsed by the greater catastrophe of the East Timor killings.

To some extent the 1998 rapes case set the scene for the following years. The women's movement was galvanised into action on the issue of public violence against women, and society gained a better understanding of the impact of violence on women and the problems of documenting it. On the other hand, military involvement in violence against women complicated the state's response to the issue, leading to a failure of state agents to conform to government rhetoric of commitment to combatting such violence.

On-going violence at the end of the century: an ineffectual state

One of the striking features of public political discourse in Indonesia in 1998–9 was the prevalence of the word *teror*: people felt that terror was being spread by unknown elements for unknown ends. In subsequent years there was no relief. In 1998 attention had focussed on violence in Java, the centre of the movement to overthrow Suharto. In the following years in Indonesia there was no centre: violence erupted in different parts of the archipelago, every region with its own dynamics and momentum. The state and the women's movement struggled to respond.

The waves of violence that broke over the archipelago after the fall of Suharto originated in disputes that dated back decades or more, but the scale of the violence took everyone by surprise. In Aceh, East Timor and Papua, attempts to separate from the Republic gained momentum with the fall of Suharto. In the cases of Kalimantan, Maluku and central Sulawesi (Poso), pre-existing tension between ethnic and religious groups flared into violence on an unprecedented scale.

The government's responses to separatism were confused. The Habibie government surprised everyone in January 1999 by agreeing to allow a referendum in East Timor, the choice being between autonomy within Indonesia or independence. As a sign of how out of touch the government was with the East Timorese society, it continued up to the last to expect that the outcome of the referendum, held in September 1999, would be in favour of autonomy. From the time that the referendum was announced, the military in East Timor, who had been outraged at Habibie's decision, took steps to ensure that the populace would be intimidated into voting for autonomy. As is now only too well known, the months leading up to and the weeks following the referendum were marked by the most appalling violence by militias backed by the Indonesian Army. The overwhelming vote by East Timorese for independence was punished by a scorched-earth campaign by the militias.

Indonesia began to accept responsibility for terror in East Timor in 1999 when it received reports from the National Commission On Violence Against Women (reporting in May on the plight of refugees in East Timor) and from a Commission of Investigation into Human Rights Violations in East Timor. The latter, a government-appointed nine-member commission included one woman, the well-known-human rights activist Nursyahbani Kacasungkana, who ensured that cases of violence against women were well reported. They included torture and public sexual humiliation by the militia and army, enforced prostititution and rape (McDonald, Ball, Dunn et al. 2002).

After the 'loss' of East Timor, it was politically difficult for any Indonesian Government to treat separatist movements elsewhere in the archipelago with any degree of sympathy. Although President Abdurrahman Wahid personally showed understanding of the grievances of people in Irian Jaya (which he permitted to be renamed Papua) and Aceh, his policies were erratic and he lacked the strength to control the army, which was adamantly opposed to allowing these provinces to pull away from the nation. Early in this century, President Megawati took a strongly nationalist stance more in line with the military. The situation deteriorated in both provinces.

In Aceh, separatist sentiments had been fuelled by resentment at Jakarta's policies. Rich natural gas deposits began to be exploited there in the 1970s, but the revenue went to the central government or into the pockets of corrupt administrators. The Free Aceh Movement (Gerakan Aceh Merdeka – GAM) was formed in 1976 as an armed separatist movement, which in turn prompted a counter-insurgency campaign by the government. In 1991 Aceh was declared a Military Operations Region. Then followed a period of terror for the local population as thousands of guerillas and civilians were tortured, killed, abducted and detained without charge, and people were displaced from their villages. As soon as Suharto fell, NGOs and the Indonesian National Human Rights Commission began to publicise the atrocities of those years, which included hundreds of sexual assaults on women, plus imposing other huge burdens on them as widows and supporters of refugee families. After Suharto, it was hoped that a fresh start could be made, and indeed the Defence Minister and Commander-in-Chief of the Armed Forces, General Wiranto, visited Aceh in late 1998 and publicly apologised for the army's behaviour, announcing that military rule would be withdrawn. For at least two reasons this did not happen. Firstly, GAM was re-energised by the offer of a referendum to East Timor in early 1999 and became increasingly active.

Secondly, military economic interests were well-entrenched in Aceh, and the army was even more determined not to lose them when its businesses in East Timor were threatened and subsequently lost. In 1999 military operations escalated and were met with increasing violence from GAM forces. Sickened by this turn of events, amongst the Acehnese population support for a referendum grew, and most observers agreed that majority opinion was in favour of independence. A spiral of violence followed, lessened only by the signing of a cease-fire agreement in May 2000. Although peace talks continued, so did violence. Again, in December 2002, another cease-fire was signed, only to falter in the months afterwards, and military rule was reimposed in 2003.

Women have been badly affected by several aspects of the violence in Aceh. Individuals thought to be associated with GAM have been raped, sexually harassed and intimidated, as many cases documented by human-rights groups have shown. To make things worse, human-rights abuses are also practised by GAM forces, leaving the civilian population defenceless. In addition there is the plight of widows and fatherless families and tens of thousands of refugee women and children. As of 2003, with the Megawati government unwilling or unable to rein in the military, the prospects for Aceh continue to look bleak.

In many ways the situation in Papua resembled that of Aceh, although the origins of its separatist movement, the OPM (Organisasi Papua Merdeka – Papuan Independence Organisation), went back to the imposition of Indonesian rule on the territory in 1969. At that time the Dutch were forced by a United Nations decision to hand over the last piece of the Netherlands Indies to the Republic, rather than develop the colony as an independent state of West Papua as they had promised the local people. Like Aceh, Papua had great mineral wealth that was exploited by outsiders, and many local people lost land to mining companies and plantations. Immigration from elsewhere in the archipelago, encouraged by the state, threatened to swamp the local population. The military had been allowed a virtually free run in the province, leading to oppression and corruption. While the level of state violence and local resistance was lower than that in Aceh, in Papua too the independence of East Timor gave renewed hope to the OPM. Although governments since the New Order have tried to win over the OPM and GAM in Aceh through promises of Special Autonomy, they do not appear to have succeeded in gaining the trust of people rendered sceptical by long years of maltreatment, and the military have made their own moves to crack down on separatists. With the greater freedom of the post-Suharto years, local organisations in Papua began to document the effect of violence on women, recording rapes, abductions and maltreatment by the armed forces (Sanggenafu 2000).

Whereas the violence in Aceh, East Timor and Papua had a long history, the communal violence that erupted towards the end of the New Order and after it came as a shock to most people. Sporadic outbreaks of anti-Christian violence had occurred in Java, but far more horrific were the waves of fighting between Christians and Muslims in Maluku and Poso, and the attacks by Dayaks on Madurese settlers in Kalimantan. Analysts are still debating the causes of these conflicts, which appear to combine grievances by local people against loss of power and resources to outsiders during the New Order and some element of external provocation or at least failure by the security forces to prevent conflict. For instance in Maluku the extremist Islamic militia, Laskar Jihad, entered the fray against Christians. In the case of Kalimantan, hundreds of Madurese were massacred and tens of thousands forced to flee the province. Starting in largely Christian Ambon in 1999, but then spreading to other parts of the region, violence in Maluku was on an even larger scale and fed on itself as Christian and Muslim groups attacked one another in spirals of revenge. In the last two years of the century, five thousand people were killed and about half a million forced to flee from what appeared to be a campaign of 'religious cleansing' which the security forces have been unable or unwilling to control. Government authorities have so far (2003) been unable to broker a lasting peace in the region.

Women's responses

Since 1998, women's organisations have been inundated by incidents of public violence against women that call for their continuing attention and assistance. The main women's organisations had little or no representation in the regions where violence is now centred, and very few had been well informed or particularly interested in events in areas like East Timor or Papua in the past. Moreover, the nationalist tradition within the women's movement made it difficult for many to sympathise with separatist movements. As shown earlier in this chapter, the Indonesian women's movement was fully behind the government's campaign to 'win back' Irian Jaya; later, in 1975, it said nothing in criticism of the annexation of East Timor or the atrocities that followed. (In this respect women's organisations were no different from others, and in New Order Indonesia it was perilous to make such criticisms.) The fact that women in these provinces were mainly Christian or animist, mostly illiterate, rural and spoke little Indonesian, only compounded the problem (Wandita 1998).

Moreover, locally based women's groups able to confront issues of violence in the main trouble spots were formed only with the end of the New Order.

Relations between Jakarta-based organisations and Aceh were somewhat better. Indeed, the province's links with the rest of Indonesia had always been far better than with East Timor and Papua, not only because the Acehnese shared a religion (Islam) with the majority of Indonesians but also because the province had a proud place in Indonesian nationalist history as a centre of fierce anti-colonialism. Acehnese women's organisations taking up the cause of the victims of state violence had emerged in the 1990s and had good links with the Jakarta-based women's movement, although Jacqueline Siapno has commented incisively on the tensions involved in this relationship (Siapno 2002). As a result, Indonesian women's organisations were more committed and successful in publicising the case of Acehnese victims of violence and lobbying the government to rein in the military. In Jakarta the Solidarity Forum for Aceh, a coalition of twenty-seven NGOs, including Kalyanamitra, was formed to provide human-rights support for the Acehnese (Barber 2000: 64). Given the history of the New Order, however, it is still highly sensitive for national, Jakarta-based, largely Javanese organisations to become involved in Aceh.

In Aceh and East Timor, one of the major problems in dealing with violence is that there is no one clear source. While the government may be held responsible for the actions of the military, some troops are outside central command, militia have taken an active role with murky links to the army, the separatist fighters are not well disciplined, and there are undoubtedly gangster elements profiting from the breakdown in law and order. Women protesting against violence may easily make enemies in any or all of these quarters and attract retaliation.

This was most notably the case in Aceh where women's organisations have been active in trying to press for peace. The best-known of these organisations, Flower Aceh, was formed in 1989. In February 2000 along with other women's groups it held a four-day conference of Acehnese women in the main mosque of the capital city, Banda Aceh. Themes for discussion were women in Islamic *syariah* and *adat* law, women and social change in Aceh, the role of women in realising peace in Aceh, their access to economic and human resources, and the role of women in the political process and decision-making. Determinedly neutral in their approach, the organisers were nevertheless venturing into highly contentious areas. Almost four hundred women attended from all but one of the districts in Aceh despite the parlous security situation. Although organisers and some participants were threatened and discussions were plagued by divisions among the women as to the future status of Aceh, the conference resulted in an institution of Acehnese women to continue working for peace, for economic progress and to distinguish 'customs that damage women' (Kamaruzzaman 2000, *Jakarta Post* 27 February 2000).

Finally, communal violence has been equally hard to tackle for Indonesian women's organisations. Most of their work has been with the hundreds of thousands of internally displaced people, who are as usual predominantly women and children. As with separatist conflicts, it has proved almost impossible for women's organisations to operate in the areas where violence reigns.

In the 1990s, women's organisations around the archipelago became better at networking. Improved and cheaper transportation, greater affluence, and encouragement from foreign-aid sources led to a greater familiarity among leaders of these organisations, some of whom received training from other women's groups. With the even greater freedom provided by the end of the New Order and the explosion of violence across the nation, it became increasingly common for women's groups to work together on advocacy issues. One of the most outstanding examples is the coordination of activities associated with the International Day for the Eradication of Violence Against Women on 25 November, which has been celebrated with especial poignancy in recent years. Marches, demonstrations, petitions and artistic performances are common in all provinces.

Among women's organisations in Indonesia today there is a very strong yearning for peace. Unlike women's movements in many other countries, the Indonesian one has not had a strong tradition of identification with the peace movement. During previous conflicts in Indonesia, many women's organisations have had a partisan commitment to one side or the other, most notably during the Revolution of 1945–9. In recent years Indonesia's conflicts have been internecine and confused, with disastrous consequences for women and children. Many women's organisations wish not only to give non-partisan assistance to victims but also to play an active role in seeking peaceful outcomes. At its conference in 2000, the conservative women's federation Kowani took the search for peace as its main theme, and its president, speaking on behalf of the 30 million women she claimed to represent, even criticised the 'political elite' for its harsh policies that violated human rights and offered no solutions but only caused further suffering for women and children (*Media Indonesia* 18 August 2000). Kowani's preparedness to speak out on political matters is a sign that it has to respond to women's changing expectations of it; it is returning to its roots.

The normal fears of sexual violence that women have, the prevailing threats of domestic violence and rape that serve to discipline and limit women's mobility and behaviour, have been heightened by an awareness that disorder is now endemic and that their bodies may be used as ways in which men score points in the political cut and thrust that accompanies the transition in Indonesia. In the rising tension between indigenous Indonesians and the ethnic Chinese, and between extremist Muslims and non-Muslims, women may be singled out as a way of targeting and intimidating a particular ethnic or religious group: violence against their women sends a clear and effective message to the group as a whole that they should leave or submit to the demands of their antagonists. In the case of the ethnic Chinese this has already produced results: many Chinese have fled the country or at least tried to get their womenfolk out. The significance of violence as a rallying point for women was confirmed in the central place it held in the historic Women's Congress held in Yogyakarta in December 1998, when a wide range of women's organisations mentioned violence as one of their foremost concerns.

Women's groups have pointed out that what Indonesian women now face is not a choice between the security of the New Order and the anarchy of democracy. The New Order always harboured an element of arbitrariness and terror that made it dangerous not only for those who defied it but also for innocent bystanders who might be sacrificed to carry a message to those who resisted or might contemplate resistance. The current regime is also held to be complicit in violence if it makes no effort to provide protection for its female citizens.

Conclusion

As elsewhere in the world, in Indonesia sexual violence was not a recognised issue until the late twentieth century. It was certainly not a subject that Indonesian women's organisations thought it appropriate to discuss publicly, however important they felt it to be. Change in attitudes starting in the West slowly permeated some layers of Indonesian society, resisted at many points by elements within the state system (particularly the military) and amongst women themselves (notably in some religious circles).

Finally, the explosion of public violence accompanying the downfall of the New Order and the stumbling onset of democracy in Indonesia brought a horrifying range of social and state-sponsored kinds of violence to the fore, many of them with gendered aspects. Communal violence, military tortures, murders and rapes forced Indonesians to acknowledge the enormous potential for violence within their society. Women's organisations came together to speak on behalf of women victims and lobby for their protection and for ways to avoid violence. Of necessity, this issue, which used to have no place in the agendas of women's organisations, is now at the forefront. The state, too, has recognised this through setting up the National Commission on Violence Against Women.

The further question remains as to what can be done, and in particular what can be expected of the state and the women's movement. Both clearly have very important roles to play in influencing social attitudes towards sexual violence. Unless society condemns all kinds of sexual violence and shows understanding and sympathy towards its victims, its incidence will never be measured let alone tackled. At the level of the state, elements that perpetrate violence, notably the military and police, need to be controlled, and the judiciary needs to prosecute effectively crimes of sexual violence. In Indonesia, the advent of democracy has made it somewhat easier to begin this task, but on the other hand the breakdown of law and order that has accompanied the democratic transition has weakened the state's ability to live up to its rhetoric. This in turn lays more responsibility on civil society to control both itself and the state. Indonesia is in the throes of this dilemma, and the fledgling women's movement, now fully aware of the extent of the problem, is struggling to rally support against sexual violence.

In Indonesia today, the issue of sexual violence is inextricably interwined with that of armed conflict. In the past, the Indonesian women's movement has avoided issues of conflict and violence and has not explored the part that women can play in conflict management, reconciliation, creating a culture of peace and ensuring that women play a part in peace negotiations and new political arrangements that emerge at the end of conflict. Nothing in Indonesia's history has prepared women for this role. In previous armed conflicts, both national and regional, Indonesian women have been mobilised to support one side or the other but have played no role in bringing about peace or in preparation for the political reforms that might follow it. In the face of conflicts like those in East Timor, Aceh and Papua, these issues have now become quite pressing. It is not just a case of dealing with on-going violence against women but a question of how, in the post-conflict situation, women will deal with the aftermath of violence (resettlement of refugees, reconstruction of family life, welfare issues associated with orphans and widows) and ensure that new arrangements address the causes of conflict to prevent renewed violence (Mar'iyah 2000).

As part of the democratic reforms of the transition period, and at the instigation of the National Human Rights Commission, the People's Consultative Assembly in 1999 passed a law calling for the creation of a Truth and Reconciliation Commission on the lines of that held in South Africa. This would be an occasion for women to bring forward issues relating to state and community violence against women, to try to work through some of the causes and influence public opinion so as to avoid a repetition of some forms of violence. Unfortunately, due to the opposition of the military and the current state of confusion in Indonesia, it seems unlikely that such a commission will be held (Putri 2003).

What is critical about the issue of violence against women at present in Indonesia is that it brings into question the whole relationship of the state to women. The state is in crisis in Indonesia; it is unable to protect many of its citizens. Whereas a basic part of the definition of the state is its legitimate monopoly of violence, in Indonesia today it is widely recognised that the executive arm of government does not control violence even by its own military forces, let alone by forces in civil society. Nor can its judiciary and administration be relied upon to punish those who illegitimately use violence. This kind of Hobbesian world had its roots in the New Order, but now state control is far more tenuous. Women are amongst the most vulnerable under such conditions (Noerhadi 2000).

Various women's organisations have taken on the tasks of working with human-rights organisations to publicise violent acts, of pressuring the law enforcement agencies to act in accordance with the rule of law, of ensuring that political parties include policies against violence in their platforms and act upon them, and of liaising with international bodies to place pressure on the Indonesian Government to bring the military under control and enforce the rule of law. The prospects of fulfilling this agenda are distant. Political parties are barely beginning to be accountable to constituencies, the Indonesian Government struggles to find factions within the military to support it in bringing the armed forces under control, and with the current international preoccupation with the War on Terror, foreign-aid donors are likely to turn a blind eye to human-rights abuses in Indonesia so long as the government keeps Islamic extremism under control. At this stage Islamic extremism does not pose a serious threat of violence against women.

The achievement of women's organisations in recent years in Indonesia in relation to violence against women is to have gained public recognition of the issue and a more sophisticated understanding of it. This is an important step in a culture where such discussion was taboo.[4] However, the major failure is that in all the efforts for peace in Indonesia today,

---

[4] Sinta Nuriyah Abdurrahman Wahid, wife of the former President, in her preface to a book compiled by the women's crisis centre of Rifka Annisa, quoted Adrienne Rich: 'Where language and naming are power, Silence is oppression, is violence' (Annisa 2000: ix).

women play only a peripheral part. In negotiations being conducted in all the trouble spots in the archipelago, women are not represented. It points again to the weakness of women's organisations at the higher political level. Although they may be active in advocacy and in assistance to the victims of violence, they are not perceived by those in power as parties to the political process.

Conclusion

From a vantage point in the early twenty-first century (January 2004 to be precise), the conclusion to this book offers a place to reflect on the past and consider the future. Two main questions will be addressed here: What lessons from the last century can be learned that are relevant for today? How is the twenty-first century likely to differ from the previous one as far as relations between Indonesian women and the state are concerned? In addition some areas that require further research will be noted.

Cutting across the thematic approach taken in most chapters, this conclusion examines the past and future through the lens of a concept basic to the study of women and of development: empowerment.[1] It is assumed that the goal underlying the struggles of women's organisations to improve the position of women is to create an environment in which they can have more power over their own lives, to fulfil their own projects. Since women cannot really be empowered by someone else, what is meant here by 'empowering women' is that certain obstacles are removed from their path and they are given more encouragement to take charge of their lives. By referring to empowerment, I do not wish to imply that Indonesian women have been completely lacking in power, but rather that most groups desire more power in certain areas of their life at certain times, and some groups are obviously vulnerable.

The state in Indonesia has rarely claimed to try to empower women. The word was too threateningly political to use until the end of the century when international fashion and changing leaders in Indonesia saw the Ministry for Women's Role symbolically change its name to Ministry for Women's Empowerment. Even before this, however, the state has, inadvertently or advertently, taken many steps towards making women more autonomous.

---

[1] There is a growing literature on this topic. It includes Afshar (1998); Datta and Kornberg (2002), and Parpart, Rai and Staudt (2002).

Lessons from the past

Reviewing the twentieth century then, for lessons about the empowerment of Indonesian women, at least two questions arise. Firstly, in what
areas have (which) women been empowered by the actions of the women's
movement and the state? Secondly, in what areas have (which) women
failed to be empowered, or even been disempowered? Understanding the
reasons will lead us into a better appreciation of the prospects for empowerment in the present century.

Progress in empowerment

It is fitting that in education, the first area on which women's organisations
worked whole-heartedly with the state, most women have reaped the
rewards. Whereas at the start of the twentieth century the overwhelming
majority of Indonesian women (and men) were illiterate, by the end of
the century virtually all children received elementary schooling. At higher
levels girls still lag behind boys, but progress has been steady. Both the
women's movement and state have played important roles in expanding
educational opportunities for girls.

Access to schooling remains a burning issue in remote regions and
among the poorest groups where less headway has been made. Gender
subordination also still lingers in educational content and pedagogy. This
is beginning to be addressed, as is the over-centralisation and stultification
of schools that resulted from New Order policies. Unsuitable, poor education is disempowering, as the high drop-out rate shows. Much remains
to be done in this important area, since women still identify education as
a key issue in their lives. It is generally recognised that education is basic
to empowering women because of the ways in which it is connected to
women's self-esteem, to their access to knowledge and employment, and
to greater power within the family.

Most Indonesian women have benefited from greater equality in marriage during the twentieth century. For much of that time two main obstacles concerned the women's movement: early marriage and the lack of
legal security for women within marriage. In particular the Islamic marriage code was a matter for dispute since according to prevailing Indonesian practice it offered too little protection for women in relation to age
of marriage, polygamy and divorce. While the women's movement was
active on this issue, the state was reluctant to tackle it. Not only could
such intervention be seen as an attack on male privilege but it would
certainly entail the wrath of organised Islam, which has seen family law

as the last bastion of Islamic law left by colonial rule. Furthermore, the women's movement was divided by religion on this issue.

Despite such obstacles, great change has occurred, in favour of women. The age of marriage rose considerably across the century. Finally in 1974 a uniform Marriage Law was achieved: monogamy became the official norm, divorce was made easier for women and more difficult for men and a minimum age for marriage was stipulated. The state appointed women as judges in religious courts. Changes in marriage patterns are as much a result of socioeconomic and attitudinal change as of legislation, which is still flouted in some areas. Both the women's movement and broader forces within Indonesian society, supported by the state, have contributed to the trends that have strengthened women's marital position. The willingness of authorities in some areas to bend the law in favour of men indicates that further work remains to be done.

Impediments to equal citizenship between men and women were progressively overcome in the twentieth century. In the early decades of this campaign, the Indonesian women's movement was influenced by Dutch suffragists and supported by democratically oriented male nationalists in its pursuit of women's rights. At independence, the Indonesian Constitution recognised equality of citizenship. Because the state has been authoritarian for most of the century, however, neither women nor men were able to enjoy citizenship rights for much of the time. Only in the 1950s and since the late 1990s have women been in a position to make real use of the vote. Some elements within the Indonesian women's movement campaigned strongly in the late twentieth century for women's rights and were supported in this campaign by the international women's movement. Male-dominated political parties and the Islamic movement have posed further hindrances to women seeking to exercise their political rights, as was made startlingly obvious by the debate about women's right to be president at the end of the century. Socioeconomic position also affects the practice of citizenship: so far the main beneficiaries of citizenship rights have been elite women, while most women are either unaware of their rights or unable to exercise them.

Most women have benefited from state intervention to assist them to control conception. Birth control gained state support from the New Order regime, which implemented a far-reaching family-planning programme assisted by foreign aid. Islamic leaders' support for the programme was skilfully negotiated by the state, which also found the cooperation of the women's movement important in extending information and services to women in villages and poor areas. Assisted by the availability of cheap and reliable contraception, the birth-rate halved in the late twentieth century, creating less drain on women's health and resources.

Where empowerment is still lacking

Most Indonesian women are overworked and underpaid, in employment that receives little or no legal protection. In the twentieth century this situation won little attention from either the women's movement or the state, apart from a few scattered cases that generated great publicity, like migrant labour. The notion of *kodrat*, which devalues women's contribution in the workforce by defining women's destiny as motherhood, has been a hindrance to women struggling for recognition as workers. There has also been pressure on the state from business (both domestic and foreign) to keep wages and conditions down. Such protective laws as there are have achieved little, because the economic and political situation is adverse for poor women workers. They share this dilemma with most male workers, but women (along with children) are at the bottom of the heap. Whereas for a small stratum of women at the top, work is a source of good income and empowerment, for most it is necessary for survival but otherwise burdensome. Indirectly the New Order state did much to promote economic growth that led to an expansion of formal employment for women, most of whom previously worked outside that sector. But women still predominate amongst the most precariously employed and worst paid.

One reason why the women's movement has been slow to take up issues related to women's economic exploitation is its dominance by better-educated, wealthier, urban women from a limited number of more 'developed' regions. The influence of the state on the women's movement has also been important. Both the colonial state and the New Order Government, which between them ruled Indonesia for most of the twentieth century, opposed the spread of organisations based on 'the masses' as too politically threatening, unless they were overtly apolitical religious groups. The women's organisations that began to take up workers' causes in the 1980s and 1990s were small groups run by well-educated young women, often with foreign funding. Unlike Gerwani in the 1950s, they have been unable to build a mass base and thus gain political leverage.

Women's health has improved over the century but remains problematic amongst the vast bulk of women, who suffer from high levels of anaemia, maternal mortality, abortions and reproductive tract infections. The family-planning programme disregarded health needs. Women's health did not receive much attention from the women's movement or the state until the late twentieth century, when it was propelled forward by international institutions. Why women are so slow to express their own health needs is an interesting question. Among poor women there is a tendency to be ignorant of health alternatives and to believe that it is more important for them to increase family income. Because Indonesia has never been a welfare state, people have also had low expectations of the state as far as health provision is concerned, depending rather on traditional healers and medicines. Furthermore, women's health problems were regarded as too close to sexual matters to be discussed publicly. Islamic opposition to legalising abortion or allowing sex education for young unmarried people has also been an obstacle to improving women's health. Since the spread of family planning and campaigns on reproductive health, however, there is now a greater willingness to prioritise women's health.

Until the end of the twentieth century, violence against women at domestic and social levels received almost no attention from the women's movement or state. It was not a matter for public discussion and no data was collected. Finally, with international backing and in response to adverse events in Indonesia it became possible, even urgent, to discuss such matters. The rape of Chinese Indonesian women in May 1998 exposed the vulnerability of some groups of women and legitimated widespread analysis of the causes and consequences of violence in Indonesia, including its gendered nature. Throughout the century, outbreaks of public violence also caused untold suffering for women in some regions like Aceh, East Timor and Papua, but these could not be confronted until the fall of the New Order. Then the state was so weak it could not enforce law and order in many areas. The women's movement is only just beginning to tackle the gendered nature of public violence, while still campaigning for attention to domestic abuse of women. Widespread violence at the close of the century has gone along with increased willingness to acknowledge it, including on the part of state, as symbolised by its creation in 1998 of the National Commission Against Violence Towards Women.

To sum up the argument of this book, there has been a coincidence of interests between the state and the Indonesian women's movement on a number of matters. Often, however, women's organisations are dissatisfied with the ways in which governments formulate and implement policies intended to address problems they have identified. At any one time, the obstacles facing women may include state gender ideology, the Islamic movement, economic interests and lack of resources. The women's movement itself has often lacked a strong basis in society and has been fragmented. Parts of it have been subject to cooption by the state in ways that weaken its ability to represent the full scope of women's interests. Increasingly, external forces have been an important source of innovation in the agenda concerning women, often proving a useful ally for the women's movement.

The power of the state and the women's movement have waxed and waned over the last century. When the state is weak, women have more freedom to organise, but they are obliged to depend more on their own resources and have less incentive to coordinate their efforts. Since the end of the century this situation has been glaringly obvious, as will be discussed below. From the point of view of achieving the movement's aims, there are advantages in women pursuing their concerns in ways that do not directly involve the state. Much can be done at the grass-roots level, through economic, social and cultural activism, to improve women's lives. Nevertheless, there will always be a need to influence state policies, at the very least to shelter women from some of their worst effects.

A note on areas requiring further research

Before examining future directions, it is worth noting the gaps in this book which limit the conclusions reached. As mentioned at the outset, study of the history of the Indonesian women's movement is still in its infancy and on many topics much research remains to be done.

Most of what has been written deals with Java and in particular with Jakarta-based organisations. An enormous amount of work is still to be done on the diversity of women's interests and organisations in the regions, particularly those in more remote areas. Even the research already done in some regions, like the Minahasa, has still to be absorbed into the national story of Indonesian women. This work is essential to counteract the tendency of writers to generalise from the Javanese experience.

Similarly, the study of Islamic women's organisations is underdeveloped. For decades these organisations maintained a low profile while working independently at the grass-roots level. They did not wish to be associated with high-level politics or to become publicly involved in debates that might put them in the position of criticising their 'father' organisations like Muhammadiyah and NU. Yet it is clear from several accounts that some interesting manoeuvres were occurring behind the scenes, as noted in the chapter on polygamy in this book. The full story is yet to be told. Moreover, in recent years new young women's Islamic groups have emerged as players within the women's movement. Their activities have been mentioned in chapters on Motherhood and Violence. What these groups show about changes within Islam on gender issues and how they have developed a more independent voice deserves further investigation, especially since Islamic women's organisations have the longest history of 'membership' organisations working among a wide range of women: they are in a good position to both reflect and influence the millions of women who identify themselves predominantly as Muslims. In addition to the well-established 'membership' women's organisations within Islam, there are also new liberal Islamic groups like Rahima, a centre for training and information on Islam and women's rights, directed by Farha Ciciek. It has been a forum not only for young women but also for *kiai* espousing standpoints that would never have been voiced twenty years ago, such as opposition to rape in marriage.

In researching this book, I have been struck by the lack of documentation on women's *experience* of some of the important issues discussed, notably in relation to polygamy. Considering how crucial this issue has been within the women's movement and in its relations with the state, it is surprising how little evidence there is of the impact of polygamy on women's lives and how this has changed over time. Similarly the high level of divorce in Indonesia and its current decline has received little attention as far as its effect on women's lives is concerned.

A fruitful area of research will be the role of the Ministry of Women's Role/Empowerment in Indonesia since 1978. We have only glimpses of the Ministers who held this position and little knowledge about the operations of the Ministry and its success or otherwise in raising women's issues within the Cabinet and in implementing policies in relation to women in conjunction with other departments. Obviously some ministers have been outstanding (notably Khofifah Parawansa) while others have been nonentities, but no detailed study has been made of the workings of the Ministry. Such a study would add greatly to our understanding of the salience of gender issues within the state apparatus and the way in which this Ministry compares with similar offices of women's affairs in other countries.

Looking to the future

Reviewing the recent past has enabled us to pinpoint some sources for and obstacles to the empowerment of Indonesian women. Some of these are ambivalent: sometimes, for instance, the women's movement has been a force behind favourable change for all women; sometimes it has offered no assistance at all, or even been a hindrance, as in confronting women's economic exploitation. Likewise the Islamic movement in Indonesia has been very supportive of some aspects of women's empowerment (such as family planning), once initial opposition dissipated. Looking at the present century, one can speculate about the probable sources of further empowerment of (which) women, and where the obstacles are likely to be. In this way we can trace the probable continuities and changes since the twentieth century. I would nominate the following forces as likely to be critical for women's empowerment. None of them has predictable outcomes.

Democratisation. The return of democracy to Indonesia since 1998 has offered great opportunities for women to place their issues on the public agenda. During the New Order there was a tendency to feel that unless the state gave its imprimatur, nothing could be achieved. With a weaker state, people are left more to their own devices. The women's movement is certainly determined to take advantage of these opportunities but is also aware of the great obstacles facing women. Events have moved very fast and women are behind in the battle to be heard by the male-dominated parties. Women who have already had political experience, like Khofifah Parawansa, are best placed to take advantage of political opportunities. In the 1999 election the lack of women candidates and the resulting decline in the number of women in parliament caused widespread concern. Even the election of Megawati as president in 2001, while a symbolic victory for women, offered little prospect of progress since she showed no interest in promoting women or their concerns.

The women's movement has been working to overcome the hurdles confronting women in the new democracy. Their campaign for quotas for women candidates has already born fruit: in 2003 the parliament passed a new electoral law that requires at least 30 per cent of candidates standing for legislatures be female, starting with the 2004 elections. This is a tremendous challenge to women to stand for election, although the electoral system still leaves great power in the hands of political parties to manipulate the candidacy requirements. Moreover, the legislation applies no sanctions to parties that do not comply, causing cynicism in some quarters. Women's organisations recognise that strenuous efforts are needed in the political education of both men and women, and to get leading women to stand for election.

As a result of democratisation, and contributing to it, women's organisations have proliferated around the country, giving voice to women in more neglected, remote and troubled areas. So far, however, these organisations lack individual and united strength, due to their weak support base. The women's federation, Kowani, has been discredited by its ties to the New Order, and no umbrella body covering most of the new organisations has yet emerged to replace it. It is probably too soon for this to happen, given the great diversity of women represented in the movement now and the legacy of resentment against Jakarta felt in many regions. To some extent this deficiency is balanced by coalitions and networking activities amongst organisations, but it is difficult for governments and political parties to relate to loose networks. The women's movement is aware of the need to learn how to lobby political parties more effectively and to encourage the process of policy-making within the parties that have so far relied more on personalities than on platforms for their appeal. To gain greater political clout, the women's movement will need to build its base and become better coordinated in its relations with governments and political parties. This is far easier said than done.

The most disappointing aspect of democratisation as it is experienced in Indonesia is that the state is weak, often unable to protect women from violence or to enforce laws. Fragmentation within the state and unstable governments are likely to make for the unreliability of government in Jakarta. Elements in the military periodically get out of hand, and the judiciary and bureaucracy are compromised by corruption.

Decentralisation. The Autonomy Law introduced by Habibie has been implemented since 2000, devolving more power to the district level in a reversal of the strong centralisation of the Indonesian state since the 1960s. It is a two-edged sword. While it offers women more spaces to be politically active, closer to home, some women find themselves discriminated against in the current resurgence of local identities and ethnonationalisms. Some reinvigorated local governments are using their power to place restrictions on women in the name of morality and tradition. For instance, there has been a trend in some places towards adopting regulations labelled '*anti maksiat*' (against immorality). Thus in Jember (East Java) a night curfew has been placed on women to keep them off the streets (*Radar Jember* 12 August 2002). Local autonomy has the ability to give women more access to decision-making but, in the present situation, it seems mainly to empower local male-dominated elites who may be even more patriarchal than the central government. It becomes necessary to fight gender battles at all levels. As with all arrangements for decentralisation, women may well encounter the old problem of confused accountability: different levels of government are likely to deny responsibility on some women's issues that they do not wish to deal with.

Globalisation is another force about which women feel ambivalent. The impact of global economic movements may be detrimental to women, as shown by the Asian financial crisis of 1997: Indonesian women were distressed by loss of employment and reduction in government subsidies and welfare spending. International Monetary Fund requirements to cut government subsidies have led to repeated demonstrations supported by some women's groups. On the other hand, Indonesian manufacturing, a major employer of women, has in the past been buoyed by foreign investment, rising levels of world trade and opening up of export markets. Female migrant labour, discussed in Chapter 7, seems likely to continue to grow, with all its attendant political problems. Sex trafficking is gaining increasing attention.

The international women's movement, one of the global forces impinging on Indonesia, has always spurred the state and the women's movement to add new issues to their agendas. This may not always be helpful
if fashions in funding cause discontinuity and neglect of basic underlying
problems of poor women.

As an example of an issue raised at the global level, sexual choice is
being advanced as a human right. If such a notion makes inroads in
Indonesia, it is likely to lead to re-thinking of simple gender categories in
Indonesia, undermining still further the notion of *kodrat*, or a fixed destiny
for women. Lesbianism has so far failed to surface as an issue in Indonesia
(see Chapter 6). At some stage in the future growing identification with
lesbianism, already being observed in a small way in middle-class circles,
may lead to new agendas within the women's movement and revision of
some notions about marriage and motherhood. The current decline in
marriage and child-bearing levels will ease the acceptance of lesbianism.

A likely counter-force to such a global influence is Islam, another agent
within globalisation. Historically, Indonesia has been subjected to waves
of influence from the Middle East. Today Islam is by no means a coherent
force: there are battles between moderate Islam and Middle-Eastern style
fundamentalism. Women are at the centre of the hostilities, that break out
over issues like abortion, dress, sex education, intermarriage with non-
Muslims, *kodrat*, lesbianism and marital rape.

Indonesia has always had a secular state that has been concerned about
Islam as source of political opposition. A new dimension has now been
revealed with the current global terrorism scare. This may well have very
important repercussions for women's relations with the state, since the
state may trade women's freedoms for Islamic support in its efforts to
repress terrorism. Despite liberal developments within Islam, so strongly
exemplified by President Wahid, it is unclear how deeply rooted such attitudes are in Indonesia. On the other hand, extremist groups have emerged
and are likely to be strengthened by international resentment of the rising power of the United States. Extremist Islamic groups have gained
support in recent years, and governments have been forced to negotiate with some of them or to turn a blind eye. In an effort to win over
the rebellious Acehnese, the central government permitted the province
to introduce *syariah* law. One of their first moves was to decree that
'proper Muslim attire for women' (covering everything except their face,
hands and feet) would be required in all urban areas of Aceh, enforced
by the police (*Jakarta Post* 5 March 2002). Similarly, one of President
Megawati's efforts to win Islamic party support involved appointing a
conservative Muslim to the position of Minister of Justice. In 2003 he proceeded to draft a criminal code bill, which involved, among other things,

punishment for extra-marital sex and homosexuality. Although unlikely to get through the legislature, the bill has certainly alarmed many groups, including women's organisations.

The women's movement is weak in relation to the state in Indonesia. It relies quite heavily on a degree of well-established respect for women that is part of the country's Southeast Asian heritage, marking the region off from other parts of Asia where women have suffered far worse indignities and injustice. International support has also been critical for feminist groups in recent years. Many trends in recent history have favoured Indonesian women's empowerment, but there is no room for complacency about the future. Indonesian women leaders are well aware that their movement will need to strengthen its membership base and learn to operate the political system to its benefit in order to face the uncertainties of the years ahead.

References

Abdullah, T. 1971. *Schools and Politics: The Kaum Muda Movement in West Sumatra (1927–1933)*. Ithaca: Cornell Modern Indonesia Project

1993. 'Kilasan Sejarah Pergerakan Wanita Islam di Indonesia', in L. M. Marcoes-Natsir and J. H. Meuleman (eds.), *Wanita Islam Indonesia dalam Kajian Tekstual dan Kontekstual*. Jakarta: INIS

Achmad, J. 1999. *Hollow Development: The Politics of Health in Soeharto's Indonesia*. Canberra: Australian National University

Acting Adviser for Native Affairs. 1921. Letter from Acting Adviser for Native Affairs, 9/8/1921. Afschrift behoorende bij den missive van de Wd. Adviseur voor Inlandsche Zaken dd. 14/6/1923 No. E/172 Geheim, Mailrapport 789x/21. The Hague: Netherlands National Archives

Adfdol. 1979. *Effectiveness of the Minimum Marriage Age Law in Bangkalan*. Singapore: Institute of Southeast Asian Studies

Adrina, K. Purwandari, N. K. E. Triwijati et al. 1998. *Hak-Hak Reproduksi Perempuan yang Terpasung*. Jakarta: Pustaka Sinar Harapan

Adviser for Native Affairs. 1922. Letter from Adviser for Native Affairs to Director for Civil Service, 9/1/1922, Afschrift behoorende bij missive van de Wd. Adviseur voor Inlandsche Zaken dd. 14/6/1923 No. E/172 Geheim. The Hague: Netherlands National Archives

1923. Letter from Adviser for Native Affairs to Director of Justice, 14/6/1923, No. E/172 Geheim, overgelegd bij Mailrapport No. 1114x/25. The Hague: Netherlands National Archives

1930. Letter from Adviser for Native Affairs (Gobee) to Governor-General, 30/8/1930 No. 1473/F-3, overgelegd bij Mailrapport No. 1114x/25. The Hague: Netherlands National Archives

1932. Letter from Adviser for Native Affairs (Gobee) to Governor-General, 9/5/1932 No. 698/F-3, overgelegd bij Mailrapport No. 1114x/25. The Hague: Netherlands National Archives

Afshar, H. (ed.) 1998. *Women and Empowerment: Illustrations from the Third World*. New York: St Martin's

'Aisjijah. 1939. *Pemandangan Terhadap Pergerakan Kaoem Iboe Oemoemnja dan 'Aisjijah Choesoesnja*. Djokjakarta: Soeara 'Aisjijah

Aj-Jahrani, M. 1997. *Poligami dari Berbagai Persepsi*. Jakarta: Gema Insani Press

Algemeene Jaarvergadering. 1934. 'Algemeene Jaarvergadering gehouden te Batavia-C. op 23 Maart '34'. *Maandblad van de Vereeniging voor Vrouwenrechten in Nederlandsch-Indie* 8(7): 1–6

Al-Haq, S. A. J. 1996. *Kedokteran dan Masalah Kewanitaan*. Solo: Khazanah Ilmu

Al-Utsaimin, M. S. 1996. *Masalah Darah Wanita*. Jakarta: Gema Insani Press

Amnesty International. 2001. *Crimes of Hate, Conspiracy of Silence*. London: Amnesty International

Andriyani, N. 1994. 'Hak Asasi Perempuan Dalam Orde Baru', in *Demokrasi Antara Represi dan Resistensi: Catatan Keadaan Hak Asasi Manusia di Indonesia 1993*. Jakarta: Yayasan Lembaga Bantuan Hukum Indonesia

1996. 'The myth of the effective little NGO'. *Inside Indonesia* (46): 22–3

Angelino, P. D. K. 1931. *Batikrapport Deel II Midden-Java*. Weltevreden: Landsdrukkerij

Annisa, R. 2000. *Ketika Ranting Patah*. Yogyakarta: SKH Kedaulatan Rakyat and Rifka Annisa Women's Crisis Centre

Atkinson, J. M. and S. Errington (eds.). 1990. *Power and Difference: Gender in Island Southeast Asia*. Stanford: Stanford University Press

Baidlowi, A. H. 1993. 'Profil Organisasi Wanita Islam: Studi Kasus Muslimat NU', in L. Marcoes-Natsir and J. H. Meuleman (eds.), *Wanita Islam Indonesia dalam Kajian Tekstual dan Kontekstual*. Jakarta: INIS

Barber, B. R. 1984. *Strong Democracy: Participatory Politics for a New Age*. Berkeley: University of California Press

Barber, R. (ed.) 2000. *Aceh: The Untold Story*. Bangkok: Asian Forum for Human Rights and Development and Support Committee for Human Rights in Aceh

Baried, B. 1990. 'Menciptakan lapangan kerja bagi kaum wanita'. *Kedaulatan Rakyat*. 15 December

BBPIP. 1939. *Boekoe Peringatan Konferensi Badan Perlindoengan Perempoean Indonesia dalam Perkawinan (BBPIP) 21–23 Juli 1939 di Mataram-Jogjakarta*. Jogjakarta: BBPIP

Bemmelen, S. van. 1982. 'Enkele aspecten van het onderwijs aan Indonesische meisjes, 1900–1940'. PhD dissertation, Utrecht University

Berita. 1931. 'Berita dari Pengoeroes Besar I.S'. *Sedar* 2(4): 5–6

Berninghausen, J. and B. Kerstan. 1992. *Forging New Paths: Feminist Social Methodology and Rural Women in Java*. London: Zed Books

Bianpoen, C. 1998. 'Dynamic plurality marks first congress in post-Suharto era'. *Indonesian Observer*. 22 December

1999. 'Indonesian Government rejects U.N. report on violence against women in Indonesia'. *Indonesian Observer*. 9 May

2000. 'The family welfare movement: a blessing or a burden?', in M. Oey-Gardiner and C. Bianpoen (eds.), *Indonesian Women: The Journey Continues*. Canberra: Australian National University

Binawas, D. 1995. 'Kebijakan dan pengawasan pemerintah terhadap pelaksanaan perundangan perlindungan pekerja wanita', in A. Sunarijati (ed.), *Pekerja Wanita, Peran Ganda dan Persamaan Hak*. Jakarta: Lembaga Wanita, Remaja dan Anak DPP-SPSI and Friedrich-Ebert-Stiftung

Blackburn, S. 1997. 'Western Feminists Observe Asian Women: An Example from the Dutch East Indies', in J. G. Taylor (ed.), *Women Creating Indonesia: The First Fifty Years*. Clayton: Monash Asia Institute

1999a. 'Winning the vote for women in Indonesia'. *Australian Feminist Studies* 14: 207–18

1999b. 'The 1999 general election in Indonesia: where were the women?', in
  S. Blackburn (ed.), *Pemilu: The 1999 Indonesian Election*. Clayton: Monash
  Asia Institute
1999c. 'Women and citizenship in Indonesia'. *Australian Journal of Political
  Science* 34(2): 189–204
2000. 'Political relations among women in a multiracial city: colonial Batavia
  in the twentieth century', in K. Grijns and P. Nas (eds.), *Jakarta-Batavia:
  Socio-cultural Essays*. Leiden: KITLV Press
2002. 'Indonesian Islamic women enter the political arena'. *Kultur: The Indonesian Journal for Muslim Cultures* 2(2): 21–46
Blackburn, S. and S. Bessell. 1997. 'Marriageable age: political debates on early
  marriage in twentieth century Indonesia'. *Indonesia* (63): 107–41
Blackwood, E. 1999. '*Tombois* in West Sumatra: constructing masculinity and
  erotic desire', in E. Blackwood and S. E. Wieringa (eds.), *Same-Sex Relations
  and Female Desires: Transgender Practices Across Cultures*. New York: Columbia
  University Press
Boerhan, D. 1941. 'Dewan Alam Minangkabau menolak kaoem Iboe?' *Isteri
  Indonesia* 5(3): 4–6
Boetzelaer, E. O. van.1933. 'Kroniek'. *Koloniale Studien* 1930(1): 321–4
Bourchier, D. 1994. 'Introduction', in D. Bourchier (ed.), *Indonesia's Emerging
  Proletariat: Workers and their Struggles*. Clayton: Monash University
Bowen, J. R. 2003. *Islam, Law and Equality in Indonesia*. Cambridge: CUP
Branson, J. and D. Miller 1992. 'Schooling and the imperial transformation
  of gender: a post-structuralist approach to the study of schooling in Bali,
  Indonesia', in R. J. Burns and A. R. Welch (eds.), *Contemporary Perspectives
  in Comparative Education*. New York: Garland Publishing
Brenner, S. 1995. 'Why women rule the roost: rethinking Javanese ideologies
  of gender and self-control', in A. Ong and M. G. Peletz (eds.), *Bewitch-
  ing Women, Pious Men: Gender and Body Politics in Southeast Asia*. Berkeley:
  University of California Press
1996. 'Reconstructing self and society: Javanese Muslim women and the veil'.
  American Ethnologist 23(4): 673–97
1999. 'On the public intimacy of the New Order: images of women in the
  popular print media'. *Indonesia* (67): 13–37
Bright, J. 1999. 'Who is co-opting whom? Historical perspectives on the fam-
  ily planning policy in Indonesia'. Paper presented at Association of Asian
  Studies Conference, USA
Brown, C. 1981. 'Sukarno on the role of women in the nationalist movement'.
  Review of Indonesian and Malayan Affairs 15(1): 68–92
Buchori, B. and I. Soenarto. 2000. 'Dharma Wanita: an asset or a curse?' in
  M. Oey-Gardiner and C. Bianpoen (eds.), *Indonesian Women: The Journey
  Continues*. Canberra: Australian National University
Budianta, M. 2001. 'Transformasi gerakan perempuan di Indonesia', in
  J. Oetama (ed.), *Demokrasi, Kekerasan, Disintegrasi – Merangsang Pemikiran
  Ulang*. Jakarta: Kompas
Budiardjo, M. 1997. Interview by Elizabeth Martyn. Jakarta
Buku Peringatan. 1958. *Buku Peringatan 30 Tahun Kesatuan Pergerakan Wanita
  Indonesia, 22 Des., 1928–22 Des., 1958*. Djakarta: Pertjetakan Negara

Butt, S. 1999. 'Polygamy and mixed marriage in Indonesia: the application of the marriage law in the courts', in T. Lindsey (ed.), *Indonesia: Law and Society*. Sydney: Federation Press.

Cammack, M. 1997. 'Indonesia's 1989 Judicature Act: Islamization of Indonesia or Indonesianization of Islam?' *Indonesia* 63: 143–68

Chan, Y.-W. F.1995. 'Feminist and scholar: the student days of Dr Thung Sin Nio in the Netherlands'. Paper delivered at the Colloquium on The Chinese Diaspora in Europe, Paris, 20–1 January

Condronagoro, R. T. (ed.) 1979. *Riwayat Laskar Putri Indonesia di Surakarta*. Solo: Wirjowitono

Congres Perempoean. 1929. *Congres Perempoean Indonesia jang Pertama, 22–25 December 1928 di Mataram*. Djokjakarta: Administratie 'Isteri'

Cooley, L. 1992. 'Maintaining Rukun for Javanese Households and the State', in S. v. Bemmelen, M. Djajadiningrat-Nieuwenhuis, E. Locher-Scholten and E. Touwen-Bouwsma (eds.), *Women and Mediation in Indonesia*. Dordrecht: KITLV and Foris Publication

Danilah, S. 1950. 'Penderitaan wanita'. *Karya* 4(8): 23–5

Datta, R. and J. Kornberg (eds.). 2002. *Women in Developing Countries: Assessing Strategies for Empowerment*. Boulder: Lynne Rienner

De Inheemsche Vrouwenbeweging. 1932. *De Inheemsche Vrouwenbeweging in Nederlandsch-Indie en het aandeel daarin van het Inheemsche meisje*. Batavia: Landsdrukkerij

Dekker, D. 1914. 'R.A. Siti Soendari'. *De Indier* 1(30): 49–51

Department of Colonies. 1932. *Departemen van Kolonien, 's-Gravenhage, 27/9/32 No. 11/97 aan Gouverneur-Generaal de Jonge*. *Archief Ministerie van Kolonien, box A55, dossier A7008*. The Hague: Netherlands National Archives

Department of Justice. 1932. *Departemen van Justitie (Dir. Schrieke) aan Gouverneur-Generaal de Jonge, 14/11/32*. The Hague: Netherlands National Archives

1936. *Departemen van Justitie (Dr K. L. J. Enthoven) aan Gouverneur-Generaal de Jonge, 14/11/32*. The Hague: Netherlands National Archives

Deventer, C. T. van. 1915. *Correspondence. Archief Vereeniging Kartinifonds*, The Hague: Netherlands National Archives

Dewantara, K. H. 1967. *Karya Ki Hadjar Dewantara*. Jogjakarta: Madjelis-Luhur Persatuan Taman Siswa

Director of Justice. 1923. *Letter from Director of Justice to Adviser for Native Affairs, 31/5/1923, Overgelegd bij Mailrapport No. 789x/21*. The Hague: Netherlands National Archives

Djaja, T. 1980. *Rohana Kudus: Riwayat Hidup dan Perjuangannya*. Jakarta: Mutiara

Djajadiningrat-Nieuwenhuis, M. 1987. 'Ibuism and priyayization: path to power?' in E. Locher-Scholten and A. Niehof (eds.), *Indonesian Women in Focus*. Dordrecht: Foris Publications

Djawas, A. A. 1996. *Dilema Wanita Karier (menuju keluarga sakinah)*. Yogyakarta: Penerbit Ababil

Djohan, B. and S. Adam 1977. *Di Tangan Wanita . . .* Jakarta: Yayasan Idayu

Djohan, E., R. Indrawasih, M. Adenam et al. 1993. 'The attitudes of health providers towards abortion in Indonesia'. *Reproductive Health Matters* 2: 32–40

Djojopoespito, S. 1940. *Buiten het Gareel*. Utrecht: Uitgeversmaatschappij W. de Haan NV

Douglas, S. A. 1980. 'Women in Indonesian politics: the myth of functional interest', in S. A. Chipp and J. J. Green (eds.), *Asian Women in Transition*. University Park: Pennsylvania State University Press

Dowling, N. H. 1994. 'O Great Goddess'. *Indonesia Circle* (62): 70–82

Dwiyanto, A. and M. Darwin (eds.), 1996. *Seksualitas, Kesehatan Reproduksi, dan Ketimpangan Gender: Implemetasi Kesepakatan Konferensi Kependudukan Kairo bagi Indonesia*. Jakarta: Pustaka Sinar Harapan bekerja sama dengan Pusat Penelitian Kependudukan Universitas Gadjah Mada dan The Ford Foundation

Dzuhayatin, S. R. 2001. 'Gender and pluralism in Indonesia', in R. W. Hefner (ed.), *The Politics of Multiculturalism: Pluralism and Citizenship in Malaysia, Singapore and Indonesia*. Honolulu: University of Hawai'i Press

Eerste Koloniaal Onderwijscongres. 1916. *Eerste Koloniaal Onderwijscongres, Stenografisch Verslag*.'s-Gravenhage

Eldridge, P. J. 1995. *Non-Government Organizations and Democratic Participation in Indonesia*. Kuala Lumpur: Oxford University Press

Elliot, J. 1997. 'Equality? The influence of legislation and notions of gender on the position of women wage workers in the economy: Indonesia 1950–58', in J. G. Taylor (ed.), *Women Creating Indonesia: The First Fifty Years*. Clayton: Monash Asia Institute

Feillard, A. 1996. 'The emergence of a Muslim feminist movement in the intellectual elite in Indonesia'. Paper presented at Second Eurames Conference, Aix-en-Provence. 4–7 July

Feillard, A. and L. Marcoes 1998. 'Female circumcision in Indonesia: to "Islamize" in ceremony or secrecy'. *Archipel* (56): 337–67

Forbes, G. 1979. 'Women and modernity: the issue of child marriage in India'. *Women's Studies International Quarterly* 2: 407–19

1996. *Women in Modern India*. Cambridge: Cambridge University Press

Ford, M. 2002. 'Whatever it takes'. *Inside Indonesia* (69): 12–13

Frederick, W. H. 2002. 'Shadows of an unseen hand: some patterns of violence in the Indonesian revolution, 1945–1949', in F. Colombijn and J. T. Lindblad (eds.), *Roots of Violence in Indonesia*. Leiden: KITLV Press

Furnivall, J. S. 1939. *Netherlands India*. Cambridge: Cambridge University Press

Gaboengan Politik Indonesia. 1939. *Parlement Indonesia!* Djakarta: Gaboengan Politik Indonesia

Gatra 1998. 'Pemerkosaan massal: Memang ada konspirasi'. 29 August

Gayatri, B. J. D. 1996. 'Indonesian lesbians writing their own script: issues of feminism and sexuality', in M. Reinfelder (ed.), *Amazon to Zami: Towards a Global Lesbian Feminism*. London: Cassell

Gerakan Wanita Indonesia. 1960. 'Pembelaan Hak-Hak Wanita'. *Buku Gerwani*. N.p.

Gooszen, H. 2000. *A Demographic History of the Indonesian Archipelago, 1880–1942*. Singapore: Institute of Southeast Asian Studies

Government of Indonesia. 1967. *Ibu Dewi Sartika: Champion of Women's Emancipation*. Djakarta: Department of Information

Government of Indonesia-UNICEF. 1989. *Situation Analysis of Children and Women in Indonesia*. Jakarta: Government of Indonesia-UNICEF

Government Secretary. 1925. *Circular to Governor of West Java and Other Heads of Regional Government from the Government Secretary, Westerouen van Meeteren, 14/12/1925, No.403x, overgelegd bij Mailrapport no.1184x/25*. The Hague: Netherlands National Archives

Grace, J. 1996. 'Healers and modern health services: antenatal, birthing and postpartum care in rural East Lombok, Indonesia', in Rice and Manderson (eds.)

Grijns, M., I. Smyth, A. van Velzen et al. 1994. *Different Women, Different Work: Gender and Industrialisation in Indonesia*. Avebury: Aldershot

Guest, P. 1991. *Marital Dissolution and Development in Indonesia*. Canberra: Australian National University

Habich-Veenhuijzen, S. D. 1920. 'Rapport betreffende de zuigelingen-statistiek/ Report on infant statistics'. *Mededeelingen van de Burgerlijk Geneeskundig Dienst in Nederlandsch-Indie* 9: 82–127

Hadiz, V. R. 1997. *Workers and the State in New Order Indonesia*. London: Routledge
  2002. 'The Indonesian labour movement: resurgent or constrained?' *Southeast Asian Affairs*: 130–42

Hafidz, W., A. Taslim, S. Aripurnami et al. 1992. 'Family planning in Indonesia: the case for policy reorientation'. *Inside Indonesia* 30: 19–20, 22

Hamdani, S. 1984. 'Riwayat Pertumbuhan Perkumpulan Wanita "Isteri Sedar"', in *Perjuangan Wanita Indonesia 10 Windu Setelah Kartini 1904–1984*. Jakarta: Departemen Penerangan RI.

Hancock, P. 1997. 'The walking ghosts of West Java'. *Inside Indonesia* 51: 16–19
  2000. 'Women workers still exploited'. *Inside Indonesia* 62: 21–2

Harkrisnowo, H. 2000. 'Perempuan dan hak asasi manusia dalam perspektif yuridis', in N. I. Subono (ed.), *Negara dan Kekerasan Terhadap Perempuan*. Jakarta: Yayasan Jurnal Perempuan

Hartono, A. B. and D. Juliantoro.1997. *Derita Paksa Perempuan: Kisah Jugun Ianfu pada masa pendudukan Jepang 1942–1945*. Jakarta: Pustaka Sinar Harapan

Hatley, B. 2002. 'Literature, mythology and regime change: some observations on recent Indonesian women's writing', in K. Robinson and S. Bessell (eds.), *Women in Indonesia: Gender, Equity and Development*. Canberra: Australian National University

Hatley, B. and S. Blackburn 2000. 'Representations of women's roles in household and society in Indonesian women's writings of the 1930s', in J. Koning, M. Nolten, J. Rodenburg and R. Saptari (eds.), *Women and Households in Indonesia: Cultural Notions and Social Practices*. Richmond, Surrey: Curzon

Heryanto, A. 1999. 'Rape, race, and reporting', in A. Budiman, B. Hatley and D. Kingsbury (eds.), *Reformasi, Crisis and Change in Indonesia*. Clayton: Monash Asia Institute

Hidayah, N. 1998. *Kontroversi Presiden Wanita*. Jakarta: Pt Pabelan Jayakarta

Hindley, D. 1964. *The Communist Party of Indonesia, 1951–1963*. Berkeley: University of California Press

Hooker, M. B. 1999. 'Islam and medical science: evidence from Indonesian *fatawa*: 1960–1995', in T. Lindsey (ed.), *Indonesia: Law and Society*. Leichhardt: Federation Press

Hugo, G. 1993. 'International labour migration', in C. Manning and J. Hardjono (eds.), *Indonesia Assessment 1993: Labour: Sharing the Benefits of Growth?* Canberra: Australian National University

2002. 'Women's international labour migration', in K. Robinson and S. Bessell (eds.), *Women in Indonesia: Gender, Equity and Development*. Singapore: ISEAS

Hull, T. H. 1987. 'Fertility decline in Indonesia: an institutionalist interpretation'. *International Family Planning Perspectives* 13(3): 90–5

1988. 'Adapting the Safe Motherhood Initiative to Indonesian society', in A. B. Saifuddin Trijatmo Rachmimhadhi, Joedo Prihartono et al. (eds.), *Bunga Rampai Gerakan KN Nasional*. Jakarta: Panitia Peringatan Dasawindu Prof. Dr H. M. Judono

1991. *Reports of Coercion in the Indonesian Vasectomy Programme: A Report to AIDAB*. Canberra: Australian National University

1994. 'Fertility decline in the New Order period: the evolution of population policy 1965–90', in H. Hill (ed.), *Indonesia's New Order: The Dynamics of Socio-Economic Transformation*. Sydney: Allen and Unwin

1999. *Indonesian Fertility Behaviour before the Transition: Searching for Hints in the Historical Record*. Canberra: Australian National University

Hull, T. H. and V. J. Hull. 1987. 'Changing marriage behaviour in Java: the role of timing and consummation'. *Southeast Asian Journal of Social Science* 15(1): 104–19

1995. 'Politics, culture and fertility: transitions in Indonesia'. Paper presented at John Caldwell seminar, 'The Continuing Demographic Transition', Canberra, August 4–11

Hull, T. H., S. W. Sarwono and N. Widyantoro 1993. 'Induced abortion in Indonesia'. *Studies in Family Planning* 24(4): 241–51

Hull, T. H., D. Widyatun, A. Raharto et al. 1999. 'Neither *dukun* nor doctor: some problems of the village midwife programme in Eastern Indonesia'. *Development Bulletin* 48: 17–20

Hull, V. J. 1996. 'Women in Java's rural middle class: progress or regress?' in P. V. Esterik (ed.), *Women of Southeast Asia*. DeKalb: Center for Southeast Asian Studies, Northern Illinois University

Hull, V. J., N. Widyantoro and T. Fetters. 1996. '"No problem": reproductive tract infections in Indonesia', in Rice and Manderson (eds.)

Hunter, C. L. 1996a. 'The National Health System and discourses of power in Indonesia'. *Asian Studies Review* 20(1): 20–34

1996b. 'Women as "good citizens": maternal and child health in a Sasak village', in Rice and Manderson (eds.)

Huzaimah, T. Y. 1996. 'Aborsi menurut hukum Islam'. *Sehat* 2: 5

Ihromi, T. O. 1973. *The Status of Women and Family Planning in Indonesia: A Study Conducted by the Research Team on the Status of Women and Family Planning in Indonesia, Preliminary Report*. Jakarta.

Ikatan Bidan Indonesia. 1996. *Profesi Bidan: Sebuah Perjalanan Karir*. Jakarta: Pengurus Pusat Ikatan Bidan Indonesia

Ilhami, H. 1995. *Buku Pintar Wanita Menjadi Pemimpin*. Surabaya: Karya Anda
Indonesia 1997. 1999. 'Indonesia 1997: results from the demographic and health survey'. *Studies in Family Planning* 30(3): 254–8
Indonesia Country Report. 1996. *Indonesia Country Report: The Implementation of the Convention on the Elimination of All Forms of Discrimination Against Women during 1985–1995*. Jakarta: Office of the Minister of State for the Role of Women, Republic of Indonesia
Indonesian Legal Aid Foundation. 1994. *A Preliminary Report on the Murder of Marsinah*. Jakarta: LBH
INGI Labour Working Group. 1991. 'Unjust but doing it! Nike operations in Indonesia'. *Inside Indonesia* 27: 7–9
Ingleson, J. 1986. *In Search of Justice: Workers and Unions in Colonial Java, 1908–1926*. Singapore: Oxford University Press
Iskandar, M. 1997. 'Health and mortality', in G. W. Jones and T. H. Hull (eds.), *Indonesia Assessment: Population and Human Resources*. Canberra: Australian National University
Isteri. 1931. 'Verslag pendek'. 3(4): 97–9
    1931. 'Motie protest meeting oeroesan Lasem di Mataran'. 3(5): 108–9
    1932. 'Pemboekaan oleh Ketoea PPII'. 11 & 12: 17–26
Isteri Indonesia. 1939. 'Djakarta Protestmeeting'. 3(9): 7
    1941. 'Kongres Perempoean IV di Semarang pada tg. 25-28 Djoeli 1941'. 5(8): 5–8
Istiadah. 1995. *Muslim Women in Contemporary Indonesia: Investigating Paths to Resist the Patriarchal System*. Clayton: Centre for Southeast Asian Studies, Monash University
Jaarverslag over 1915. 1915. *Jaarverslag over 1915 van de Afdeeling Batavia van de Vereeniging voor Vrouwenkiesrecht*. Batavia
Jaarverslag over 1918. 1918. *Jaarverslag over 1918 van de Afdeeling Batavia van de Vereeniging voor Vrouwenkiesrecht*. Batavia
Jaarverslag over 1919. 1919. *Jaarverslag over 1919 van de Afdeeling Batavia van de Vereeniging voor Vrouwenkiesrecht*. Batavia
Jaiz, H. A. 1998. *Polemik Presiden Wanita*. Jakarta: Pustaka Al-Kautsar
Jakarta Post. 1998. 'Government condemns gang rapes during riots'. 11 July
    1998. 'Letter to editor (E. Busri)'. 13 July
    1999. 'May riot rape victims scared into silence: UN'. 27 March
    1999. 'I belong to the nation: Megawati'. 22 October
    2000. 'Acehnese women map future'. 27 February
    2000. 'Doctors demand ruling on legal abortion to curb illegal practice'. 3 April
    2000. 'Aisyah ponders new gender awareness in Islam'. 22 April
    2001. 'Population policy'. 8 January
    2001. 'Indonesian maids slam exploitation in Hong Kong'. 21 July
    2001. 'Comfort women an awkward issue'. 26 October
    2002. 'Aceh to start enforcing Islamic dress code this month'. 5 March
    2003. 'Citizenship bill protects women more than ever'. 9 February
    2003. 'Women activists urged to join political parties'. 10 March
    2003. 'Workers protest against new labour laws'. 26 March
    2003. 'Contraceptive users down, birth control endangered'. 14 July

2003. 'We are against polygamy!' 30 July

2003. 'Rights activist calls for revision of marriage law'. 27 August

Jennaway, M. 2000. 'Bitter honey: female agency and the polygynous household, North Bali', in J. Koning, M. Nolten, J. Rodenburg et al. (eds.), *Women and Households in Indonesia: Cultural Notions and Social Practices*. Richmond: Curzon

Jeumpa, B. and Ulil. 2001. 'Quo vadis, lesbians? Lesbians want to be themselves'. *Inside Indonesia* 66: 13

Jolly, M. 1998. 'Introduction: colonial and postcolonial plots in histories of maternities and modernities', in K. Ram and M. Jolly (eds.), *Maternities and Modernities: Colonial and Postcolonial Experiences in Asia and the Pacific*. Cambridge: Cambridge University Press

Jones, G. W. 1994. *Marriage and Divorce in Islamic South-East Asia*. Kuala Lumpur: Oxford University Press

Jones, G. W. 2001. 'Which Indonesian women marry youngest, and why?' *Journal of Southeast Asian Studies* 32(1): 67–87

Jones, G. W., E. Sulistyaningsih and T. Hull. 1995. *Prostitution in Indonesia*. Canberra: Australian National University

Jones, S. 1996. 'Women feed Malaysian boom'. *Inside Indonesia* 47: 16–18

Jordaan, E. 1984. 'The mystery of Nyai Lara Kidul, goddess of the southern ocean'. *Archipel* 28: 99–116

Jumawar. 1952. 'Taman Muslimaat'. *Adil* 6 (23): 6

Jurnal Perempuan: Newsletter Jaringan Suara Ibu Peduli. 1998. 'Aksi Damai Ibu-Ibu yang Peduli'. 2: 1–2

1998. 'Ibu, Masak Apa Hari Ini?' *Supplemen Journal Perempuan* (6): 1–2

Kahin, A. 1999. *Rebellion to Integration: West Sumatra and the Indonesian Polity*. Amsterdam: Amsterdam University Press

Kamaruzzaman, S. 2000. 'Kekerasan, pengungsian dan dampaknya terhadap perempuan di Aceh'. Paper delivered at Conference of Asian Studies Association of Australia, University of Melbourne. July

Kandiyoti, D. (ed.) 1991. *Women, Islam and the State*. Houndmills: Macmillan

Kartini, R. A. 1911. *Door Duisternis tot Licht: Gedachten van Raden Adjeng Kartini*. 's-Gravenhage: C.G.T. van Dorp en Co.

1974. 'Educate the Javanese!' *Indonesia* 17: 83–98

1992. *Letters from Kartini, An Indonesian Feminist, 1900–1904*. Clayton. Monash Asia Institute

1995. *On Feminism and Nationalism: Kartini's Letters to Stella Zeehandelaar 1899–1903*. Clayton: Monash Asia Institute

Kartinifonds. 1939. *Herdenking van het 25-jarig bestaan der Vereeniging Kartinifonds*. N.p.

Kartowijono, S. 1977. *Perkembangan Pergerakan Wanita Indonesia*. Jakarta: Yayasan Idayu

1983. *Mencari Makna Hidupku*. Jakarta: Sinar Harapan

Katjasungkana, N. 1992. 'Engendering a new order: endangering democracy; a reflection on the use of women in New Order Indonesia'. Paper presented at Indonesian Democracy conference, Monash University, Clayton, December.

1993. 'Kedudukan wanita dalam perspectif Islam', in L. M. Marcoes-Natsir and J. H. Meuleman (eds.), *Wanita Islam Indonesia dalam Kajian Teskstual dan Kontekstual.* Jakarta: INIS

1995. 'Peranan LSM dan perjuangan persamaan hak', in A. Sunarijati (ed.), *Pekerja Wanita, Peran Ganda dan Persamaan Hak.* Jakarta: Lembaga Wanita, Remaja dan Anak DPP-SPSI and Friedrich-Ebert-Stiftung

1996. 'Hak Reproduksi di Indonesia: Antara Hukum dan Realitas Sosial', in A. Dwiyanto and M. Darwin (eds.), *Seksualitas, Kesehatan Reproduksi, dan Ketimpangan Gender: Implementasi Kesepakatan Konferensi Kependudukan Kairo bagi Indonesia.* Jakarta: Pustaka Sinar Harapan bekerja sama dengan Pusat Penelitian Kependudukan Universitas Gajah Mada dan The Ford Foundation

1997. 'Pandangan Islam tentang posisi perempuan dan laki-laki dalam keluarga', in D. S. Anshori, E. Kosasih and F. Sarimaya (eds.), *Membincangkan Feminisme: Refleksi Muslimah atas Peran Sosial Kaum Wanita.* Bandung: Pustaka Hidayah

2001. 'Aspek hukum kekerasan terhadap perempuan', in N. Katjasungkana, L. Soetrisno and A. Gaffar (eds.), *Potret Perempuan: Tinjauan Politik, Ekonomi. Hukum di Zaman Orde Baru.* Yogyakarta: Pustaka Pelajar

Katoppo, M. 1996. 'Angka Kehidupan Ibu'. *Suara Pembaruan.* 23 Desember

Katz, J. S. and R. S. Katz. 1975 'The new Indonesian Marriage Law. a mirror of Indonesia's political, cultural and legal systems'. *American Journal of Comparative Law* 23(4): 653–81

Kolibonso, R. (ed.) 1998. *Perempuan Menuntut Keadilan.* Jakarta: Mitra Perempuan

Komnasham. 2001. *Diskriminasi terhadap Perempuan dalam Pendidikan.* Jakarta: Komisi Nasional Hak Asasi Manusia

Kompas. 1996. 'Angka kematian ibu Indonesia di atas ratarata negara berkembang lainnya'. 17 December.

1997. 'Meski tidak mudah, ada harapan penurunan AKI'. 19 February

1997. 'Hasil Uji coba yang Menggembirakan'. 10 March

1998. 'Pemerintah Alpa dan Perlu Minta Maaf'. 10 July

1998. 'Pemerintah bentuk tim independen'. 14 July

1998. 'Pemerintah kutuk aski kekerasan'. 16 July

1998. 'Sebanyak 781 orang tewas, 163 hilang'. 25 August

2000. 'Ada 2.3 Juta Aborsi di Indonesia Setiap Tahun'. 3 March

2000. 'PKBI Promosikan aborsi Aman'. 26 August

2000. 'Angka kematian ibu di Indonesia tertinggi di Asia Tenggara'. 3 September

2001. 'Khofifah Indar Parawansa: UU Perkawinan Patut Direvisi'. 8 January

Koning, J. 1996. 'Family planning acceptance in a rural Central Javanese village', in P. Boomgaard, R. Sciortini and I. Smyth (eds.), *Health Care in Java: Past and Present.* Leiden: KITLV Press

Konsorsium. 2002. Konsorsium Pembela Buruh Migran Indonesia. *Laporan Situasi Buruh Migran Indonesia Tahun 2002.* Jakarta: Konsorsium Pembela Buruh Migran Indonesia.

Krisnawati, T. 1995. 'Pekerja migran perempuan Indonesia: perlindungan dan kesejahteraannya', in A. Sunarijati (ed.), *Pekerja Wanita, Peran Ganda dan*

Persamaan Hak. Jakarta: Lembaga Wanita, Remaja dan Anak DPP-SPSI and Friedrich-Ebert-Stiftung

Krulfeld, R. 1986. 'Sasak attitudes towards polygyny and the changing position of women in Sasak peasant villages', in L. Dube, E. Leacock and S. Ardener (eds.), *Visibility and Power: Essays on Women in Society and Development.* Delhi: Oxford University Press

Kusyuniati, S. 1998. 'Strikes from 1990 to 1996: an evaluation of the dynamics of the Indonesian labour movement.' PhD dissertation, Swinburne University of Technology

Kuypers, S. 1993. 'Profil Organisasi Wanita Islam Indonesia: Tinjauan dari Dalam', in L. Marcoes-Natsir and J. Meuleman (eds.), *Wanita Islam dalam Kajian Tekstual dan Kontekstual.* Jakarta: INIS

Lelo, S. M. 1914. 'Anak perempoean'. *Soenting Melajoe* 3(25): 1–2

Lev, D. 1996. 'On the other hand?' in L. J. Sears (ed.), *Fantasizing the Feminine in Indonesia.* Durham: Duke University Press

Liem, S. T.-O. 1936. 'De Indo-Chineesche Vrouw en het Vereenigingsleven', in Schreven and Boomkamp (eds.)

Lim, R. and M. Kemp. 1994. 'Modernisation and maternity in Bali'. *Inside Indonesia* 39: 15–17

Locher-Scholten, E. 2000. *Women and the Colonial State: Essays on Gender and Modernity in the Netherlands Indies, 1900–1942.* Amsterdam: Amsterdam University Press

Locher-Scholten, E. and A. Niehof. 1987. 'Introduction', in E. Locher-Scholten and A. Niehof (eds.), *Indonesian Women in Focus: Past and Present Notions.* Dordrecht: Foris Publications

Logsdon, M. 1985. 'Gender roles in elementary school texts in Indonesia', in M. J. Goodman (ed.), *Women in Asia and the Pacific: Towards an East-West Dialogue.* Honolulu: University of Hawai'i Press

Lombard, D. 1977. 'Apercu sur les associations feminines'. *Archipel* 13: 193–210

Lucas, A. 1996. 'Wanita dalam Revolusi: Pengalaman Selama Pendudukan dan Revolusi, 1942–1950'. *Prisma* 25(5): 17–28

Madjelis Departement Pergerakan Isteri PSII. 1940. *Boekoe Peringatan 'Pergerakan Isteri PSII' 1918–1940.* [Jakarta?], Pergerakan Isteri PSII

Manderson, L. 1996. *Sickness and the State: Health and Illness in Colonial Malaya, 1870–1940.* Cambridge: Cambridge University Press

Mangoensarkoro, S. 1946. *Riwayat Pergerakan Wanita Indonesia.* Yogyakarta: Penerbit Wanita Rakyat

Mangunpuspito, S. S. 1984. 'Organisasi Wanita Dimasa Pendudukan Jepang', in *Perjuangan Wanita Indonesia 10 Windu Setelah Kartini 1904–1984.* Jakarta: Departmen Penerangan RI

Manning, C. 1998. *Indonesian Labour in Transition: An East Asian Success Story?* Cambridge: Cambridge University Press

Manoppo-Watupongoh, G. Y. J. 1991. 'Sejarah Kaum Ibu Gereja Masehi Injili Minahasa'. *Warta Studi Perempuan* 2(1): 12–17

Marcoes, L. 2002. 'Women's grassroots movements in Indonesia: a case study of the PKK and Islamic women's organisations', in K. Robinson and S. Bessell (eds.), *Women in Indonesia: Gender, Equity and Development.* Canberra: Australian National University

Marcoes-Natsir, L. 2000. 'Aisyiyah: between worship, charity and professionalism', in M. Oey-Gardiner and C. Bianpoen (eds.), *Indonesian Women: The Journey Continues*. Canberra: Australian National University

Mar'iyah, C.2000. 'Violence, democracy and human rights: women's peace building initiatives in Indonesia'. Paper presented at conference on Violent Conflict in Indonesia: Analysis, Representation, Resolution, University of Melbourne. 6–7 July

Martyn, E. 2001. 'Gender and nation in a new democracy: Indonesian women's organisations in the 1950s'. PhD dissertation, Monash University

Ma'shum, S. and A. Sawawi (eds.), 1996. *50 Tahun Muslimat NU Berkhidmat untuk Agama dan Bangsa*. Jakarta: Pucuk Pimpinan Muslimat Nahdlatul Ulama

Mather, C. E. 1983. 'Industrialization in the Tangerang Regency of West Java: women workers and the Islamic patriarchy'. *Bulletin of Concerned Asian Scholars* 15(2): 2–17

McBeth, J. 2001. 'Labour leader forges ahead'. *Far Eastern Economic Review*. 8 March

McDonald, H., D. Ball, J. Dunn et al. 2002. *Masters of Terror: Indonesia's Military and Violence in East Timor in 1999*. Canberra: Australian National University

McVey, R. 1967. 'Taman Siswa and the Indonesian National Awakening'. *Indonesia* 4: 128–49

Media Indonesia. 1992. 'RUU Kesehatan Merugikan'. 17 February

    2000. 'Program kesehatan reproduksi akan dilaksanakan semua daerah'. 8 August

    2002. 'Kongres Wanita Indonesia serukan "Damai Bangsaku"'. 18 August

    2002. 'Perjuangan buruh perempuan diadang kekerasan'. 23 October

Milner, A. (ed.) 1996. *Comparing Cultures*. Melbourne: Oxford University Press

Moedinem. 1931. 'IS terhadap pada pekerdjaan kaoem perempoean di Indonesia'. *Sedar* 1(11/12): 5–9

Moghadam, V. (ed.) 1994. *Gender and National Identity: Women and Politics in Muslim Societies*. London: Zed Books

Mohamad, K. 1998. *Kontradiksi dalam Kesehatan Reproduksi*. Jakarta: Pustaka Sinar Harapan bekerjasama dengan PT Citra Putra Bangsa dan The Ford Foundation

Molyneux, M. 2001. *Women's Movements in International Perspective: Latin America and Beyond*. Houndsmills: Palgrave

Muchtar, D. 1999. 'The rise of the Indonesian women's movement in the New Order state'. MPhil. thesis, Murdoch University

Mufti, S. H. S. 1996. 'Strategi Kowani Menuju Kemandirian', in M. Oey-Gardiner, M. Wagemann, E. Suleeman et al. (eds.) *Perempuan Indonesia: Dulu dan Kini*. Jakarta: Gramedia

Mulia, M. 1999. *Pandangan Islam tentang Poligami*. Jakarta: Lembaga Kajian Agama dan Gender dengan Perserikatan Solidaritas Perempuan dan The Asia Foundation

Murray, A. J. 1999. 'Let them take ecstasy: class and Jakarta lesbians', in E. Blackwood and S. E. Wieringa (eds.), *Same-Sex Relations and Female Desires: Transgender Practices Across Cultures*. New York: Columbia University Press

Muthali'in, A. 2001. *Bias Gender dalam Pendidikan*. Surakarta: Muhammadiyah University Press

Nasution, A. B. 1992. *The Aspiration for Constitutional Government in Indonesia: A Socio-Legal Study of the Indonesian Konstituante 1956–59*. Jakarta: Sinar Harapan

Netherlands Indies Government. 1914. *Onderzoek naar de mindere welvaart der Inlandsche bevolking op Java en Madoera, Vol. IXb3: Verheffing can de Inlandsche Vrouw*. Batavia: Drukkerij Papyrus

1922a. *Volksraad Afdeelingsverslag*. Batavia

1922b. *Volksraad Handelingen*. Batavia.

1927. *Circular on Child Marriages, 26/8/1927, No. 1753/A2, overgelegd bij Mail-rapport No.1954/27*. The Hague: Netherlands National Archives

1930. *Volkstelling 1930* (8 vols.). Batavia: Landsdrukkerij

1932. *Circular on Combating Child Marriage, 1/6/1932, No.144/a, overgelegd bij Mailrapport No.778/32*. The Hague: Netherlands National Archives

1937. *Ontwerp-regeling voor een monogaam huwelijk voor hen, wier huwelijksrecht niet bij algemeen verordening is vastgesteld, Mailrapport 309/20*. The Hague: Netherlands National Archives

1940. *Verslag van de Commissie tot Bestudeering van Staatsrechtelijke Hervormingen* (2 vols.). Batavia

Netherlands Indies Government. 1941. *Volksraad Handelingen*. Batavia

Niehof, A. 1998. 'The changing lives of Indonesian women: contained emancipation under pressure'. *Bijdragen tot de Taal-, Land- en Volkenkunde* 154(2): 236–58

Noerhadi, T. H. 2000. 'Kekerasan negara terhadap perempuan', in N. I. Subono (ed.), *Negara dan Kekerasan Terhadap Perempuan*. Jakarta: Yayasan Jurnal Perempuan

Nordholt, H. S. 2002. 'A genealogy of violence', in F. Colombijn and J. T. Lindblad (eds.), *Roots of Violence in Indonesia: Contemporary Violence in Historical Perspective*. Leiden: KITLV

Nurliana, N., M. P. B. Manus, G. A. M. Ohorella et al. 1986. *Peranan Wanita Indonesia di Masa Perang Kemerdekaan 1945–1950*. Jakarta: Departemen Pendidikan dan Kebudayaan

Oey-Gardiner, M. 1992. 'Gender differences in schooling in Indonesia'. *Bulletin of Indonesian Economic Studies*: 57–91

1997. 'Educational developments, achievements and challenges', in G. W. Jones and T. H. Hull (eds.), *Indonesia Assessment: Population and Human Resources*. Canberra: Australian National University

Ohorella, G. A., S. Sutjiatiningsih, M. Ibrahim et al. 1992. *Peranan Wanita Indonesia dalam Masa Pergerakan Nasional*. Jakarta: Departemen Pendidikan dan Kebudayaan, Direktorat Sejarah dan Nilai Tradisional, Proyek Inventarisasi dan Dokumentasi Sejarah Nasional

Op de Uitkijk. 1926. 'Op de Uitkijk'. *De Vrouw in Huis en Maatschappij* 1(5): 1

Orleck, A.1996. 'Tradition unbound: radical mothers in international perspective', in A. Jetter, A. Orleck and D. Taylor (eds.), *The Politics of Motherhood: Activist Voices from Left to Right*. Hanover: University Press of New England

Overveldt-Biekart, S. van. 1928. 'Aan de Leden'. *Maandblad van de Vereeniging voor Vrouwenkiesrecht in Nederlandsch-Indie* 3(2): 1–3

Panitia Penasehat. 1957. Panitia Penasehat Perkawinan dan Penjelesaian Kotapradja Djakarta Raya. *Laporan.* Djakarta

Panitia Peringatan. 1958. Panitia Peringatan 30 Tahun Kesatuan Pergerakan Wanita Indonesia. *Buku Peringatan 30 Tahun Kesatuan Pergerakan Wanita Indonesia, 22 Des., 1928–22 Des., 1958.* Djakarta, Pertjetakan Negara

Parawansa, K. I. 2002. 'Institution building: an effort to improve Indonesian women's role and status', in K. Robinson and S. Bessell (eds.), *Women in Indonesia: Gender, Equity and Development.* Singapore: Institute of Southeast Asian Studies

Parker, L. 1993. *Gender and School in Bali.* Canberra: Gender Relations Project, Australian National University

Parpart, J. L., S. M. Rai, and K. Saudt (eds.) 2002. *Rethinking Empowerment: Gender and Development in a Global/Local World.* London: Routledge

Pergerakan Isteri PSII. 1940. *Boekoe Peringatan 'Pergerakan Isteri PSII' 1918–1940.* N.p.: Pergerakan Isteri PSII

Pijper, G. F. 1937. 'De strijd om de monogamie'. *Koloniale Studien* 5: 476–90

Poeradiredja, E. 1939. ' Lezing van Mevr. E. Poeradiredja'. *Maandblad van de Nederlandsch-Indische Vereeniging voor Vrouwenbelangen en Gelijk Staatsburgerschap* 10(10): 6–8

Poerwandari, E. K. 2000. 'Christian women's organisations: the way ahead', in M. Oey-Gardiner and C. Bianpoen (eds.), *Indonesian Women: The Journey Continues.* Canberra: Australian National University

Poeze, H. A. 1986. *In het Land van de Overheerser. Vol.1: Indonesiers in Nederland 1600–1950.* Dordrecht/Cinnaminson: Foris Publications

Polan, R. 1998. 'Tim Relawan jajaki PBB sebagai "watchdog"'. *Merdeka.* 3 August

Pontianak. 1919. 'Pontianak'. *Encyclopaedie van Nederlandsch-Indie.* 's-Gravenhage: Martinus Nijhoff. III: 450–1

Postel-Coster, E. 1985. *Het Omheinde Kweekbed. Machtsverhoudingen in de Minangkabausche Familleroman.* Delft: Eburon

Prae-Adviezen. 1916. *Prae-Adviezen van het Eerste Koloniaal Onderwijscongres.* 's-Gravenhage: Drukkerij Korthuis

Price, S. 1983. 'Rich woman, poor woman: occupation differences in a textile producing village in Central Java', in L. Manderson (ed.), *Women's Work and Women's Roles: Economics and Everyday Life in Indonesia.* Canberra: Australian National University

Pringgodigdo, A. K. 1949. *Sedjarah Pergerakan Rakjat Indonesia.* Djakarta: Pustaka Rakjat

Pringgodigdo, S. 1937. *Perlindoengan dalam Perkawinan.* Batavia: Kenanga

Putri, A. 2003. 'Hiding the truth'. *Inside Indonesia* 73: 26–7

Rachmat-Ishaya, F. A. 1990. 'Indonesian women's organizations during the Japanese Occupation 1942–1945'. MA thesis, Universiteit van Amsterdam

Radar Jember. 2002. 'Satpol PP tetap berlakukan jam malam berkeliaran hingga larut, perempuan bisa ditangkap'. 12 August

Rafiah. 1912. 'Roedingan dari hal bermadoe'. *Soenting Melajoe* 1(25): 1

Rahardjo, Y. 1997. 'Women's role in demographic transition and human resource development', in G. W. Jones and T. H. Hull (eds.), *Indonesia Assessment: Population and Human Resources.* Canberra: Australian National University

Rahman, A. 2000. 'Moslem women's organisations: their role in attaining the benefits of development', in M. Oey-Gardiner and C. Bianpoen (eds.), *Indonesian Women: The Journey Continues*. Canberra: Australian National University

Rasid, G. 1982. *Maria Ullfah Subadio: Pembela Kaumnya*. Jakarta: Penerbit Bulan Bintang

Reid, A. 1988. *Southeast Asia in the Age of Commerce 1450–1680. Volume One: The Lands below the Winds*. New Haven: Yale University Press

Reid, A. 1998. 'Political "tradition" in Indonesia: the one and the many'. *Asian Studies Review* 22(1): 23–38

Republika. 1998. 'Kasus perkosaan dimanfaatkan untuk sudutkan Islam'. 22 July

1998. 'Perkosaan massal jangan terulang'. 23 July

1998. 'Kerusuhan Mei, sedikitnya ada 168 perkosaan'. 14 July

1998. 'DPR harus desak pemerintah bentuk TPF kerusuhan Mei'. 21 July

1998. 'Benarkah terjadi perkosaan massal'. 2 August

1998. 'Kiprah Tim Relawan, memadukan pelayanan sosial dan investigasi'. 24 August

Rice, P. L. and L. Manderson (eds.), 1996. *Maternity and Reproductive Health in Asian Societies*. Amsterdam: Harwood Academic Publishers

Robinson, K. 1989. 'Choosing contraception: cultural change and the Indonesian Family Planning Programme', in P. Alexander (ed.), *Creating Indonesian Cultures*. Sydney: Oceania Publications

1991. 'Housemaids: the effects of gender and culture on the internal and international migration of Indonesian women', in G. Bottomley, M. de Lepervanche and J. Martin (eds.), *Intersexions: Gender/class/culture/ethnicity*. Sydney: Allen and Unwin

1994. 'Indonesian national identity and the citizen mother'. *Communal/Plural* 3: 65–81

1997. 'Indonesian women: a survey of recent developments'. *Review of Indonesian and Malaysian Affairs* 31(2): 141–62

2000. 'Gender, Islam, and nationality: Indonesian domestic servants in the Middle East', in K. M. Adams and S. Dickey (eds.), *Home and Hegemony: Domestic Service and Identity Politics in South and Southeast Asia*. Ann Arbor: University of Michigan Press

Rochaida, E., B. Wicaksono and W. Tamtiari. 2001. 'Perdagangan perempuan pencari kerja di Tawao, Kalimantan Timur', in A. N. Abrar and W. Tamtiari (eds.), *Konstruksi Seksualitas: Antara Hak dan Kekuasaan*. Yogyakarta: Ford Foundation and Pusat Penelitian Kependudukan Universitas Gadjah Mada

Roeswo, N. 1932. 'Propaganda PPPPA'. *Isteri* (11 & 12): 68–9

Sadli, S. 1998. 'Tuntaskan'. *Merdeka*. 5 August

Sahly, M. 1994. *Etika Sexual*. Pekalongan: C.V. Bahagia

Salmon, C. 1977. 'Presse feminine ou feministe?' *Archipel* 13: 157–91

Sanggenafu, S. 2000. 'Pelanggaran HAM, perempuan, dan aparat militer di Irian Jaya', in N. I. Subono (ed.), *Negara dan Kekerasan Terhadap Perempuan*. Jakarta: Yayasan Jurnal Perempuan

Saptari, R. and A. Utrecht. 1997. 'Gender interests and the struggle of NGOs within and beyond the state: the experience of women organizing in Indonesia'. *Journal für Entwicklungspolitik* 13(3): 319–39

Sardjono, U. 1955. *Meluaskan Organisasi Gerwani dan Kerdjasama Organisasi2 Wanita.* Djakarta: DPP Gerwani

Sawitri, C. 2001. 'Women in Indonesia's military'. *Latitudes* 10: 1–10

Schild, V. 1997. 'New subjects of rights? Gendered citizenship and the contradictory legacies of social movements in Latin America'. *Organization* 4(4): 604–19

Schreven, M. A. E. van Lith van and J. H. H.-v. L. Boomkamp (eds.). 1936. *Indisch Vrouwen Jaarboek 1936.* Jogjakarta: Kolff-Buning

Schultz-Metzer, C. H. R. 1936. 'I.E.V. Vrouwenorganisatie', in Schreven and Boomkamp (eds.)

Sciortino, R. and I. Smyth. 1997. 'The triumph of harmony: the denial of domestic violence on Java'. *Journal für Entwicklungspolitik* 13(3): 299–317

Sedar. 1930. 'Iboe'. 1(5): 5–6

1931. 'Berita dari Pengoeroes Besar I. S.'. 2(4): 5–6

1932. 'Poetoesan2 dari Congres'. 2(12): 25

Sehat. 1998. 'Islam dan Hak Reproduksi di Indonesia'. 4(21): 2–4

Sejarah Muslimat. 1979. *Sejarah Muslimat Nahdlatul Ulama.* Jakarta: PP Muslimat NU

SERUNI. 1999. *Seruan Kaum Ibu dan Seluruh Perempuan Indonesia.* Jakarta: SERUNI.

Shiffman, J. 1999. 'Policy and diffusion in public health transitions: Indonesia in global perspective'. PhD dissertation, University of Michigan

Shiraishi, T. 1990. *An Age in Motion: Popular Radicalism in Java, 1912–1926.* Ithaca: Cornell University Press

Siapno, J. A. 2002. *Gender, Islam, Nationalism and the State in Aceh: The Paradox of Power, Co-optation and Resistance.* London: RoutledgeCurzon

Siegel, J. T. 2001. 'Thoughts on the violence of May 13 and 14, 1998, in Jakarta', in B. R. O. G. Anderson (ed.), *Violence and the State in Suharto's Indonesia.* Ithaca: Southeast Asia Program, Cornell University

Singarimbun, M. and S. Sairin. 1995. *Lika-Liku Kehidupan Buruh Perempuan.* Yogyakarta: Yayasan Annisa Swasti Yogyakarta

Sissons, M. E. 1997. *From One Day to Another: Violation of Women's Reproductive and Sexual Rights in East Timor.* Melbourne: East Timor Human Rights Centre

Siwidana. 1981. 'Kasus Lumajang: pemecehan atas masalah perkawinan bawah umur'. *Pelita.* 22 December

Smyth, I. 1991. 'The Indonesian family planning programme: a success story for women?' *Development and Change* 22: 781–805

Smyth, I. and M. Grijns. 1997. 'Unjuk Rasa or conscious protest? Resistance strategies of Indonesian women workers'. *Bulletin of Concerned Asian Scholars* 29(4): 13–22

Soebadio, M. U. 1981. *Perjuangan untuk mencapai Undang-undang Perkawinan (Suatu Pengalam).* Jakarta: Yayasan Idayu

Soebagio, I. N. 1982. *S.K. Trimurti: Wanita Pengabdi Bangsa.* Jakarta: Gunung Agung

Soedomo, N.R. W.1954. 'Polygami (dipandang dari segala sudut oleh fihak jang pro dan kontra)'. *Suara Perwari* 4(11): 13

Soenting Melajoe. 1913. 'Bermadoe'. 2(23): 1

1914. 'Sekali lagi seroean dari Betawi'. 3(23): 1

Soetomo. 1928. *Perkawinan dan Perkawinan Anak-Anak*. Batavia: Balai Pustaka

1934. *Kenang-Kenangan*. Surabaja

Stivens, M. 1990. 'Thinking about gender and the state in Indonesia', in A. Budiman (ed.), *State and Civil Society in Indonesia*. Clayton: Monash University

Stoler, A. 1995. *Race and the Education of Desire*. Durham: Duke University Press.

Stuers, Vreede-de C.. 1960. *The Indonesian Woman: Struggles and Achievements*. 's-Gravenhage: Mouton & Co.

Suara Merdeka. 1982. 'Perkawinan dan kehamilan wanita muda usia perlu penangan serius'. 16 October

Suara Pembaruan. 1998. 'Koalisi Perempuan melancarkan protes ke Departemen Hankam'. 20 July

Sukarno. 1963. *Sarinah: Kewadjiban Wanita dalam Perdjoangan Republik Indonesia*. Jakarta: Panitya Penerbit Buku-Buku Karangan Presiden Sukarno

Sullivan, N. 1994. *Masters and Managers: A Study of Gender Relations in Urban Java*. St Leonards, NSW: Allen and Unwin

Sumargono, H. A. 1998. *Siaran Pers: Kecerobohan Majalah 'Jakarta-Jakarta'*. Jakarta: Komite Indonesia untuk Solidaritas Dunia Islam

Sunindyo, S. 1998. 'When the earth is female and the nation is mother: gender, the armed forces and nationalism in Indonesia'. *Feminist Review* 58: 1–21

Supomo, R. 1960. *The Provisional Constitution of the Republic of Indonesia*. Ithaca: Cornell University Modern Indonesia Project

Surabaya Post. 2000. 'Nursyahbani Katjasungkana Prihatinkan Juugun Ianfu'. 21 November

Surastro, S. 1959. 'Kedudukan buruh wanita Indonesia'. *Kedudukan Wanita Indonesia* 1(10): 23–33

Surya-Hadi, I. S. 1959. *Wanita Pro dan Contra Poligami*. Semarang: Jajasan Gedung Wanita

Suryakusuma, J. I. 1987. 'State Ibuism: the social construction of womanhood in the Indonesian New Order'. Master of Development Studies thesis, The Hague: Institute of Social Studies

1996. 'The state and sexuality in New Order Indonesia', in L. J. Sears (ed.), *Fantasizing the Feminine in Indonesia*. Durham: Duke University Press

Suryochondro, S. 1984. *Potret Pergerakan Wanita di Indonesia*. Jakarta: Rajawali

2000. 'The development of women's movements in Indonesia', in M. Oey-Gardiner and C. Bianpoen (eds.), *Indonesian Women – The Journey Continues*. Canberra: Australian National University

Suyono, H., N. Piet, F. Stirling et al. 1981. 'Family planning attitudes in urban Indonesia: findings from a focus group'. *Studies in Family Planning* 12(12): 433–42

Suwondo, N. 1981. *Kedudukan Wanita Indonesia dalam Hukum dan Masyarakat*. Jakarta: Ghalia Indonesia

Taj, A. M. 1990. 'Gender intergenerational relations and marriage patterns in Indonesia'. PhD dissertation, University of Michigan

Taylor, J. G. 1996. 'Images of the Indonesian Revolution', in J. Drakard and J. Legge (eds.), *Indonesian Independence Fifty Years On*. Clayton: Monash Asia Institute

Tempo. 1973. 'RUU Perkawinan, aksi dan reaksi'. 8 September: 6–9

1998. 'Fakta lain tentang pencari fakta'. 16 November: 26–7

Thalib, M. 1995. *40 Petunjuk Menuju Perkawinan Islami*. Bandung: Irysad Baitus Salam

Thayib, A. 1994. *Struktur Rumah Tangga Muslim*. Surabaya: Risalah Gusti

Thomson, J. 1995. 'Blind spot'. *Inside Indonesia* 45: 13–14

Tim Relawan. 1998. Tim Relawan untuk Kemanusiaan Divisi Kekerasan terhadap Perempuan. *Kerusuhan Mei 1998 dalam Perspectif: Memahami kekerasan terhadap perempuan dan mencari pemulihan bersama*. Jakarta: Tim Relawan untuk Kemanusiaan

Tjoeng, T. F. 1948. *Arbeidstoestanden en Arbeidsbescherming in Indonesie*. 's-Gravenhage

Tobing, M., M. Hartiningsih, A. M. Dewabrata et al. 1990. *Perjalanan Nasib TKI-TKW*. Jakarta: Gramedia

Toemenggoeng, C. S.D. 1936. 'Bestrijding van den vrouwenhandel', in Schreven and Boomkamp (eds.)

(ed.) 1958. *30 Tahun Menentang Polygami*. Djakarta: Penerbit Chailan Sjamsoe

Toer, P. A. 1975. *A Heap of Ashes*. St Lucia: University of Queensland Press

2001. *Perawan Remaja dalam Cengkeraman Militer*. Jakarta: Kepustakaan Populer Gramedia

Tri, S. K. 1950. 'Perlindungan buruh wanita dan anak-anak'. *Wanita* 2(10): 171–2

Tsuchiya, K. 1987. *Democracy and Leadership: The Rise of the Taman Siswa Movement in Indonesia*. Honolulu: University of Hawai'i Press

UNDP. 2001. *Human Development Report 2001*. New York: Oxford University Press

UNICEF. 1994. *Situation Analysis on Children and Women in Indonesia*. Jakarta: UNICEF

Verdoorn, J. A. 1941. *Verloskundige Hulp voor de Inheemsche Bevolking van Nederlandsch-Indie*. 's-Gravenhage: Boekencentrum NV

Vereeniging Kartinifonds. 1938. *Jubileum-Verslag uitgegevan ter gelegenheid van het 25-jarig bestaan der Vereeniging Kartinifonds door den Raad van Beheer, 1912–1938*.N.p.

Von Benda-Beckmann, F. 1994. 'Comments and discussion: custom, state law and the problem of selective enforcement'. *Law and Society Review* 28(3): 508–9

Wal, S. L. van der. (ed.) 1963. *Het Onderwijsbeleid in Nederlands-Indie 1900–1940: Een bronnenpublicatie*. Groningen: J. B. Wolters

Wandita, G. 1998. 'The tears have not stopped, the violence has not ended: political upheaval, ethnicity, and violence against women in Indonesia'. *Gender and Development* 6(3): 34–41

Warwick, D. P. 1986. 'The Indonesian Family Planning Program: government influence and client choice'. *Population and Development Review* 12(3): 453–90

Wasmukan, Waskito, P. Reksonotoprodjo et al. (1995). *Permasalahan Haid, Nifas dan Istihadlah*. Surabaya, Risalah Gusti

Weix, G. G. 2002. 'Resisting history: Indonesian labour activism in the 1990s and the "Marsinah" case', in B.S.A. Yeoh, P. Teo and S. Huang (eds.), *Gender Politics in the Asia-Pacific Region*. London: Routledge

Wertheim, W. F. 1986. 'Indonesian Moslems under Sukarno and Suharto: majority with minority mentality'. *Kabar Seberang* 17: 31–52

Wessel, I. and G. Wimhofer (eds.). 2001. *Violence in Indonesia*. Hamburg: Abera

White, B. 1993. 'Industrial workers on West Java's urban fringe', in C. Manning and J. Hardjono (eds.), *Indonesia Assessment 1993: Labour: Sharing the Benefits of Growth?* Canberra: Australian National University

White, B. and E. L. Hastuti. 1980. *Different and Unequal: Male and Female Influence on Household and Community Affairs in Two West Java Villages*. Bogor: Bogor Agricultural University

Wieringa, S. 1992. 'Ibu or the beast: gender interests in two Indonesian women's organizations'. *Feminist Review* 41: 98–114

1999. 'Desiring bodies or defiant cultures: butch-femme lesbians in Jakarta and Lima', in E. Blackwood and S.Wieringa (eds.), *Same-Sex Relations and Female Desires: Transgender Practices Across Cultures*. New York: Columbia University Press

2002. *Sexual Politics in Indonesia*. Houndsmills: Palgrave Macmillan

Wiriaatmadja, R. 1983. *Dewi Sartika*. Jakarta: Departemen Pendidikan dan Kebudayaan

Wolf, D. L. 1992. *Factory Daughters: Gender, Households Dynamics, and Rural Industrialization in Java*. Berkeley: University of California Press

World Bank. 1999. *Safe Motherhood and the World Bank: Lessons from 10 Years of Experience*. Washington: World Bank

Yuval-Davis, N. 1997. *Gender and Nation*. London: Sage Publications

Zahr, C. A. and E. Royston (eds.), 1991. *Maternal Mortality: A Global Factbook*. Geneva: World Health Organization

Index

For EU product safety concerns, contact us at Calle de José Abascal, 56–1°,
28003 Madrid, Spain or eugpsr@cambridge.org.

www.ingramcontent.com/pod-product-compliance
Ingram Content Group UK Ltd.
Pitfield, Milton Keynes, MK11 3LW, UK
UKHW010038140625
459647UK00012BA/1459